HANDBOOK
TO
TRAIN TRAVEL
IN EUROPE

by GEORGE PANDI

Berlitz Guides

Editor
AMANDA HOPKINS

Designer
PHILIPPE AQUOISE

Station Plans
HAI-TOH LIM

TABLE OF CONTENTS

PREFACE

Whether for business or pleasure, travel ought not to be a chore but a pleasant interlude. That's what trains offer. Born in a more leisurely era, trains have kept to a high standard of comfort. Unlike planes or buses, where you sit with elbows stuck in your own or your neighbor's ribs, trains give room to shift, stretch, prop up your feet and read, or walk around. Meals are served on solid china, wine is poured into glasses and you get adult-sized cutlery, not plastic toys. A railway car is not just a metal crate for moving live cargo, but a rolling living room, café, or bedroom. Read a book, lean back and watch the view of the Rhine or the Alps roll past while sipping a glass of wine. Or sleep if you like, an afternoon nap or a night between sheets while you get where you want to be the next day.

But rail's appeal goes beyond pleasure or nostalgia. It is also quite practical: European trains are winning the race against planes and cars, in both speed and cost.

It makes sense to fly only if you are an executive who visits, say, Stockholm and Rome without any stops between. A more usual itinerary would call for 200- to 400-mile trips. In that range you travel faster by rail than by air because trains go directly between city centers; planes may move faster in the air but their passengers spend more time sitting in airport buses struggling in and out of city traffic. And your travel time is freer on a train: you don't waste it with transfers, hauling baggage and then waiting for it, and standing in line at every turn. And planes in Europe cost 3-4 times more than trains.

What about the car, convenient, always ready to go? So are trains. In Europe, rapid transit trains leave downtown every 10–30 minutes for the suburbs. If you decide on an impulse to visit another city, intercity trains depart hourly, often half-hourly. Then trains easily beat cars at average speeds from 100 mph to the TGV's 185.5 mph. Their tracks lead straight into the heart of the city with a clear right of way; expressways skirt around suburbs, then funnel your car into a snail-slow maze. And do you really want to vacation in a car, whiteknuckling for long hours on the highway, trying to read signs with one eye on the road, the other on the map?

In your own car the cost of gas (at $3-4 a gallon in Europe) may not be more than the train fare for the whole family. But when rental is added, you can do better on the train with reduced family fares. For one or two people, driving is sheer folly, especially in big cities; parking alone costs more than a tourist pass for unlimited use of the entire city transit system.

During the past 40 years Europeans have not only replaced their war-wrecked network, but built a modern system; one that can compete with the car and the plane, attracting passengers by offering more creature comforts aboard and more special services away from the trains. Rolling stock has been rejuvenated with new cars and fast engines, more and more of them electric-powered. Smooth welded rails and improved suspension systems provide a quiet and safe ride at higher speeds. The new developments were so impressive even twenty years ago that the U.S., once exporter of technology, bought French turbo trains. In 1955 speed records of 205 mph opened the way for passenger trains averaging 125 mph. Today the French TGV has pushed the record over 300 mph.

North Americans don't trust trains, and with reason. Their rail service may be better today than ten years ago, but far from what it could be, were it not treated as the Cinderella of transportation. Once there were grand expresses, reliable suburban trains and workhorses whistlestopping at all the small towns. One could travel anywhere in reasonable comfort and at convenient times. But then the freight-happy railways decided to get rid of passenger trains. Into the gap stepped the national rail passenger corporations, Amtrak in the U.S. and VIA Rail Canada. They have put in gleaming new trains, but not enough of them; the connections are not convenient, and the fares are high. They suffer from ineffi-cient management, overmanning, and road lobbies attacking from all direc-tions! North Americans deserve an economical, non-polluting, efficient, safe, comfortable transport system. Until they get their own, for a taste of how it could be, they come and try some of the good ones in Europe. This book was written to help in that.

The world of trains seems complicated to first-time users. Rail travel is a do-it-yourself job: you pick out your train from the timetable, get your ticket and reservation, look for the track or platform, find the train and search for your car and seat. If you also want to forward your bag, change money, and grab a snack, then departure becomes quite a task. At the station, as the experts cleave the crowd and grab the right train, you, a beginner, are still trying to sort out exits from entrances, wishing that someone would show you the way. I often felt that way until I had had enough and decided to take a short crash course in getting around.

When I began in 1979 there was no such course. I had to write the curriculum as I went, learning what was needed to cope. In the process I visited fifty-seven stations in fifteen countries as a "professional passenger" with a day in each place, to take an inventory of the services. To save time I traveled at night. My itinerary let me get a good night's sleep while going from one city to the next. I arrived in time for a shower and breakfast, then checked in my bag and, ready with notebook, did the rounds. Later I had time for a little sightseeing, a stop at the tourist office, a quiet hour in a cafe to go through my notes and have an aperitif; then dinner, reclaim the suitcase, and into bed on the next train out. Trains were my bedroom, stations my hotel. I lived on wheels for three months; covered over 25,000 miles, or once around the world; spent 530 hours in motion, 66 working days at stations, 45 nights in couchettes. Halfway through I took a vacation and, for sanity's sake, carefully avoided anything that rolled or whistled.

Five years later, then again in 1989, I was back for updates and rode the rails across Europe from Helsinki to Lisbon and back again.

It's a convincing testimony for trains that I still feel they are the only civilized way to travel. The answers to your next two questions are (1) no, I would not recommend such trips to everybody, (2) yes, I would and probably will do it again.

After this introduction it may come as a surprise that I am not a train buff. I have never taken a nostalgic museum ride with photo opportunities. The sound of a steam whistle leaves me cold; all I care about engines is that they should be quiet and clean—I am happiest with electrics. To the romantic clickety-clack of old tracks I prefer welded rails. I appreciate the fine craftsmanship in venerable wagons-lits, but favor the quiet of a new TEN sleeper.

To sum up, my interest in trains is that they are good transportation. They offer you more than just going from A to B: along the way you can sleep, dine, study for an exam, plan a company takeover, start a romance or make a phone call to end one. Life on fast tracks—enjoy it.

About this guide and how to use it

How can you find it if you don't know it's there? Visitors to Europe often miss out on the museum to see, the perfect hotel, the best fish soup in the country, and so on. Travelers often miss out on the perks and frills of rail travel, and suffer from being unprepared. Back home they can always buy a sandwich on the train, and a redcap takes the bags to the taxi. In Europe a family travels at half price, the train may have a fine restaurant on wheels or no food at all, and the last porter died but the railway will deliver baggage to the hotel.

This book is both a planning aid and on-the-spot guide to railways, cities, stations, and airports in Europe.

The choice of countries covers Western Europe and Hungary, where Eurailpasses are valid, and Britain where a BritRail Pass gets you around. We help you in all the important destination cities and their railway stations. The part on the 'great routes' cuts through borders, like the international trains, and suggests the fastest and most comfortable way to travel.

What did we leave out? Nostalgic rides and railway museums. This book is about travel today, not how it was. Rail fans should ask overseas railway agencies and tourist offices about steam-drawn excursions, usually not covered by regular tickets or passes.

What did we add? The airways to Europe and the airports where you arrive. Those complete this guide as a single source of information about European travel. We also describe shipping services, ferries and river boats, that complement or can be substituted for trains.

The information will help travelers from North and South America, Australia, and Japan, who are used to different railway systems. Many British and Irish readers may be familiar with European trains, but we hope to be of assistance to those who have difficulties finding out about reduced fares in the small-print introduction of a Portuguese or Norwegian timetable; they should skip the chapter on Britain and Ireland—or send us corrections.

The following is a summary and guide to the guide.

Part 1: Travelcraft introduces you to the moving world: how to plan, how to get there, and how to travel by train in Europe. We explain tickets, passes, reservations, baggage, timetables, additional services. Find out what you can expect on a train, at a station, in a sleeping car, what kind of passes and tickets there are, and how to say "first class" in Finnish.

Part 2: Travel manual contains everything you need to know, but didn't know where to ask—or couldn't speak the language. For each country you find a description of the railway, local information for each city, a map showing the principal rail routes from the city, floor plans of the major stations together with lists of services and their working hours, and the way through gateway airports.

The section on each **national railway** begins with an overview and an evaluation based on experience. The occasional criticism is not a sign of pique: it warns the uninitiated traveler what to expect and it may even prompt the improvement of a currently poor service.

Information: Sources at railway stations and aboard trains.

Schedule changes: Holidays when some trains may run at different times. Check a current timetable! For movable holidays see page 54.

Fares: Prices in local currency and in US dollars for tickets bought overseas.
Supplements: Increased fare on special or fast trains.
Reduced fares: Discounts for children, youths, seniors, families, individuals with low-fare cards, return tickets.
Go-as-you-please passes: International and national tourist passes.
Tickets: Rules for purchase, validation, stopover.
Reservations: Seat reservation conditions, time limits, fees.
Baggage: Forwarding, pickup and delivery, coins needed in lockers.
Meal services: The fare aboard trains and at stations.
Night travel: Accommodation in sleepers and couchettes.
Other services: Car and bicycle rental, train telephones, etc.
Assistance: Help for the handicapped; whom to contact in case of emergency.
City information is limited to what you need when you arrive (for sights, history, cuisine, and other information, take along a Berlitz travel guide).
Tourist information: City tourist offices.
City transit: How to use the local public transport, especially with tourist passes. Instead of prices, which may change, we list what passes save over single tickets.
Post office, telephone: Where to find permanent or late service.
Help in emergencies: Police, ambulance, physician, dentist, pharmacy on 24-hour duty, the lost property office.
Airport: The nearest international airport and how to get there.
Rail connections: Cities which can be reached by direct train in 5-6 hours, by day or overnight.
Boat connections: Ferries that connect to or substitute for trains.
For each **railway station** you find an inventory of services and facilities (shops, restaurants), their working hours and locations keyed to a floor plan. 'All hours' means service while the station is open (passengers with tickets may enter when the station is closed at night).
Travel center: Office for one-stop shopping: information, tickets, reservations, and other services.
Train information: Where to ask about schedules and fares.
Tickets, reservations: Inland and international services.
Baggage: Where to forward, pick up, or store baggage.
Lost & found: For property lost on the train or at the station.
Emergencies, first aid, police: Where to get help in a hurry.
Handicapped help: Where to request assistance.
Nursery: A place to change and feed babies. May also have a rest place for ill passengers.
Toilets, bath, shower, waiting room: In case you spend more than five minutes at the station or want to face the city refreshed.

Restaurants with table service, self service cafeterias, bars, buffets and kiosks for snacks and drinks.

Provisions, pharmacy, shopping: Where to find necessities in or near the station.

Tourist information, accommodation: The city tourist office at the station.

City transit information: Maps and passes for public transport.

Foreign exchange, post, telephone offices at the station.

To other stations, to airport: Best access from the station.

For the gateway airports, where you might arrive or leave, find a walk-through guide between plane and city, and a list of services and their locations.

Part 3: The **Great Routes** are the paths that travelers followed before there were rails, and where the great trains have run, some of them for a century. You'll find information on the quality of trains and on-board services, and recommendations when to take a day train for scenery and when to sleep through a long stretch. Read these before you buy your tickets so that you can plan the best trip.

Acknowledgments

The material for this guide was collected during many months of research. I received much-needed cooperation from the national railway companies, and want to thank those officers who helped my work with personal attention: Renate Pelz-Nakladal (Austria), Hugo Vanherle (Belgium), Seija Petman (Finland), Fridolin Schell (Germany), Annemieke Blom (The Netherlands), and Daniele Colomba (Switzerland).

Lufthansa German Airlines extended generous assistance by providing transatlantic transportation.

Travel in Europe was assisted by national railway companies, the Eurailpass Executive Committee, Silja Lines, and the KD German Rhine Line.

Toshiba Canada Ltd kindly provided computer equipment for organizing the data and preparing text en route.

I worked with a competent and helpful team at Berlitz Guides.

And thanks are due to Maggie MacLelland for her patience and encouragement.

G.P.

TRAVELCRAFT IN PLANNING

Planning a trip is a skill that leisure-lovers pursue as an art and timetable buffs raise to a science. It's best learned by planning, and then putting the plan into practice, but why not benefit from others' experience? Travelers love to talk about their exploits and their own clever, practical ways of coping on the road. Your friends will overwhelm you with advice. Many travelers also write, as proven by the crowded travel shelves in bookstores. You can study your way through Europe, spending many delightful winter evenings reading about it, to find the place familiar when you get there.

Consider how many questions you ask when buying a stereo or trading in your car. A trip that costs anywhere from $2,000 to your particular ceiling deserves to be looked at just as carefully.

If you want a really leisurely trip, work hard on planning it; then you can relax when on the road. Don't make your itinerary too tight; if you leave it flexible then little hitches don't wreck the entire schedule. Expect to miss a train or two, and have some idea of what to do when stranded in Metz at midnight. Flexibility, a blank day or two, also gives you the luxury of doing just what you please.

When should you start getting information and making plans? If you travel once a year, then start a year ahead.

Homework: guide books, timetables
Bookstores have stacks of nostalgic picture books on steam engines, but only a few guides to the use of trains—how to be a passenger. Among these, the upmarket writers disdain cheap couchettes and don't list discounts, assuming that everyone has a Eurailpass. Others write for backpackers living on pizza and burgers. Some pad their text with timetables that go out of date in months.

For information about what to see and do when you get there, consult a Berlitz travel guide. In pocket-sized form, the guides contain sightseeing itineraries, historical notes, tips on food and drink, data on climate, useful addresses and even vocabularies. The Berlitz Phrase Books (similarly compact) provide introductions into the culture, customs, and cuisine of each country, in addition to their comprehensive vocabularies on all needed subjects.

Excellent and free sources of maps and brochures are the national tourist offices and airlines in your home country. Get what you can at home, do your reading, then choose the most useful to take with you. Once you know where you want to go, it's time to get down to some serious planning with a timetable. Read TIMETABLES (page 52).

Advance information about railways

Few travel agencies keep their railway information up to date. Contact one of the European railways' offices with questions about routes, fares, passes, and for general tourist information. You can also buy tickets and make reservations through them.

US East

BritRail Travel International	630 Third Avenue, New York, NY 10017. Tel.: 212/599-5400.
Italian State Railways	666 Fifth Avenue, New York, NY 10103. Tel.: 212/397-9300.
French Rail, Inc.	610 Fifth Avenue, New York, NY 10020. Tel.: 212/582-2816.
GermanRail	625 Statler Office Bldg. Boston, MA 02116. Tel.: 617/542-0677.
GermanRail	747 Third Avenue, New York, NY 10017. Tel.: 212/308-3100.

US Central

Italian State Railways	500 N. Michigan Avenue #1310, Chicago, IL 60611. Tel.: 312/644-6651.
French Rail, Inc	11 East Adams Street, Chicago, IL 60603. Tel.: 312/427-8691.
GermanRail	9575 W. Higgins Road, #505, Rosemont, IL 60018. Tel.: 312/692-4209.

US West

BritRail Travel International	6800 South Hope Street, #603, Los Angeles, CA 90017-4697. Tel.: 213/624-8787.
Italian State Railways	15760 Ventura Blvd, #819, Los Angeles, CA 91436 Tel.: 213/728-7245.
French Rail, Inc.	360 Post Street, #606, San Francisco, CA 94108. Tel.: 415/982-1993.
French Rail, Inc.	9465 Wilshire Blvd., #713, Beverly Hills, CA 90212. Tel.:213/272-7967.
GermanRail	11933 Wilshire Blvd., Los Angeles, CA 90025. Tel.: 213/479-2772.

US South

BritRail Travel International	Cedar Maple Plaza, #210, 2305 Cedar Springs, Dallas, TX 75201. Tel.: 214/748-0860.
French National Railroads	2121 Ponce de Leon Blvd, Coral Gables, FL 33134. Tel.: 035/445-8648.
GermanRail	3400 Peachtree Road NE, Lenox Towers, #1229, Atlanta, GA 30326. Tel: 404/266-9555.

Canada

BritRail	94 Cumberland Street, #601, Toronto, ON M5R 1A3. Tel.: 416/929-3333.
BritRail	409 Granville Street, Vancouver, BC V6C 1T2. Tel.: 604/683-6896.
Italian State Railways	2055 Peel Street, #102, Montreal, PQ H3A 1V4. Tel.: 514/845-9101.
Italian State Railways	13 Balmuto Street, Toronto, ON M4Y 1W4. Tel.: 416/927-7712.
French Rail, Inc.	1500 Stanley Street, Montreal, PQ H3A 1R3. Tel.: 514/288-8255.
French Rail, Inc.	55 University, #600, Toronto, ON M5J 2E7. Tel.: 416/368-8639.
French Rail, Inc.	409 Granville Street, #452, Vancouver, BC V6C 1T2. Tel.:604/688-6707.
GermanRail	1290 Bay Street, Toronto, ON M5R 2C3. Tel.: 416/968-3272.

Britain

French National Railways	179 Piccadilly, London W1V OBA. Tel.: 1/493-9731.
Italian State Railways	10 Charles II Street, London SW1Y 4AB. Tel: 1/930-6722.

Other countries

Australia	Italian State Railways in Adelaide, Brisbane, Melbourne, Sydney.
	Thomas Cook in Adelaide, Brisbane, Charleston, Geelong, Hobart, Melbourne, Perth, Sydney.
New Zealand	Thomas Cook in Auckland.
Japan	Japan Travel Bureau in Kobe, Kyoto, Nagoya, Sapporo, Sendai, Tokyo.

When to go and where

In the spring or fall, air fares and hotel prices drop, and both cities and trains are cooler and less crowded. In July and August, Europe is on vacation and train seats are reserved months in advance.

Visit a few places each time. Those constantly on the move retain only confused, blurred images from their whirlwind city tours. But a few days in a city lets you explore and enjoy it fully. And it's more pleasant not to have to live out of a suitcase, but to unpack and settle down for a while.

Big cities can be expensive and hectic. A nearby small town has its own quiet charm and you can better appreciate the attractions of the metropolis on daily visits from a more relaxed place. Rapid transit trains quickly reach the city centre; for example, the S-Bahn from Mainz or Wiesbaden to Frankfurt, the RER from Saint-Germain-en-Laye to Paris.

Day or night travel

To decide whether to take a night train, figure out the total travel time. To the train time add two hours for packing, checking out, getting to the station; add more time to reach the hotel at your destination. If it is 350 to 400 miles away, you'll spend most of your waking hours getting there. But if you take a night train, you can add that day to your vacation. For example, going from Frankfurt to Paris you should start at 8 to catch the 10:00 train. You arrive at 16:50 when the thundering herd of commuters fills the station. Then you crawl through rush-hour traffic to reach your next residence at about 6 p.m. The day is gone. But if you take a night train, you can add that day to your vacation. Leave Frankfurt at 22:52 and arrive in Paris at 7:04, ready for a new day.

The cost? While a single compartment is an expensive luxury, a double or tourist triple may not cost more than a hotel. A couchette can save a lot of money. Add a few dollars for a shower at the station in the morning. See NIGHT TRAVEL (page 38).

Choosing first or second class

The choice between first and second class depends not so much on your budget, but on the country where you travel. In northern Europe the new second-class cars are as comfortable as old first-class ones. In the more crowded south, first class is often a must unless you want to learn to hate trains and your fellow man. Fortunately, fares are lower there and the money that only buys second class in the north will get you comparable comfort on first around the Mediterranean.

Pass or tickets?

The great advantage of a pass is the convenience: hop on a train when you like, backtrack or go in a circle, without the limitation of point-to-point tickets. You can also save money: for example, two long trips between Hamburg and Rome can cost you as much as a two-week Eurailpass. On the other hand, if you make short trips or spend several days in one place, the cost of the pass per trip works out to be high. With the appropriate ticket, especially if you travel with family or a small group (as few as three people), you benefit from reduced fares. Youths under 26 should check low-priced point-to-point tickets sold by Transalpino Ltd. (See FARES, page 41). For details on international passes, see PASSES TO GO AS YOU PLEASE (page 45). National passes and reductions are described in each country's chapter.

Advance tickets and reservations

Advance purchase saves waiting in line at stations. Tickets are sold six months in advance by overseas railway offices but at a premium, since Eurailtariff, calculated in US dollars, may be higher than local fares (see FARES, page 41). It's just as easy to invest an hour or so at the start of your trip and buy all tickets—and make reservations—at a big European station with competent and multilingual staff.

You can also reserve seats, couchettes or sleepers several months in advance and should do so if you travel during the summer or at holiday times. See RESERVATIONS (page 49), NIGHT TRAVEL (page 38), and country chapters for local conditions.

Health

Napoleon's army traveled on its stomach and so do tourists who worry about food and water when going abroad. They are partly right: plagued by an upset stomach is no way to spend a holiday. But Europe is not a jungle; the water is fine, and no one with normal care should fall victim to any bug. Read about medication in WHAT TO PACK (page 16). If you are not in good health, contact one of the organizations which supply lists of English-speaking physicians around the world.

Help for the handicapped

All railways provide special facilities but to varying degrees. They supply personal assistance through railway staff, police, Red Cross or similar organizations. Most stations loan wheelchairs, many have lifts or ramps. Many trains have space for wheelchairs. Some Scandinavian trains even have compartments with non-allergenic bedding. We have tried to list the available services and how to request them at each railway and station. But the best way is to make advance arrangements; that's how the railways prefer it to provide good service. Send an itinerary to each railway, they will be prepared to assist you.

Taking off

Make a list of what to do before departure, don't try to remember a dozen things when you are about to lock the door. An idea worth trying is to start your vacation a day early. Say goodbye, drop the routine, check out, relax. Go to a movie, eat out (don't drink too much), have a good sleep. This will help you adjust to a different pace. The break will do wonders to ease jet lag and help you cope with the demands of the first hectic day in another land.

What to pack

Even the most seasoned travelers tend to carry too much. You repeatedly trim the list of essentials, only to find after the trip that several items were never used.

It's wise to be prepared for emergencies but silly to gear for a survival exercise when going to Europe for a few weeks. Where trains go, there are shops. Saving weight should start with small things; ounces multiply rapidly to pounds with every minute of carrying the bag. Only four aspirins need to be carried, because by the time more are needed, there'll be a place to get them. Of course, aspirins are nothing, but a glass bottle weighs a lot more than a plastic pack.

Clothes

Making a list will save money you would spend on forgotten things, and save time and nerves in the last minutes. Write down what you wear in a week. Combine items: you can use your raincoat as bathrobe, sandals as slippers, T-shirts as pajama tops. Have enough underwear to last between laundry stops. Forget the advances of modern chemistry: synthetics next to the skin will make you hot and itchy during a day of touring around; wear wool and cotton. Shirts and blouses of mixed polyester are comfortable and easy to take care of. Sweaters should be mostly wool, especially when going near lakes or the sea. Slacks, skirts and coats should be synthetic to resist creasing and soiling.

Toilet articles

Instead of family-size jars, buy shampoo, toothpaste, and detergent in small travel packs (they are more available in Europe), or transfer some into suitable containers.

Medication

Your resistance tends to be lower while traveling and you may encounter new varieties of bugs. The best basic defense is vitamins. Carry aspirins, Band-Aids, antacid, anti-diarrhea tablets and, since most people suffer from the opposite problem, a mild laxative. No sedatives unless prescribed! A muscle relaxant like Gravol works wonders against tension, fatigue-induced headache, and motion sickness. If you wear glasses, you should always carry a spare pair since it may take several days to replace lost or broken ones.

Practical things

A Swiss army knife. A small fork lets you enjoy a salad in a civilized manner. A drinking glass, even a plastic one, makes beer or the local plonk taste better. An alarm clock is essential to avoid worry about missing trains. Pocket timer/calculators have calendar, clock and alarm, and are useful to convert metric measures and currencies. Dedicated train riders will pick a model with 24-hour clock. A small penlight will be handy to find light-switches. And always have a supply of paper tissues—they have a multitude of functions!

The office
Passport, tickets, credit cards, traveler's checks, ready cash in foreign money, timetable, guidebook, phrase book, map. Keep what you don't need in the suitcase, where it's less easy to lose.

If you travel with a Eurailpass, keep the counterfoil card separately (as you do traveler's check records); write down the name and cable address of the agency where you bought it, in case you need to get a replacement.

Photography
Serious photographers never listen and will suffer under tons of equipment. Others will be sensible enough to take a small camera and a lightweight flash. An excellent aid is a camera clamp which substitutes for a tripod. The think-small principle could be relaxed when packing film, which can be very expensive in Europe (both Kodak and Fuji are imported). Customs permit a 'reasonable quantity,' which is interpreted liberally to mean several dozen rolls.

Money
The safest way to carry money is in traveler's checks; the 1% fee is worth the security. You'll have to pay, though, for cashing them. While banks have better rates than hotels or shops (if you want cash and not just to pay for services or goods), they charge commission for exchange. The cost varies with the strength of the local currency: in stable Switzerland and Germany the commission is nominal, in inflation-prone countries high; for unexplained reasons you'll get gouged (up to 9%) in Britain and France. But traveler's checks in the country's currency are cashed without commission. When dealing with a *bureau de change* at an airport or station, find out the cost first; some charge atrocious commissions. Some of your traveler's checks should be in low denominations: if you need just a little money before departure (to get the baggage out of storage or reserve a seat) and have to cash a large check, then you lose money when exchanging the leftover in the next country.

Credit cards are widely accepted, not only in hotels and boutiques but sometimes even at unlikely places like street stalls. In most countries the ticket windows at railway stations accept Visa, Master Charge, American Express, Access and Eurocard. You can also get local currency from automatic teller machines, but your card may not work in some countries; phone your credit card center to find out in advance.

Many railway ticket offices accept foreign currency for tickets and give you enough change in local money to buy a drink on the train.

When exchanging cash, you usually gain when you sell foreign money for local and lose when buying foreign. But before leaving a country you should buy some currency of the next country. You'll need coins on arrival: before you can get to a bank you may need to feed a pay phone or a locker, or buy a tram ticket. Having money at hand will save a lot of tramping about weighed down with baggage. The best idea is to have a packet of coins before you leave home. Some banks and exchange offices (like Deak) sell change in an array of different currencies. And you can keep leftover coins for the next trip.

Passports, visas

A valid passport is required in all Western European countries (ID-cards are sufficient for citizens of the EC countries). Visas are not needed by citizens of Australia, Canada, and the United States.

Suitcases and bag

Maximum two suitcases and that's already stretching it. One case and a spacious shoulder bag should hold everything and leave you one hand free to open doors. The shoulder bag should have pockets for your train guide, a tourist guide, map, camera, and a section big enough to hold the makings of a picnic meal. The suitcase shouldn't be larger than 26" or it won't fit luggage racks nor lockers. Soft sides pack better than hard ones. Get one with built-in wheels; strap-on wheels are too cumbersome. Backpacks belong in the hills. They take up more space than is allotted to a passenger and getting them up steps and through doors usually entails battering innocent bystanders. If you insist on looking rugged, find a portage pack that may be carried on the back or by its top handle.

Across the Atlantic

If you have a lot of time set aside for travel, you might want to shop around for a freighter that takes passengers. If you have a lot of money as well as time, you should take a cruise ship and sail on to the next chapter. The rest of us will fly.

Until the return of airships with real beds, there won't be true luxury travel by air. Sitting up all night is a pain, not much eased—perhaps postponed—by champagne. The best you can do is save on the fare for a comfortable hotel on your first day in Europe to recover from jet lag.

About fares

The airlines' fare structure could be learned by a diligent travel agent in a few months—if it didn't change during that time. It's a confusing system: the cost of a ticket depends on season (high, low and shoulder), when it is bought (immediate or advance), then the day of departure (weekday, Friday, weekend), length of stay, and day of return. The regulations are modified as competition demands—and are put aside when an airline panics and announces a seat sale. The following, though, should give you a general idea of what to choose—subject to change. First, some fictitious numbers, in dollars, for comparison (two figures where low and high season fares are different):

SuperAPEX	550–770
APEX	720–930
Excursion	900–1040
Full fare economy	1800
Business class	1900
First class	3400

High season is from mid-May to mid-September and the Christmas-New Year period; low season is the rest of the year.

Without an expense account, forget full fare. Savings begin with excursion. With an excursion fare the minimum overseas stay is two weeks, the maximum six months. Up to two stopovers are allowed at some extra cost. No advance purchase is necessary and you can cancel without penalty.

Airlines make more money with full planes and can afford to drop the price of tickets bought in advance. So plan ahead and reserve early. At APEX (Advance Purchase EXcursion) and SuperAPEX fares the minimum stay is seven days, the maximum is six months. No stopovers are allowed. With APEX you may go and return with different airlines, and have to pay the full cost within a week of reservation; SuperAPEX is usually by the same airline for both trips, you have to make a deposit when you reserve and pay the balance a week before departure. A change of dates costs about $100.

APEX fares apply from anywhere in North America to any international airport in Europe, even if there are no direct flights; you take a connecting flight from the airport where you first land in Europe. For example, you can go to Venice with Lufthansa, changing planes in Frankfurt, or with British Airways via London. Stopovers are not allowed when you change planes.

When business is slow, airlines put on seat sales, discounting fares to below SuperAPEX price for a limited period, usually a month or two. These are advertised about two months in advance. If you reserved earlier for that period, your fare should be reduced to the seat-sale price. The minimum stay is usually seven days, the maximum about a month but you must return within the seat sale period. You can find even cheaper special discount flights through student travel agencies and stand-by clubs; read the tiniest ads in the newspapers' travel sections. You'll get the best price, if not the best service, although you'll need to be flexible in your dates and times.

Open jaw

With the 'open jaw' option you can return from a different city from where you landed, even by a different airline. The advantage is that you can travel on the ground in one direction and not have to double back to catch the return flight. The cost is the average of the two APEX return fares. Find out about the various fares first, as it may influence your choice of cities for arrival and departure.

Reserving and buying the ticket

With all due respect to hardworking travel agents, few of them are up to date on the best fares; blame the information lag on the airlines' constant rule changes. The best way is to deal directly with the airline. Phone late at night when the agent has time to look up the various routes and special fares. Make your reservation directly with the airline. You'll get a file number with which you can pay for your ticket at any travel agent. If you like one, pay there, so he can get the commission. An advantage of reserving with the airline is that if their clerk quotes a lower price by mistake, they'll honor it; if the travel agent makes a mistake, you pay.

Read the ticket carefully and have errors corrected immediately. Write down the number of the ticket, so a duplicate can be issued if you lose it.

Baggage

The baggage allowance on transatlantic flights is by piece and size. You are allowed two pieces, the size is calculated by volume; any reasonable suitcase you can lift should be within the limit. You may carry one bag aboard but only if it fits under the seat or in the overhead compartment. Reserve this for valuables, camera and other fragile items; find space for toilet bag and some clothes for the first day in case your suitcase does not turn up (that is more likely to happen coming back; European airports keep better track of baggage). If your case is damaged, report it to your airline's desk or the airport baggage office before leaving the baggage pick-up area. Note that on most flights within Europe a weight limit applies, usually 20 kg (44 lbs). Check this in advance and avoid the high cost of overweight baggage.

Seat selection

The basic choice is smoker/nonsmoker. Then you can ask for aisle, center or window seat, close to the movie screen, over the wing, as you like. Note, however, that families with small children are usually seated near a bulkhead; you may want to sit elsewhere.

Special requirements

All special requests should be made as far in advance as possible, at least two days before departure both on the outgoing and returning flights. Handicapped or elderly passengers and mothers with infants get assistance at boarding and arrival, including being driven in electric carts to and from the plane at large airports. For the handicapped, most airlines prefer to supply a wheel-chair, but the passenger's wheelchair will be carried without charge. Special meals include infant, kosher, Moslem, low sodium, diabetic, low cholesterol, low calorie, Hindu (vegetarian or not), hypoglycemic, pure vegetarian, and gluten-free. We have heard of some non-religious passengers who asked for a kosher meal and were served some tasty smoked-meat sandwiches, just to get away from the usual tired chicken.

Coping with jet lag

Your body follows a rhythm. Physical and mental functions wax and wane during the day/night cycle. Crossing time zones too fast for adaptation disturbs this pattern. You cannot avoid jet lag completely, but there are ways to lessen it. Here is some advice from the physicians of the Lufthansa Medical Center.

Adjust the sleep period to the time at destination. Go to sleep and get up daily one hour earlier when going east, or later when going west, working up to the number of time zones to be crossed. On Days 3 and 1 before the flight, have high-protein breakfasts and lunches, followed by high-carbohydrate dinners. On Day 2 before and on the day of the flight keep meals light. On the last day avoid carbohydrates till 6 p.m. Start the day on arrival with a high-protein breakfast.

Jet lag is also affected by eating and drinking on the way. Eat lightly and avoid hard drinks. Enjoy some champagne but drink mostly juices and water to replace fluids lost to the dry air—about 3% humidity as opposed to 30% on the ground. One trick is to breath occasionally through a wet face towel: this revives parched mucous tissue. Above all, don't smoke.

After the flight the body's inner watch must be set to the new time. Rest helps, so get sufficient sleep on the first night after arrival. An easily digestible carbohydrate meal and/or muscle relaxation exercises will help you sleep, but if the body rebels, use a short-acting sleeping pill. The minimum recovery time may be calculated from a formula published by the ICAO:

Departure time coefficient	+	Travel time 2	+	Crossed time zones	+	Arrival time coefficient	=	Rest time (in tenths of day)

Time periods:	Departure time coefficient	Arrival time coefficient
08:00 to 12:00	0	4
12:00 to 18:00	1	2
18:00 to 22:00	3	0
22:00 to 01:00	4	1
01:00 to 08:00	3	3

For example, if you depart New York at 18:30 (3 points), fly for $7\,^1/2$ hours (3.75) crossing 5 time zones (5), and arrive in Frankfurt at 8:00 (4), the total is 15.75 points, equaling over a day and a half. The return flight leaves at 10:00 and arrives at 12:00; the count is 10.5, little over one day. But you may recover even faster after westbound flights which give you a longer day; this is because the day/night cycle of the body is naturally longer than 24 hours. The time varies, of course, with age and health. For full recovery you may need a day for every two hours of time change.

If you take medication, you should adjust the dosage to accommodate the changed intervals between administrations. Your physician should prescribe an intermediate adjusting dose to be taken at the normal interval after the last pre-flight dose. The amount should be lower than the normal when going eastbound, higher on westbound trips. After arrival, medication may be taken at the usual hours by local time.

Travelcraft en route

You board the Riviera Express in Brussels at six in the evening, finish your dinner in Luxembourg at nine, get ready for bed in Metz at 10:30, turn over in Basel at two a.m., and arrive next morning in Milan. In one night the train takes you through five countries.

You seldom notice borders when you ride a train. Sometimes, while standing in the station, your train twitches when engines are switched; then, under way again, between two stops—and two countries—an official saunters through the car to glance at passports. Long before Europe started planning its 1992 union, the railways formed a network without borders. This makes it easy to learn travelcraft that you can put to good use in most countries (find the details about national railways in PART 2).

Information at stations

Self-confidence is not a good trait in a traveler. It's better to be dumb and ask everything twice than to miss a train. Help is there for the asking.

The big blue letter **i** marks the information office where you find multilingual staff and brochures of train schedules and fares. This office sometimes also handles reservations and international tickets, and can get very crowded. At many stations information officers, distinguishable by an orange or yellow band on their caps, are positioned near entrances and on platforms. They help with departure times and track numbers, but for complicated questions about routes and connections the main office is the place.

Timetables are displayed on posters, yellow for departing and white for arriving trains. Track numbers may change, so check your train on the large indicator board in the station concourse. There may also be overhead indicators on each platform, showing the next train's departure, route and destination. Also on the platforms, boards show the composition of major trains, where the different classes, types of car (compartment or saloon) and dining car are. If you stand under the letter sign that corresponds to the position of the car you want to board, it will stop right in front of you.

Unlike airlines, railways don't use English as a common language. But English is spoken in northern Europe by all staff dealing with tourists. In France, some French may be needed away from the major routes or indeed in Paris if you run into an uncooperative clerk, French can come in useful in Italy and Portugal. Spain can still be difficult.

The international language of the railways is pictograms. Symbols have been replacing written signs to solve the language problem. Germany, Switzerland, the Benelux and Scandinavian countries have almost entirely dispensed with words, and others gradually follow.

Tickets and reservations

Check the details on your ticket and reservation. If the clerk made a mistake, he can correct it immediately on the computer; trying to argue it out on the train may not work.

In most countries tickets are not checked at the station but by the conductor aboard the train. If the ticket is not valid (not dated for travel on that day or not validated), the conductor collects a stiff surcharge, a fine by any other name. However, if you didn't have time to buy a ticket before boarding but volunteer to pay before the conductor asks you, there's only a small service charge. Seat and couchette reservations also cost slightly more when made on board.

Boarding your train

Most long-distance trains are split several times along the way, and adjacent cars may end up at opposite ends of the country. Find the car with the number on your reservation. If you don't have a reserved seat, check the route board on the side of the car to make sure that you sit in the car that goes to your destination. For a list of possibly confusing city names in English and the local language, see page 55.

Information on board

Conductors are seldom great linguists. If you have questions, northern and central Europe present few problems, but elsewhere you may have to find a fellow passenger who wants to practice his English.

On EuroCity and InterCity trains loudspeakers announce the stations in advance in several languages. There are also leaflets in every compartment that give the full schedule of the train: arrival times at all stops, departure times of connecting trains, services on board (restaurant, telephone, secretary).

Bed and board
See MEALS (page 35) and NIGHT TRAVEL (page 38).

Passenger etiquette
Your fellow passengers are your temporary roommates. "Do unto others..." should be your motto. Show the consideration you expect for yourself.

Your ticket entitles you to a seat and the space just above and below it for your baggage; don't crowd out the others. Extra baggage should be forwarded.

Smokers and non-smokers are separated on trains; reserved seats are assigned accordingly. Since one of non-smokers' complaints is the persistent smell, you are not allowed to smoke in a non-smoking section even when alone. Smoking in dining cars is allowed only at certain tables and never during meal times. In sleeping and couchette cars there is no smoking in the compartments when the beds are made up for the night.

Use the ashtrays and wastebaskets. Throwing anything out of the window is dangerous and can result in a stiff fine.

Of course, you personally would never do any of these things, but while you are not a boor nor a fool, a surprising number of your fellow tourists become one or the other as soon as they leave home. Perhaps you could help them with their manners.

After arrival: city transit
We suggest a good look at the city pages in PART 2. Travel agents and writers seldom suggest the use of public transport; they either don't know about it or simply assume that everyone wants to crawl bumper-to-bumper through narrow streets in a taxi or the obligatory rented car.

Consider the alternative. Buses, trams, and metro usually run from about 5:00 until after midnight; some provide limited service throughout the night. The lines cover the city and extend through the suburbs practically into the countryside. These extensions often belong to the railway. Municipal and national rail services are integrated in rapid transit systems with easy transfers between lines. Passengers can use the same ticket or pass to get to the center from 25 to 30 miles away, and then move about above or below ground as they please.

Single tickets are expensive to discourage cash payment on buses and trams: it wastes the drivers' time and slows down traffic. But regular passengers never pay the high single fare. They buy blocks of tickets for six to twelve rides at up to 60% discount.

The best deals are the tourist passes for unlimited travel on all lines. A 24-hour pass usually costs the equivalent of four trips. It will pay for itself if you visit only two sights a day, and save quite a bit of money if you are the mobile type. A great advantage is the simplicity of use: once you have bought the pass at a tourist or transport office or a vending machine—and validated it—the city is yours to ride in without further formalities.

Most trams and buses don't have conductors. Passengers without tickets board in front and pay the driver, others enter in the middle or the back and validate their cards or passes in punch-clocks next to each door. It seems easy to slip in without a ticket, or save it for another time. But the honor system gets an occasional close look by plainclothes inspectors. Playing dumb or being truly ignorant of the language is no escape: the culprit is handed a folder which explains in several languages why he is charged 10 or 20 times the normal fare.

Air connections

Many cities have direct plane-to-train connections, saving you the bother of bus transfer. At Amsterdam, Frankfurt, Geneva, London Gatwick, Zurich and other gateways to Europe, passengers can board trains an escalator ride away from the arrival hall. From some airports you can even forward your luggage to anywhere in Europe as soon as you step off the plane or, going home, have your suitcases checked at any train station to meet you at the airport.

Cities without rail links usually run trams, metro or buses as inexpensive alternatives to airport limousines.

Telephone

Long-distance calls may be made from pay phones, including those on trains. Have a stack of coins at hand to pay as you talk: there is no operator to grant you extra seconds, the automatic timer will cut you off after the warning signal. Or use a telephone card which is magnetically coded so that the phone subtracts the charge second by second as you talk; you can use the card for several calls. The phone warns you to insert a new card when the full value is used up. Cards are sold at post and telephone offices, kiosks, and some railway ticket windows.

If you don't trust yourself with unfamiliar automats, go to a post or telephone office where the operator will place a long-distance call for you and collect the charge afterwards. Beware of calling from hotels—they collect a generous surcharge for the service.

And after...

Personal experience is the best teacher. But there is so much to learn on a trip that many of the little details may be forgotten, so it is a good idea to keep some record. Pick up pamphlets at the information offices and add your own notes on the margins. Or scribble in this book. The reminders of pitfalls and escape routes will help you plan an even smoother journey next time.

Trains

The quality of European train travel falls somewhere between the fantasy of the marble bathtub in Lucius Beebe's private carriage and the reality of cracked plastic seats in commuter cars. You may find the latter on some branch lines, but most European trains surpass any jet in comfort. Of course, modernization allows fewer frills—no bathtubs, although some new sleeping cars do have showers.

Railway cars have been reshaped to answer the demands of efficiency, but still offer traditional comfort and space. Economy demanded more passengers per car, so seats in the open-plan French *Corail* and some other new models face one way, in the anti-social pattern of airline seating. The British build saloon cars of a friendlier type: four or two seats face each other with a table between them. When the tables are set, the place converts into a spacious dining car; food is served from a galley in the next car. In most Continental carriages, only in the middle of the car can you find facing seats (try to reserve these if you travel with friends). Traditional, cozy compartments are getting harder to find except on German InterCity trains. There are six seats per compartment in either class, a welcome change from the eight seats in old second class.

Cars built in the last 10 to 15 years have far more space than airplanes but similar comforts: adjustable seats, individual reading lights, carpeted floors. They are air-conditioned and sound-proofed with double-sealed windows. Automatic doors add convenience and safety. Improved suspensions contribute to comfortable travel even on old tracks. But the rails, too, are being rebuilt. Gone is the nostalgic clickety-clack; on the welded rails the sound now is the swoosh of steel on steel, conducive to quiet conversation or sound sleep.

Steam power has disappeared from all commercial service, except for a few museum trains. And, at the rate electrification progresses, in a decade or two the nostalgic will have to look hard for a diesel engine. Huffing and puffing behind the faster and stronger electrics, the diesels will survive only until the overhead wires go up everywhere. Travel on the main lines, mostly already electrified, has quietened down a lot and the air smells better (a Deutsche Bundesbahn poster shows two electric locomotives under the slogan, "Our engines have given up smoking").

Distances and speeds

The speed of a train depends much on the demography of its route. In France, where population centers are far apart, *rapides* run non-stop for hundreds of kilometers and you may have to change to a local train if your destination is a smaller town. In Germany, cities are closer together and the InterCity trains halt often; travel time is longer but the stops are more convenient. EuroCity trains sprint through countries to stop only in the capitals and major cities.

Short distances around metropolises and between small towns are served by local or suburban trains. These are often diesel or electric railcars with one-class seating. On short runs there is no need for services aboard, although in the morning and afternoon a mini-bar trolley may dispense refreshments.

The sensible tourist never hurries, but taking a slow regional train is a mistake. These omnibuses are not for leisure travel, they merely serve as point-to-point transport. Try to catch a long-distance runner at the nearest stop; it will have more spacious seating, a buffet or dining car.

Long distance expresses

We may reckon the golden age of rail from October 4, 1883, the day the Orient Express first departed from Paris to arrive 81 $^1/_2$ hours later in Istanbul. The imagination and perseverance of Georges Nagelmackers, founder of the Compagnie Internationale des Wagons-Lits et des Grands Expresses Européens, had made it possible to cross frontiers without changing trains along the route. Soon a whole parade of grand expresses conveyed tourists, royalty, and businessmen along the length and breadth of the continent. Engines were slow then and the journeys lengthy, but trains offered all the comforts of a better hotel, much appreciated on voyages of well over a day and a night.

Paradoxically, the increase of speed contributed to the demise of the transcontinentals. As travel times grew shorter, more and more passengers could reach their destinations within a day. Most of the legendary hotels-on-wheels have disappeared.

The surviving international expresses now stop more often to serve the smaller towns. At night they crawl or even halt for an hour: they are timed to arrive at a convenient hour in the morning. Night trains are still the choice for destinations 10 to 12 hours' travel away. But economy reduced the luxuries of old. It has become forbiddingly expensive to haul a dining car with a full staff outside meal times. Night trains that leave after dinner time and arrive just before breakfast may not have any meal service. Even during the daytime one cannot rely on regular service. Who hasn't heard horror stories of vacationers waving money in vain, the only supplies on board being crackers and mineral water? Consult the fine print of footnotes in the timetable to see what is offered.

The old cars are not what they once were but they are spacious and comfortable. Regular expresses are appreciated by the nostalgic and, supplements being small or nil, by the budget-minded.

InterCity trains

A practical alternative to driving even short distances between major cities is offered by frequent and fast trains that deliver passengers from downtown to downtown. The best example is the German InterCity Network. Passengers may choose leisure or work en route, have a meal or a drink, dictate letters to the train secretary, send telegrams, make phone calls, order a rented car to wait on arrival or reserve a seat on another train. There are hourly trains from every city of importance to every other, from six in the morning till eleven at night. Most IC trains are timed to meet at junctions, and since they always stop at designated IC platforms, changing trains is more convenient than transferring in a subway: usually a matter of walking a few feet across the platform.

Other countries operate similar services, differing only in frequency according to local demands, usually hourly or even every half hour at peak times. In France, the *trains d'affaires* used to be bunched in the morning and afternoon, but the TGV runs hourly. Some intercity networks send trains across borders: Basel is included in the German, Brussels in the Netherlands' system. All InterCity trains carry two classes. The supplement includes the fee for reservations; seats are assigned automatically when tickets are issued.

In Memoriam: Trans-Europ-Expresses

The train of kings and king of trains, the Orient Express died in the sixties. But pretenders to the throne were already born in 1954: the Trans-Europ-Expresses, brain children of Dr. den Hollander, president of the Netherlands Railways, answered the need of the newly forming European Community for fast international passenger transport. These trains could compete for the top of the market: the VIP or businessman willing to pay premium fare for the kind of speed, comfort and convenience that until then only airlines could supply.

TEEs sped across borders as passport and customs checks were done aboard. Railways cooperated to move the trains through Europe without change of cars or engines and tackled the problem of outdated rolling stock. To be awarded TEE status, a train had to meet strict standards of passenger comfort and safety at high speeds.

In the race to supply the best, a new generation of luxury trains was born. Italy, for example, followed up on the futuristic Settebello with state-of-the-art *gran confort* stock, still in service as InterCity trains. They are fully air-conditioned and soundproofed. Outside doors are remote controlled, those between cars open automatically. Venetian blinds between the panes of sealed double windows are raised and lowered with the flip of a switch. Compartments have plate-glass sliding doors, dimmable ceiling lights, reading lights, carpeting and fine upholstery.

More important than luxury was speed and reliability. TEEs had priority and 'green roads': no red lights along the way. The railways put their effort into maintenance and not making excuses. The trains moved, and there were no hard-luck stories about frozen switches, hot boxes or power losses.

But TEEs were expensive, both to operate and to ride. Because of the high fare—first class plus supplement—they often ran empty. A multi-thousand horse-power engine would pull a dozen cars with one or two businessmen or

Eurailpassing vacationer in each compartment. Their total fares couldn't have paid for the energy to air-condition the train, let alone move it. The taxpayers footed the bill, even though the typical prosperous TEE patron didn't need social assistance to buy comfort. Operating exclusive glamour trains at public expense couldn't be justified. Railway managements realized this and cut the all-first-class trains. In 1980 there were 36 TEEs, 14 in 1984. In 1989 the last four ran in inland service in France.

EuroCity trains

When someone hooked second-class cars to TEEs, the international intercity trains were born. Many of these ran on the previous TEE routes and used the original rolling stock. But often the IC name, a mark of quality, was misapplied. The IC-Ligure, once a proud TEE, ran any old cars and slowly; a Madrid-Valencia train was named *Interciudad* with no perceptible increase in speed. Something had to be done.

In 1988, the UIC, the organization of European railways, introduced EuroCity, the designation for international trains that replaced the TEEs and international ICs. These also include the French TGVs that run into Switzerland and several night trains.

To qualify for EuroCity designation, a train must meet strict quality standards. The minimum average speed is 90 km/h, stops at stations no more than five minutes. Delays up to five minutes are tolerated, but the train must keep to schedule on at least 80% of all trips. Cars must be less than 15 years old, or rebuilt in the past 10 years. The diner or buffet car must be accessible to all passengers. Train staff must be able to use at least two languages, staff at stations along the route to make announcements in several languages. Passport and customs checks should be done aboard. Other requirements include on-board announcements, timetables, telephones, coordinated reservations and so on. Trains not meeting these standards lose the EuroCity designation (the InterCity name may not be used on international trains anymore).

The EuroCity concept completed the 'democratization' of speed and comfort. The modest supplement is fixed or altogether waived in some countries. And, of course, it no longer takes a first-class ticket to buy speed.

Night riders, the TENs

TEN stands for Trans-Euro-Night (Nuit, Notte, Noche, Nacht), the sleeper version of Trans-Europ-Express, and designates sleeping cars built to the uniformly high standards of comfort specified by the UIC.

For the railways the practical advantage of the TEN cars is in the flexibility of internal arrangement. Any compartment may be used as a single, double, or triple; all but the bottom berth fold into the wall when not needed. Compartments may be opened together to accommodate families of up to six. Second-class passengers also benefit from the new design. Double compartments used to be reserved for first class; now there are tourist doubles at second-class fares.

High-speed trains—present and future

Three hours from London to Paris or from Barcelona to Marseille? Yes, and by train, not plane. It's not a dream but a resolution of the European Community to develop a high-speed rail network. In the next decade, billions will be invested in a system to meet the demands of the 21st century.

High-speed trains still run on steel wheels on steel rails. They can use existing stations and old tracks at conventional speeds; to run at full speed, tracks and signal systems must be upgraded or rebuilt. New technology consists of increased power (electric engines), lighter cars, better suspension, and tilting bodies that lean into curves. The world rail record, set by a French TGV in December, 1989, is 301 mph, the speed of most turboprop planes.

Currently high speed means above 125 mph and up to 187 mph. This translates into travel times like the three-hour London–Paris service, due to start in 1993. The trains will run on new high-speed track in France and existing slower track in Britain. When the British section is rebuilt, the trip will take little over two hours, only an hour more than from London to Dover today. In the 1990s travel between Barcelona and Madrid or Paris and Frankfurt—now night trips—will be reduced to three-hour hops.

Until recently the railways worked mainly on speeding up domestic services, concentrating on improving connections between major cities. But the planners have kept an eye on the routes leading out of the country. The European high-speed network will develop gradually as domestic fast services are extended to other countries.

Europe's first high-speed train, the French TGV (train à grande vitesse) started in 1981 between Paris and Lyon, and more than proved the viability of rail. About 50% of air and 25% of road travelers switched to the train within months. The attraction of a two-hour trip (instead of four) also brought new passengers who had not taken the trip before. Since then, the TGV Sud-Est has expanded to the Mediterranean and into Switzerland. The TGV Atlantique to Brest and Le Croisic opened in 1989 and will be extended to Bordeaux in 1990. The next project is the TGV Nord. This route will run from Paris to Lille, there branching off to London via the Channel Tunnel, and to Brussels, sending one line to Amsterdam and another to Cologne. Still under study is the TGV Est from Paris to Karlsruhe and Frankfurt.

Germany's high-speed train, the ICE, or InterCity-Experimental, tested out at 252 mph (406 km/h). Named InterCity-Express and integrated in the existing InterCity System, trains will run at tamer speeds, 155 to 175 mph, on upgraded and some new tracks.

Italy races to build tracks and let loose the new electric trains. The ETR 450 with a top speed of 156 mph has been in service since 1988; the next generation ETR 500 will do 190 mph in 1993. To accommodate these trains on the overcrowded main routes new tracks are being built alongside the old ones.

Britain doesn't plan to set records, but the East Coast InterCity trains will soon be accelerated to 140 mph. This speed is feasible without new road and signals; tracks will be straightened in places and some junctions and stations rebuilt. Eventually new tracks will connect the Channel Tunnel to London. But while the Chunnel is being built, there are still discussions with H.M. Customs about examinations aboard a moving train. It's something that Europeans have been doing for decades, but in Britain the bureaucrats may not agree that passengers' convenience is worth changing centuries of practice.

Other countries have more modest programs, determined by geography and market, aiming at 125-mph services within the next five to ten years.

Austria is upgrading the Vienna-Salzburg line. In Switzerland's Rail 2000 program, tracks are being upgraded to allow 125 mph between major centers. Denmark expects to complete the fixed link (bridge and tunnel) across the waters of the Great Belt in 1993, and raise the commercial speed of its new IC3s. There are discussions about a fixed link between Denmark and Sweden, to be completed in 1995. In Sweden new trains on upgraded tracks will cut the Stockholm-Göteborg travel time to three hours in 1990. In Spain the next big step is the construction of a new line for TGV trains between Madrid and Seville for the 1992 World's Fair. And both Spain and Portugal will convert to standard gauge on their main routes with international traffic.

A few years ago cautiously optimistic railway officials looked to the 21st century for the high-speed European network. Yet, as the effort in each country continues to accelerate, a transcontinental day trip is definitely within sight before the year 2000.

Stations

In North America the demise of passenger trains hastened the deterioration of cities: cars on freeways moved people from the core to the suburbs. But in Europe railways have kept cities alive by moving a constant flow of humanity through the stations in the centers.

A station is more than a terminal. It serves the railway as the heart and brains of its organism. It is a central gateway to the city, the single most important point of access.

Within the walls of a major station the traveler can find virtually everything he needs. There are shops, bars, restaurants, hotel, post office, bank, telephone, bath, cleaners, nursery, clinic, pharmacy, travel agency, perhaps a cinema and a chapel. Even the railway's competitors, car rental and airline offices, have homes in this small city. And, as in every strange town, the traveler needs a guide. You find floor plans and lists of services in PART 2.

While the station invites townspeople as well as travelers to its shops and entertainment, the platforms are usually restricted to passengers with tickets. The essential services are available at any time but most stations close for a few hours in the early morning. Passengers with tickets are allowed in if they want to wait, but they will be alone with the cleaning staff and vending machines.

Railway services

Travel centers have appeared in large stations for the convenience of long-distance and international passengers. Instead of having to line up at various windows, you find information, tickets and reservations in one place. The staff speak several languages and have computer terminals at hand for instant information on schedules and fares, and to make out tickets and reservations. The office often houses a city tourist desk or the railway clerks may have local maps and transit information. Travel centers do not keep late hours.

Information offices try first of all to steer inquirers to the right place for information: the railway's office posts large 'NO tourist information. Trains only' signs; the tourist bureau next door advertises the opposite. Read those signs and the following.

Train information offices, marked with a blue letter **i**, are concerned only with railway matters, not only information but complaints and emergencies. At large stations the same pictogram appears over information kiosks where simple questions are answered.

Tourist information is not handled by the railway but the city tourist organization. The offices, marked with a green **i**, are staffed by multilingual clerks. Either the same office or one next to it handles hotel and private room reservations. They also distribute maps and guides, and sell tickets for concerts, theater and other events.

Ticket windows may be in the dozens. Find the right one for inland or international tickets, reservations, extensions, changes, refunds, immediate or same-day departure or advance purchases, suburban tickets. Inland tickets are usually sold around the clock but international services may close before midnight.

Reservations are handled at the travel center or at a ticket window marked with **R** or pictograms showing a seat, a couch, or a bed (for seat, couchette, or sleeping car berth). When these are closed, you can reserve at a late-service ticket window.

Baggage offices are often split into two parts. One office may handle only forwarded baggage, the other storage. The latter also looks after the lockers; ask there for change or to get a jammed lock opened. The few porters still in business congregate there too, but luggage carts are easier to find.

The lost property office is usually open only during working hours, not at night or weekends. However, if you are really desperate to retrieve something before departure, the baggage office or the stationmaster will send someone to open it up.

In **emergencies** look for the duty officer. The man in the red cap will not carry your luggage: he is an assistant stationmaster or platform supervisor who looks after trains and not passengers. But he is in charge and will summon the needed help with his radio. He also answers questions about schedules when the information office is closed.

First aid posts are marked with the red cross. Many large stations have clinics with a doctor, trained nurse or paramedic, some even have an ambulance standing by. Elsewhere the first aid post may be the railway employees' medical department which keeps short hours; in that case go to police or the stationmaster's office where the officer on duty is trained to deal with medical emergencies and will summon a physician or ambulance if needed.

Security is handled by police, urban or national or the railway's own. Every station has a police post, as well as patrolling officers. Public safety is good; while the crowds may be thicker than in the streets outside, the additional surveillance stops all but the hungriest pickpocket. The policemen seldom get to chase thieves, more often they are occupied helping old ladies on and off trains. Officers speak English in Scandinavia, the Netherlands, and in the large German and Swiss cities. Elsewhere the information office is the place to run to for an interpreter in an emergency.

Handicapped passengers find it easy to get about in new or modernized stations. These have wide-door toilets, low telephones, elevators to bypass stairs, call buttons at entrances to summon assistance. In older buildings, where personal help is needed, the police or porters should be called.

The old, ill, lost, and the very young are helped by organizations somewhat like the American Travelers' Aid. The *SOS Voyageurs* in France and the *Bahnhofsmission* in German-speaking countries provide places to rest and have a coffee while problems are solved. The volunteer staff will take care of babies (often there is a nursery), dispense medication and meals, provide escorts for elderly or handicapped passengers, and generally act as good mother. These shelters have immediate access to medical aid if needed, and to social agencies to help moneyless or lost passengers contact their families or consulates.

Communications and transportation

Post offices are always close to the station since most of the mail moves by train. For the same reason, the branch with continuous day and night service is usually the one at the station.

Telephone and telegraph belong to the post office in most countries. Offices for international calls or telegrams are open for long hours at the station. The French and Italian railways operate their own communications systems and these may be used by the public when the post office is closed.

City transit information is given either at the tourist office or, in large cities, in the city transit company's own office, where you can also buy bus/tram tickets and tourist passes.

Car rental is available through either the railway's own or a contract agency at the station.

Airlines and railways are friends in Europe. The major carriers maintain offices at the more important stations, as well as shuttle buses to the airport. The gesture is reciprocated in cities like Frankfurt, Düsseldorf, Zurich, and others where rail links take the trains right to the planes.

Conveniences, concessions

Waiting rooms have largely been eliminated to discourage loitering. Instead, bona fide passengers with tickets may sit in reserved sections of restaurants or cafeterias. They do not have to order and may even bring their own food. Since the free tables are not always marked, ask the waiter where to sit. Sometimes the waiting sections for first and second-class passengers are in different restaurants, plush for the first, simple for the second class. Either in the restaurants or in regular waiting rooms, tickets are occasionally checked by security officers; take the intrusion with good grace. These visits are in the interest of your safety.

Toilets are public but not always free. An attendant collects an admission fee, supposedly in payment for keeping the place clean. Unfortunately, hygiene is often lacking. If there is a choice, use the toilets in the bath or restaurants.

Baths and showers can be found at most large stations. The rooms are big enough to take in all your belongings, change clothes and repack the suitcase. The attendant supplies towels and sells soap, shampoo, razor blades, etc.

Restaurants with table service, self-service cafeterias and bars are many, catering to all budgets. Their hours are staggered so that at least one of them is open at any time.

Food shops, including supermarkets, delicatessen, bakeries, groceries, and fruit stands at the station are often the only ones in the whole city to keep open 16-18 hours on weekdays, up to 12 hours on Sundays.

Drugstores of the North American kind are seldom seen in Europe; you may have to go to different shops to find all necessities. In stations, cosmetics and toiletries are sold at the barber's shop, the bath, or the pharmacy.

Pharmacies in stations keep long hours.

Books, newspapers, photo supplies are sold in kiosks with extended opening times or in shops which keep regular hours.

A shopping arcade is often next to or right underneath the station. Many large stations expanded their underground passages, originally built to connect to subways or across the street, into shopping galleries of boutiques and restaurants. Prices are the same as outside, regulated by the landlord—the railway—or the city; while you may not find fire-sale bargains, you won't be horribly overcharged.

The foreign exchange may be a regular bank branch or run by the railway or the city tourist office. The exchange rate is sometimes slightly, but not significantly, worse than in a regular bank. When the office is closed, limited amounts of currency may be changed at a designated ticket window.

Meals

Sound eating habits are part of good travelcraft—easier said than acquired. Few travelers manage to eat properly. Some starve to save money but most overeat. The temptation to sample all the local dishes is strong. Sometimes a long wait at the station drives people through the gamut of fast-food stands. Soon, Montezuma's or Bismarck's revenge strikes. The simplest defense is to keep track of meals and cut down on impulsive snacking.

Where to eat? Dining in motion is a treat but be warned—dining cars charge more than restaurants. Trains cater only as a sideline and the extra labor adds to costs. Picnic meals aboard save money and help break the monotony of long rides; the quality is up to your shopping skills. Station restaurants usually serve good food at reasonable prices.

Meals on wheels
Check the footnotes in the timetable to avoid disappointments; see what kind of meal you can expect and when. Dining cars are often dropped off soon after mealtimes.

Dining cars with full table service (marked in timetables with the crossed knife and fork symbol) are carried on EuroCity and InterCity trains and many long-distance expresses. Their style and standard occasionally evoke a more leisurely past, and a moving feast can be a memorable experience, worth the occasional splurge. Real aficionados will carefully time their meal so that their after-dinner coffee and cognac will be complemented by suitably fine scenery rolling past the window.

The host aboard most trains is the Wagons-Lits Company (CIWL). This is a diverse international organization and the quality of service depends on the standards of the country that provides staff and supplies. You may be in for some rude surprises on the outskirts of this empire. Home base for CIWL is Belgium and France, and here is where the best meals are served in high style. Tables should be reserved or you may have to wait a hour or more for the next sitting. Stewards call at each compartment soon after departure to take orders.

Outside CIWL territory and on inland routes the national railways do the catering. Dining is cheaper and less formal. The atmosphere is more that of a coffeehouse where you are free to drop in anytime, and stay as long as you like.

In Germany your perfect host is the Deutsche Service Gesellschaft (DSG). It serves fresh rolls with the hefty breakfast, tasty and substantial lunches, dinners and a good variety of snacks at medium prices. At mealtimes tables are reserved for diners. The new Bord-Restaurant cars offer a dining section and a bar to take up the overflow. A very pleasant way to travel is to settle into a corner with magazines, timetables, postcards, order a half bottle of Mosel, and while away the time. The friendly DSG believes in *Gemütlichkeit*.

At-seat meal service (marked by crossed knife and fork above a seat) eliminates dithering over menus: you order your meals in advance when you reserve your seat and it is brought to you on a tray. In most cars a meal at your seat may be as cramped as on a plane. But in the more spacious British and Scandinavian cars, there are generously-sized tables, suitable for dining.

Self-service buffet cars (marked by knife and fork in a circle) provide light, inexpensive meals. The savings are on labor and not the quality of meals which can be as good as in a dining car, if somewhat simpler. A French Gril-Express may offer a variety of hors d'oeuvres, main dishes, cheeses, desserts, wine, cognac, juices, etc. In the new German Bistro Café, carried on InterRegio trains, you find a good choice of drinks and snacks in a setting that verges on the luxurious. An advantage of self-service is that the buffet is always open while the train is running; you pick your mealtime.

Mini-bars (vending carts, marked with a stemmed glass) are mentioned as a desperate last resort to stave off hunger. Their wares are plastic-wrapped sandwiches, crackers and cheese spread, old cakes, and what's probably the world's worst coffee. The prices are quite outrageous.

Better night trains usually have a dining car in the evening until about eleven; it is attached again in the morning for breakfast. But if the train leaves after dinner-time and arrives before eight, then often the attendant's pantry is the most you can hope for. The selection and quality are not much better than that of the vending carts. The DSG makes more of an effort, serving fresh bread, boiled eggs and hot frankfurters. And we must mention a fine contribution to civilized mornings: some sleeping cars have reintroduced steam on trains in the shape of espresso machines.

Station restaurants

When stagecoaches rattled across Europe, every post was also an inn, restoring the travelers. Railways continued the custom and did much to improve it. Station restaurants have an excellent reputation for good food at affordable prices. No one should be surprised to see families of townspeople dining out at their local *Bahnhofsrestaurant* or *Buffet de la gare*. In Copenhagen the main station sets one of the finest smorgasbords in town; at any large Swiss or Italian station as many as three good places may be competing. In Germany, the DSG runs 'InterCity' restaurants in the larger stations: they look and feel expensive, but their prices beat the ones outside the station.

When you choose a place to eat according to your budget, you should know that quite often both the first and second-class restaurants are served from the same kitchen; the only difference is in the tablecloth and the bill.

In a higher realm are some restaurants which have risen above the simple functional role of the inn, and their cooking often surpasses that of the best hotels. In fact, the Relais Gastronomique at the Gare de Luxembourg, which the chef deigns to open only for lunch, supplies the fine hotel across the street. And Le Train Bleu, upstairs in the Gare de Lyon in Paris, has more than crystal chandeliers, gilt mirrors and velvet curtains: the fare attracts regular visits from gourmet critics. The price is high, but you pay for the best in taste and service, not for name and fame.

Picnics

A fine meal can turn a possibly dreary ride through some industrial wasteland into a pleasant time of leisure. The most economical way of doing it is to pack a picnic meal. Not much planning is needed and shopping is easy.

Around any station you'll find shops. One store carries all: cold cuts, cheeses, patés, breads, pastries, beer, wine, and spirits in flasks from one ounce to a liter. But a word of advice: try to control the urge to sample everything or you end up eating stale leftovers for days after.

To turn a picnic from just a snack into a lunch or dinner, a few props are needed. Besides the essential Swiss army knife, take along a small fork, tempered unbreakable wine glass, and a linen napkin to set the table. The tiny extra weight is worth carrying for that touch of style you will enjoy.

A warning about water

For some obscure reason, remote in the murky past in the age of thirsty steam engines, it's quite difficult to find drinking water aboard trains. Apart from happy exceptions, like the elegant glass decanter in its niche on Swedish trains, taps carry a warning sign that the water is for washing only. Unprepared travelers can suffer agonies of thirst in overheated sleepers where there is literally no way to get anything to drink.

Bottled mineral water is the answer. It is usually available on board from the couchettist or sleeper attendant. (Water costs a few cents more than beer, no one knows why.) Bring your own bottle in case the stock runs out.

Night travel

Traveling at night is slower than in the daytime, but it can add an extra day to your vacation and save money as well. Granted, you'll miss the view while asleep, but there are few routes scenic enough to entertain you for eight hours. Set aside the nice spots for short trips.

If your destination is six or more hours away, then most of your day will be spent in transit. The special advantage of night travel is the morning arrival. There is ample time to take a leisurely look at the city and find just the right hotel in a suitable quarter. Much better than taking, sight unseen, a room picked by a travel agent 3,000 miles away.

What will it cost?

The cheapest way to travel at the night is in a seat. It's also the worst. Do it only if you are under 25 and expect to spend the next day sprawling on a beach. Even on a low budget a couchette is not a luxury, but an affordable way to avoid a miserable day after the night before. A berth in a sleeping car costs more but isn't necessarily extravagant. The supplement on international routes is high, but some of the inland routes are quite affordable. It's not indulgent to sleep in a made-up bed in Scandinavian countries, Portugal, or Spain where sleepers cost about the same as international couchettes.

The following Eurailtariff prices in US dollars are given only for comparison; these prices are set for the year and do not vary with the exchange rate. The local price may be slightly higher or (usually) lower.

	Triple	Double	Special	Single
International	42	63	105	146
France	43	66	110	154
Italy	38-45	44-52	64-75	93-111
Germany	34	52	86	121
Sweden	18	26	–	81
Norway	14	28	–	55
Denmark	–	25	–	47
Spain	15-20	18-24	30	46-61
Finland	13	20	–	39

Couchettes cost $14 in either class, $19 in a four-berth second-class compartment; slightly higher without reservation.

Reserve berths well in advance. Couchettes fill up quickly. Sleeping cars seldom sell out, but the vacancies could all be expensive first-class singles.

Couchettes

In couchette cars, seats convert to berths. The first-class couchettes—four per compartment—are more comfortable; unfortunately, they are seldom found outside France and Italy. Second-class couchettes are usually six per compartment, but for a higher supplement you can reserve in a four-berth.

You get sheets, blanket, and pillow. Each berth has a light, and a net for clothes. The ladder used to get to the upper berths has hooks on which to hang clothes. A collapsible table, kept under or behind the seats, can be set up for breakfast after the berths have been folded up. At both ends of the cars are washrooms with sink, mirror, soap, paper towels, hot water and electric razor outlet (220 volts).

Couchette cars are operated by national railways; comfort and cleanliness vary accordingly. By far the best are the French first class. The berths are wide and soft and, these cars being recently built, the ride is smooth. Second-class cars have less space but the service is excellent in Austrian, Belgian, Scandinavian, German, and Swiss cars. The attendants (couchettists) are multilingual, polite and prompt, the blankets are soft and warm. In contrast, in Spain and Italy the coarse blankets, and the attendants, appear to be army surplus. The cars are noisy, drafty, and seemingly never cleaned. Washrooms have more water on the floor than in the tap. Lots of room for improvement.

Sleeping cars

Some of the old plush wagons-lits are still in good enough shape to run, but you'll find mostly new Trans-Europ-Night (TEN) sleeping cars. These are air-conditioned and soundproofed. The wide beds have proper mattresses, sheets, two blankets and two pillows. Each bed has its adjustable reading light, switches for ceiling light and blue night light, call button for the attendant.

There are towels, soap, toothmugs, and even a shoeshine kit. The wash basin has hot and cold water; find drinking water in the medicine chest. Underneath is a chamber pot which cleverly empties into the dark night outside when replaced in its slot. Some new cars have showers, a rebirth of old-style luxury for the next generation of travelers.

The furnishings are the same on both classes, but a first-class ticket and higher supplement buy more space and privacy. Singles are first class, doubles may be first or second, three-bed tourist compartments second class. Some cars have 'specials,' smaller and cheaper singles. First-class doubles have beds side by side, second-class one above the other. Not all types of accommodations are available on all trains. Check the timetable: first-class special singles are marked Sp., second-class doubles or triples T2 and T3.

Hints and tips for night travel

An early departure gives you time to relax and prepare for bed comfortably. But it may be followed by a cruelly early awakening and mad scramble to pack and get off. At the last stop the passengers are usually allowed to sleep till about 7:30, but this may not be easy in the din of a busy station.

Couchettes are popular and should be reserved. Even if there is a vacant berth, the charge is higher on the train. Reservations are taken from two months to between two and five hours before departure. Computers assign berths according to their own pattern unless a special request is made. Top berths are warmer, with more head room, more space for your luggage within reach (on the shelf above the corridor), and—being out of the way—more privacy. It's a good idea to change into night clothes or you'll spend the night and next day crumpled and itchy. Since men and women may be in the same compartment, the railways suggest that passengers take turns undressing while the opposite sex waits outside. Changing in the washroom may preserve modesty but requires unusual gymnastics.

Sleeping car berths are assigned according to sex unless a couple or family reserve a compartment together.

Security is an increasing concern, especially when you are alone in a compartment. But simple precautions, the same as at home, will suffice. Lock the door when everybody is in bed. In many cars, especially Italian ones, there are two locks: the regular latch and a heavy safety bolt which cannot be opened from the corridor, not even by the conductor (these were installed after too many passkeys had been stolen). In an emergency, the safety lock can be opened from outside but it's a noisy process which thieves wouldn't undertake. Keep valuables close to you or give them to the attendant who has a safe.

In the evening, the attendant collects tickets and, on international routes, passports and customs declarations. The police check these at night without disturbing the passengers.

In the morning, the attendant wakes up each passenger about 30 minutes before reaching his destination. Some new sleepers have telephones next to each berth; the attendant calls you when it is time to get up and asks if you want breakfast. The great disadvantage of this fine new technology is that the squawk of the phone wakes up everybody in the compartment; in the less progressive couchette cars a gentle tap on the shoulder is the more civilized way of being woken up.

The attendant stocks snacks and drinks and serves coffee in the morning. If there is a dining car or buffet on the train, you can order breakfast to be served in bed.

Etiquette
Smoking is forbidden in sleepers and in couchette compartments when the berths are in the sleeping position. The ceiling light should, of course, stay off (awkward though this can be) when others are sleeping. (A pocket penlight can often be useful.) If you go in a couchette, extra baggage should be forwarded to your destination, because there is less room in a compartment with the berths down than during the day.

Fares, supplements, reductions

The European tariff structure differs from the North American. In the United States and Canada the basic fare buys coach; a fixed extra charge adds the comfort of a club car. The rate is the same on all trains, regardless of speed. In the European system the increase for first class (equivalent to club) is not a fixed charge but a percentage, usually 50% of the basic second-class fare; there may also be a supplement on fast trains.

Fares and classes
Fares vary widely; between neighboring countries the difference may be up to 300%. But a simple distance-for-dollar comparison is misleading since it ignores the quality of travel. In southern countries the basic fare buys an uncomfortable seat on a slow train; you have to pay much more for a little more comfort, a little more speed. North of the Alps the railways charge higher fares but more equitably: the difference between classes is much less marked and quality is more uniform.

Once upon a time trains had three, even four classes, to suit passengers from prince to peasant. The world has changed, trains with it. Fourth-class cars are seen only in museums, third class survives in Asia and Africa.

The policy of Western European railways has been to equalize comfort. Current design standards provide as much space in second as in first class. In the future the only difference will be the fare which will keep first class emptier. A bit like the Paris metro where some pay a little more to ride in the same type of car but away from the madding crowd.

The fare structures reflect social attitudes as well as economics. The democratic principles of the northern countries do not tolerate great inequalities. Their railways—with comfortable and spacious second class—charge only 50% more for first class on their fastest trains.

In the southern countries, the attitude is somewhat feudal. The Latin world (Italy, Spain, and even France) maintains wide differences between classes, both in the price and in what money buys. First-class travel in Italy and Spain is posh—for up to 170% more in surcharges; those who cannot pay the price have to travel slowly in rat-traps. The tourist should remember this when balancing cost and comfort.

Eurailtariff 1989 fares for 200 km distance, 2nd class, in US dollars:

Austria	22	Ireland	20
Belgium	19	Italy	15
Britain	30	Netherlands	22
Denmark	19	Norway	30
Finland	15	Portugal	10
France	20	Spain	14
Germany	29	Sweden	22
Greece	10	Switzerland	31
Hungary	15		

Supplements

Supplements above the regular fare are charged on some fast trains. In France, Italy and Spain supplements are charged by distance and category (air-conditioned trains cost extra in Spain). On EuroCity and most InterCity trains a fixed supplement is payable, regardless of distance. There are no supplements charged in Switzerland, the Benelux and Scandinavian countries. On some special expresses in Finland and Sweden seat reservations are obligatory at a fee that is high enough to be considered a supplement.

Seat reservations may be included in the supplement. The cost of sleeping accommodation is charged on top of the fare.

Reduced fares

Railways offer many reductions, most of which apply only in inland services; those available in each country are listed in PART 2. In some countries the reduced fares only apply on low-fare days and off-peak hours. The railways issue calendars showing these times. Here are the types of domestic and some international discounts.

Family reductions given to relatives traveling together can save up to 50% of the total fare. Depending on the local rules the family may be as large as eight or as small as three. The **Rail Europ Family card** is good for reduced fares throughout Europe: the card holder pays full fare, others 30 to 50% less, children 5 to 11 pay half of the reduced adult fare. Buy it at stations; about $10 for a year.

Seniors' discount of 50% is given to passengers over 60 or 65. Proof of age is needed for an ID-card issued at stations. If you hold a European national senior card, you can buy a **Rail Europ Senior** card for 30 to 50% discounts in Western Europe, Greece, Hungary, and Yugoslavia.

Return tickets are usually offered at discounts between 10 and 50%.

Low-fare or **half-fare** cards entitle you to a 40 to 50% reduction on fares, useful if you travel frequently in one country. Figure out whether the savings are worth the price of the card.

A **kilometerbank** is an account with the railway. You buy travel for a total distance. Several people can use the ticket at once: the distance is multiplied by the number of users and deducted from the balance.

Youth fares offer reductions of 30 to 50%. Eligibility varies from country to country. Youths under 26 may travel from Britain to hundreds of destinations on the Continent for up to 50% less with tickets from Transalpino Ltd. Tickets may be bought two months in advance and are valid for two months with unlimited stopovers. For further information, contact Transalpino Ltd, 71-75 Buckingham Palace Road, London SW1 (tel. 236-2507) or their branch offices in Birmingham, Liverpool, Oxford, Edinburgh, Glasgow, Belfast, and Dublin.

Ticket validity, stopovers

Tickets are valid either on the day of issue or, if bought in advance, on the date marked on the ticket. In Spain tickets must be validated at a ticket window, in France they must be stamped in the orange punch clock *(composteur)* when you enter the platform area.

Tickets are not sold in advance for short distances (usually less than 200 km). They are dated when issued and are valid for only that day. Stopovers are not allowed with short-distance tickets.

Long-distance tickets are valid for up to two months. Stopovers are usually allowed. In some countries the ticket must be endorsed when breaking and again when resuming the journey. See Part 2 for local rules.

International and long-distance tickets may be bought and reservations made up to two months ahead. If you have a firm schedule you can do all that in advance through a railway agency in North America or Britain (see Travelcraft in Planning, page 12 for addresses).

Ticket control

In most countries tickets are not checked at the station before boarding but by the conductor on the train. If the ticket is not dated for travel on that day or not validated as required, the conductor collects a fine, politely called a service charge. At many British, Italian, and Spanish stations you can enter platforms only with a valid ticket (or platform ticket for visitors).

Refunds

To get a refund you have to prove that the ticket was not used. This is taken for granted when the ticket is returned at the issuing station before the day of validity. Elsewhere the use of other means of travel has to be shown. Plane tickets and car rental bills are good evidence, witnesses to hitchhiking are not. Usually 10 to 15% of the ticket's value is withheld as a service charge.

Eurailtariff tickets

The European railways sell tickets in advance outside Europe. The fares are guaranteed for a year, immune from local increases but not from a drop in the value of the US dollar. Whether or not this works to your advantage depends on the currency situation in the previous year when the fares are fixed.

The real advantage of advance purchase is the one-stop shopping for a whole trip. Given a detailed itinerary the travel agent can get all tickets and reservations from the nearest European railway office.

The disadvantage is that you can't save through local reductions (return fares, family tickets, etc.). Look through these discounts for each country to see if it's better to buy tickets locally.

Eurailtariff rules

When you buy a Eurailtariff ticket these uniform rules override the discrepancies between regulations in different countries:

- Tickets are valid for six months.
- Stopovers are allowed without restriction (in Spain tickets must be endorsed before resuming the trip).

- Children under four travel free. Children between four and twelve are charged half fare but pay full reservation fees and supplements.
- The itinerary may be changed at any railway office or station.
- For a refund the ticket should be endorsed at the station where the journey was interrupted. The cancellation fee is 15%. Seat reservations are not refundable.
- There are special rates for groups of 10 or more, free tickets to one person in a group of 15 or more. The itinerary should be submitted six weeks in advance.

Passes to go as you please

Nothing smooths the road more than a pass. No waiting in line to buy tickets, no confusion with prices and currencies. Just hop on any train, any class, any category, and a flash of the card takes care of it all. These magic carpets come in lengths of validity from one day to a year, in widths from a district to a continent, and in prices to suit.

Worth and cost
The value of a pass depends on how far it will take you and for how long. The cost is commensurate with the quality of travel offered: a month on spartan second class in Greece costs a quarter of the price of luxury in France.

Compare passes by their daily cost. Passes for longer periods cost less per day: the 15-day Eurailpass costs $22.66 a day, the 3-month Eurailpass only $10.11. Of course, the less a pass is used, the higher the cost of each trip. It becomes expensive to stay in one place; the pass ticks away in your pocket, using up precious travel dollars while you rest. The solution is at hand: a flexipass that's used only on certain days selected within a longer period, so it's not wasted when you don't travel. For example, the 15-day Eurail Flexipass is valid on any five days within fifteen; the daily cost is only $13.20 when spread over the whole period.

To decide where to buy a pass and where tickets, check the fares along your route and in the countries where you'll spend most of your time. If you take even one long trip between countries, then a Eurailpass could save you money—and add the convenience. If the country is inexpensive, then even daily travel might not be worth buying a network pass. The Greek one-month pass costs the same as 128 km a day; you would get your money's worth only if you traveled 2 hours 20 minutes each day. The one-month *Swiss Pass* costs the same as 59 km a day; you could travel that in 41 minutes.

Types of passes

International passes let you travel through several countries without wasting a single moment at a ticket window. Currently on offer are a variety of Eurailpasses and Inter-Rail Cards, the Nordtourist Ticket for Scandinavia, the Benelux-Tourrail Card for Belgium, the Netherlands, and Luxembourg, and the BritFrance Railpass for Great Britain and France.

National network passes give you the freedom of one country. Most visitors have about three weeks to spend and the wise ones don't try to see all of Europe in that time. The best use of the pass is to see the country, settle for a rest when it expires, then—if you have more time—move on to the next country with a single ticket, starting a new pass from the border.

Regional network passes usually cover an area of touristic interest, like Britain's Southwest or Switzerland's Ticino, and are valid for a week or two. They effectively make the district your turf where you can come and go at will.

Route passes allow unlimited travel back and forth on a designated route. Residents use the weekly or monthly pass to go to work. But you can put one to good use if you decide stay in a quiet and inexpensive place outside a big city and just commute for sightseeing.

We review international passes in the rest of this chapter. See each country in PART 2 for national and regional passes.

Eurailpasses

These supercards allow unlimited travel in seventeen countries: Austria, Belgium, Denmark, Finland, France, Germany, Greece, Hungary, Ireland, Italy, Luxembourg, Netherlands, Norway, Spain, Portugal, Sweden, and Switzerland. They are good on trains, buses and ferries run by the railways, ferry crossings (France-Ireland, Denmark-Sweden, Finland-Sweden, Italy-Greece), the lake steamers in Switzerland, many ships on the Rhine and Danube, some mountain cog railways and cable cars. Many private operators give fare reductions to pass holders.

Eurailpasses are sold only to those resident outside Europe and North Africa by travel agents and railway offices. You can also buy them in Europe at Eurail Aid offices and major railway stations for 10% more than the overseas price if you have a non-European passport. British subjects are Europeans and excluded, even though Britain does not honor the Eurailpass.

Eurailpasses for adults are valid on first class, the **Eurail Youthpasses** for youths between 12 and 26 on second (but may be used on first class by paying the difference). Children between four and twelve pay half price, under four travel free. All supplements are included. Reservations must be made on trains where it is obligatory (on express trains in Spain you need a boarding pass; show your Eurailpass at the ticket window). Charges for reservations, couchettes and sleepers have to be paid.

Eurail Flexipasses allow you to choose your days of travel during a longer period: 5 days in 15, 9 days in 21, or 14 days in a month. This obviously takes the sting out of paying for the right to travel on days when you don't go anywhere.

The Eurail Saverpass is a discounted 15-day pass for people traveling together (at least two off-season, before March 31 and after October 1, at least three people between April 1 and September 30).

The pass has to be used within six months of purchase and validated before its first use. This may be done in advance, as soon as you know when you are going to begin traveling. To validate, a railway official at a station enters the first and last days of use, as well as your passport number (train conductors may ask to see your passport as proof of ownership). Check these numbers carefully before leaving. There is a charge of about $5 for validation aboard a train (except when traveling from airports without a railway ticket office). If you use a Flexipass, you have to enter each day of use before boarding the train.

Each pass is issued with a counterfoil card also filled out at validation. Detach this card and carry it separately: it is your proof of purchase and may be requested by conductors.

You can have a lost card replaced if you prove its purchase with the counterfoil card and the agency that sold the pass confirms the pass number and date of issue. The procedure by telex or cable may take more than a day. Damaged or improperly validated cards will also be replaced. Ask the train information people for the appropriate office at major stations.

Prices for Eurailpasses in 1990 are the following (US dollars):

	15 days	21 days	1 month	2 months	3 months
Eurailpass	340	440	550	750	930
Saverpass	240/person				
Youthpass			380	500	
Flexipass	198	360	458		
	(5 days)	(9 days)	(14 days)		

Inter-Rail Cards

This pass is sold only to youths under 26, European residents or visitors with six months of proven residence. It is valid on the trains (second class) of 22 countries: Austria, Belgium, Denmark, Finland, France, Germany, Great Britain, Greece, Hungary, Ireland, Italy, Luxembourg, Morocco, Netherlands, Norway, Portugal, Romania, Spain, Sweden, Switzerland, European Turkey, and Yugoslavia.

The Inter-Rail Card is issued for one month. It's good for half-fare tickets in the country where bought, unlimited travel elsewhere, and 50% reduction on many ferries. **The Inter-Rail+Boat** adds free travel on some of the ferries between the participating countries. **The Inter-Rail-Flexi** allows you to choose ten days of travel within a calendar month. Mark each day before boarding the train. **The Inter-Rail 26+,** for adults over 26, is sold only in Scandinavia. It's similar to the youth card but includes half fare on ferries: Helsinki/Turku-Stockholm (Silja Line), Göteborg-Frederikshavn (Stena Line), Trelleborg-Travemünde (TT Line).

The cards are priced in European currencies. The listed US dollar figures may vary with the exchange rate.

Inter-Rail	270
Inter-Rail+Boat	316
Inter-Rail-Flexi	250
Inter-Rail 26+	370

Benelux-Tourrail Card

The card allows unlimited travel by train in Belgium, Luxembourg, and the Netherlands, and by bus in Luxembourg, on any five days chosen in a 17-day period. Supplements are included. Mark the card each day of travel before boarding the train. Travel agencies and stations in the three countries sell the card. You can also buy it from Netherlands Board of Tourism, 225 North Michigan Ave, # 326, Chicago, IL 60601. Tél.: 312/819 03 00. Youths under 26 may buy the cheaper Junior card.

	Adults		Youths	
	1st class	2nd class	1st class	2nd class
Belgium BF	3740	2490	2690	1790
Luxembourg LF	3740	2490	2690	1790
Netherlands f	210	140	148	99
Overseas US$	105	70	75	50

BritFrance Railpass

This flexipass allows unlimited travel by train in Britain and France on any five days in a fifteen-day period or ten days in a month. All supplements are included. Also included is round trip crossing by hovercraft (regular ferry in bad weather) between Dover and Boulogne; reservation is obligatory. Have the pass validated at any railway station on the first day of use, then enter the date on each day before use.

The pass is sold only by travel agencies outside Europe to travelers residing outside Europe. It must be used within six months of purchase or turned in for refund within a year (cancellation costs 15%). Children under four travel free, between four and twelve pay half price.

Prices in US dollars:

	1st class	2nd class
5 days in 15	269	199
10 days in a month	399	299

Nordturist Ticket

Valid in Denmark, Finland, Norway, and Sweden for 21 days, this pass allows unlimited travel on trains, ferries owned by the railways, ferries between Stockholm and Turku (Silja Line), Göteborg and Frederikshavn (Stena Line), Kristiansand and Hirtshals (Fred. Olsen Lines/KDS). It offers 50% reduction on ferries between Stockholm and Helsinki (Silja Line), Copenhagen and Oslo (Scandinavian Seaways), and hydrofoils between Copenhagen and Malmö. It is sold at Scandinavian railway stations and overseas rail and tourist offices. The price is lower for youths aged 12 to 16. Children under four travel free, between four and eleven pay half of the adult price.

	Adults		Youths	
	1st class	2nd class	1st class	2nd class
Denmark Dkr	2325	1550	1740	1160
Finland FIM	1350	900	1010	675
Norway Nkr	2120	1410	1590	1060
Sweden Skr	2035	1355	1525	1015
Overseas US$	321	214	242	161

Reservations

Seat reservation is a must on busy routes and during holiday periods: without it you may have to stand. Off-season and away from the main routes, reservations are not essential but still advisable. There may be an unexpected onslaught, caused by a little-known Mediterranean feast day, which fills up all southbound trains with large families. The usual fee of about $3 is cheap for the guarantee of a comfortable trip.

The reservation fee is included in the supplement for EuroCity and InterCity trains. With Eurail or other passes the reservation fee has to be paid. The fee is not refundable.

If you have not reserved in advance, do it for the next leg of your trip on arrival, before you even leave the station. The farther ahead you reserve, the better, especially for trips in the summer. Railways take reservations by mail 2 to 3 months in advance; address requests to the reservation office in major stations. Telephone reservations are accepted five days in advance, in person from two months to a day or, rarely, a few hours before departure. Small stations may not be able to assure seats on trains originating elsewhere, unless reservations are made a day before. At larger stations the limit is usually two hours; for TGVs until a few minutes before departure. Note: These time limits count from the train's departure from the station of origin.

Reservations are optional on trains marked with **R** in the timetable. The framed ℝ means that reservation is obligatory. On these trains, seats are assigned when tickets are sold, but if you travel with a pass or already have a ticket (continuing after a stopover) then you have to make the reservation yourself.

Seats are assigned by the computer according to a programmed pattern unless you have a preference. The reservation clerk can request a window seat from the computer which will then search through the whole train to find a vacant one. This can be done quickly and easily, so don't hesitate to ask. Also mention how many people are traveling, otherwise the computer in its kindness will disperse your party through the train (to avoid crowding, it hands out the four corner seats in each compartment first, then starts on the middle ones).

Always check the reservation card as soon as it is issued; corrections can be made only until the time limit for reservations.

Baggage

Your ticket entitles you to one seat and the space above and below it. The rule is not enforced when there are vacant seats. But if the compartment is full and your second suitcase crowds out someone else's, then you have problems. The extra piece should be in the baggage car. That way you also save yourself the strain, sprains and bruises, wrestling bags up steps and through narrow doors and aisles.

Porters are fewer and more difficult to find every year. At some stations they are called by phone or signal button from platforms and entrances. Luggage carts are the speedier alternative.

Forwarding

Take your baggage to the forwarding office at least 30 minutes before departure. If sent late, it may go on another train and you will be delayed on arrival. To make life easier on traveling day, you can send baggage a day ahead, and pick it up after you have reached your destination. The forwarding charge includes several days of storage. Many railways offer house-to-house delivery. Call the station a day before departure for pickup and have the baggage either taken to your next address or, if you have yet to find a place, stored until you tell the destination station where to deliver it.

From airports with train stations you can forward baggage to anywhere along your train route. When leaving Europe from Germany or Switzerland, the railway will take your baggage and put it on the plane for you (Swissair will check it right through to your home airport).

Storage

Deposit offices usually keep open from 6:00 till midnight or later (check when you hand in your luggage). Lockers are accessible practically round the clock (even small stations close for only a few hours at night). The cost varies from country to country, from 75 cents to a few dollars a day. Lockers come in several sizes at different cost. Have the right coins ready; only large stations have change machines. For security reasons, in Italy and Spain the locker areas are guarded and your baggage is X-rayed before being deposited.

Customs

The European Community is getting rid of customs barriers but traffic in alcohol and tobacco is still restricted. Depending on whether you enter from overseas, a non-EC, or a member country, the limits vary between 1-2 liters of spirits, 2-3 liters of wine, 200-400 cigarettes or equivalent in tobacco. However, examinations on trains are rare.

Forwarded baggage has to be cleared but usually the written declaration (green slip) is sufficient. Since customs officers at stations keep civil service hours, your baggage may not be released during lunch time, evenings and public holidays.

Additional railway services

Railways go beyond running trains and handle other aspects of travel. These services are offered conveniently at many stations.

Travel agency

Some agencies handle hotels, car rentals, excursions, package tours, train, bus, ship, and airline tickets. The advantage is one-stop shopping and savings on many package deals with reduced rates.

Train + Hotel

Railways have always provided the passenger with bed and board at their own hotel just across the street or right above the station. In the Train + Hotel arrangement, a room may be reserved at the other end of an excursion or a one-way trip, usually at a discount.

Train + Auto

Some railways run their own car-rental business, others contract outside. The rates for rail passengers are usually reduced. A car may be reserved from any station before departure or from the train if it has a telephone aboard. It will be waiting at the station on arrival. Return it at any other station that has a car-rental office.

Train + Velo

A sporty version of Train + Auto, available mostly in rural touristic areas. Bicycles can be rented at stations and returned elsewhere, at the other end of a scenic route.

Telephones

On most InterCity trains there are pay phones linked by radio to the national network. Long-distance, even overseas calls may be made en route for the usual charge or a small supplement. Have lots of change or a telephone card.

Ships

Railways don't stop where the tracks end. Ferry services are integrated with trains in countries with lakes or seashore. In Scandinavia the trains are shipped across the water, and passengers have the run of the ship's restaurants and duty-free shop. In Finland and Switzerland lake steamers connect between trains. In Germany and Austria the Rhine and Danube ships are alternate choices to the trains that follow the river's course.

Timetables

National timetables are hard to find outside of the country in question. Use one of the international timetables for planning.

The International Union of Railways (UIC) publishes a pocket timetable, Through Europe By Train. The 160 pages contain all the intercity schedules you may need and some local ones as well. It's available free from the European railways' overseas offices; you also receive a copy with a Eurailpass, but usually too late for planning.

The most comprehensive reference is the Thomas Cook European Timetable that has full details of all international and hundreds of national routes in Europe.

Previous editions, the venerable classic Continental Timetable (published 1873-1976) listed North Africa and Asia, the International (1977-1980) the entire world. The schedules of Nile steamers, of Le Train Bleu, of the Punjab Mail or the Grand Trunk Express were readings verging on the romantic.

Cook now issues two editions. Services outside Europe are listed in the bi-monthly Overseas Timetable. Europe is covered in the European Timetable, published monthly. The key issues are May and September which contain both the summer and winter schedules. A copy costs £5.85 from Thomas Cook Ltd., P.O.Box 36, Peterborough PE3 6SB England, or $19.95 from Forsyth Travel Library, P.O.Box 2975, Shawnee Mission, KS 66201 USA. It's also sold by a few travel book shops and at principal Thomas Cook offices in Europe (Amsterdam, Brussels, Paris, Zurich) but the latest issue usually arrives around the 12th of the month and is gone by the 20th.

Some warnings

Europe changes to daylight saving time in March; the Continent goes back to standard time in September, Britain and Ireland in October. Many trains' timings change then and you should make sure that you are working with the appropriate timetable. Also, check the timings on both sides of the border when traveling between countries not on Central European Time: Britain, Ireland, and Portugal are an hour earlier, Finland and Greece an hour later.

Check all the symbols and read the footnotes when choosing your train to see if it operates every day, just on workdays or only on holidays. Watch out for exceptions, such as national or movable holidays.

In the long columns of large tables, connections may be mistaken for through trains. Read the footnotes to check what cars go to your destination; this is especially critical when picking couchette or sleeper cars.

If you have to change trains, look up the name of the station where you arrive and check if you depart from there, too. Some cities (Budapest, Lisbon, London, Lyon, Madrid, Milan, Paris, Vienna) have several stations, not all touched by arriving or departing trains. You may have to cross the town to make a connection. Leave enough time!

Finally, timetables may be wrong. Typographical errors are rare, but sometimes a too recent schedule change has not been entered. There could be temporary reroutings or retimings of trains. Always check departure times locally. Neither the timetable publishers, nor the railways will accept responsibility for delay or inconvenience caused by misinformation.

How to read them

Many people are daunted by timetables. Yet some have even mastered income tax forms. Timetables are simpler because they are logical. And the symbols make them readable in any language.

Times are given in the 24-hour system. Midnight arrivals belong to the previous day, so they are marked down as 24:00; departures in the same second appear as 00:00, the beginning of the next day. (See THE 24-HOUR CLOCK, page 54.)

In the Cook timetables, the single tables show one route each, the large ones several trains which leave from different cities, then merge and divide again to go to different destinations. Each column may show several trains that make connections. In the heading you find the train number, category (D, EC, IC, Rap), available classes (1, 2), symbols for services (dining car, sleeper, couchettes), and—if the train doesn't run daily—a letter or number indicating the days when it runs. The symbols are explained in the introduction of the timetable. Letters at the head of the column or next to timings refer to more details in the footnotes. Footnotes indicate the through cars (which you want to find to avoid transfers). If a city has more than one station, the departure station appears in parentheses after the city name. The following number refers to other tables where service to that station may appear in more detail.

Calendar of moving holidays

Legal holidays are listed for each country in PART 2. The movable holidays fall on different dates from year to year. On these days trains may run on different schedules.

	1990	1991	1992	1993
Shrove Tuesday	27 Feb	12 Feb	3 Mar	23 Feb
Ash Wednesday	28 Feb	13 Feb	4 Mar	24 Feb
Good Friday	13 Apr	29 Mar	17 Apr	9 Apr
Easter Sunday	15 Apr	31 Mar	19 Apr	11 Apr
Easter Monday	16 Apr	1 Apr	20 Apr	12 Apr
Ascension Day	24 May	9 May	28 May	20 May
Corpus Christi	14 Jun	30 May	18 Jun	10 Jun

The 24-hour clock

In Europe not only railways but shops, cinemas, and offices use this system. No special skill is needed to handle numbers above 12 and you'll soon appreciate the unambiguous straight scale without the a.m. and p.m. tags. The civilian version is more legible than the military: a colon or the letter 'h' separates the hours and minutes, for example, 6:15 p.m. is written 18:15 or 18h15.

In conversation the 12-hour clock is used. When inquiring about departure times find out whether day or night was meant!

TRAVEL VOCABULARIES

Timetable and station indicator boards show city names in the local language. We list below major city names that are quite different from their English version, and that you may need to recognize when trying to locate them from somewhere using another language.In the following section, we give travel vocabularies in thirteen languages, in alphabetical order of language, as an aid to getting round stations and asking for what you want in the way of services.

City names

Åbo (Swedish)	Turku	Helsingfors (Swedish)	Helsinki
Aix-la-Chapelle (French)	Aachen	Hoek (Dutch)	Hook (of Holland)
Aken (Dutch)	Aachen	Köln (German)	Cologne
Anvers (French)	Antwerp	Köpenhamn (Swedish)	Copenhagen
Atene (Italian)	Athens	København (Danish)	Copenhagen
Athinai (Greek)	Athens	Lisboa (Portuguese)	Lisbon
Baile Atha Cliath (Irish)	Dublin	Londres (French)	London
Bâle (French)	Basel	Mailand (German)	Milan
Basilea (Italian)	Basel	Marsella (Spanish)	Marseille
Bécs (Hungarian)	Vienna	Monaco (Italian)	Munich
Bucuresti (Romanian)	Bucharest	München (German)	Munich
Bruxelles (French)	Brussels	Napoli (Italian)	Naples
Den Haag (Dutch)	The Hague	Parigi (Italian)	Paris
Firenze (Italian)	Florence	Tukholm (Finnish)	Stockholm
Genova (Italian)	Genoa	Venedig (German)	Venice
Genf (German)	Geneva	Venezia (Italian)	Venice
Ginevra (Italian)	Geneva	Wien (German)	Vienna
Göteborg (Swedish)	Gothenburg	Zurigo (Italian)	Zurich

English/Danish

arrival	ankomst
baggage	bagage
baggage cart	bagagevogn
baggage forwarding	indskrevet bagage
baggage locker	bagagebokse
baggage pick-up	udlevering
baggage store	bagageopbevaring
couchette	liggeplads
couchette car	liggevogn
danger	fare
departure	afgang
dining car	spisevogn
entrance	indgang
exit	udgang
first aid	førstehjælp
first class	første klasse
forbidden	forbudt
foreign (country)	udland
foreign exchange	vekselkontor
information	oplysning
inland	indland
local (train)	regionaltog
long-distance (train)	fjerntog
lost/found	hittegods
men	herrer, mænd
one-way (ticket)	enkelt
platform	perron
porter	drager
refund	tilbagebetale, refundere
reservation	bestilling
return (ticket)	tur retur
seat	siddeplads
second class	anden klasse
sleeping car	sovevogn
sleeping berth	soveplads
smoker	rygere
station	banegård, station
supplement	tillæg
ticket	billet
ticket office	billetkontor
timetable	køreplan
to	til, mod
track	spor
train	tog
wagon	vogn
waiting room	ventesalvogn
women	damer, kvinderwagon

Danish/English

afgang	departure
anden klasse	second class
ankomst	arrival
bagagebokse	luggage lockers
bagageopbevaring	baggage store
bagagevogn	baggage cart
banegård	station
bestilling	reservation
billet	ticket
billetkontor	ticket office
damer	women
drager	porter
enkelt	one-way (ticket)
fare	danger
fjerntog	long distance train
forbudt	forbidden
førstehjælp	first aid
første klasse	first class
herrer	men
hittegods	lost/found
indgang	entrance
indland	inland
indskrevet bagage	baggage forwarding
kvinder	women
køreplan	timetable
liggeplads	couchette
liggevogn	couchette car
mod/til	to
mænd	men
oplysning	information
perron	platform
regionaltog	local train
rygere	smoker
siddeplads	seat
soveplads	sleeping car berth
sovevogn	sleeping car
spisevogn	dining car
spor	track
tilbagebetale	refund (to)
tillæg	supplement
tog	train
tur retur	return (ticket)
udgang	exit
udland	foreign (country)
udlevering	baggage pick-up
vekselkontor	foreign exchange
ventesal	waiting room

English/Dutch

arrival	aankomst
baggage	bagage
baggage cart	lorrie
baggage forwarding	bagage en expeditie
baggage locker	bagagekluis
baggage pick-up	bagage en expeditie
baggage store	bagage-depot
couchette	couchette
couchette car	ligrijtuig
danger	gevaar
departure	vertrek
dining car	restauratie
entrance	ingang
exit	uitgang
first aid	eerste hulp
first class	eerste klas
forbidden	verboden
foreign (country)	buitenland
foreign exchange	geldwisselkantoor
information	inlichtingen
inland	binnenland
local (train)	stoptrein
long-distance (train)	intercity/doorgaande trein
lost/found	gevonden voorwerpen
men	heren
one-way (ticket)	enkele reis
platform	perron
porter	kruier
refund	terugbetaling
reservation	bespreking/ reservering
return (ticket)	retour
seat	zitplaats
second class	tweede klas
sleeping berth	bedplaats
sleeping car	slaaprijtuig
smoker	roken
station	station
supplement	toeslag
ticket	plaatsbewijs/kaartje
ticket office	loket
timetable	spoorboekje
to	naar
track	spoor
train	trein
wagon	wagon
waiting room	wachtkamer
women	dames

Dutch/English

aankomst	arrival
bagage	baggage
bagage en expeditie	baggage forwarding
bagage en expeditie	baggage pick-up
bagage-depot	baggage store
bagagekluis	baggage locker
bedplaats	sleeping berth
bespreking/reservering	reservation
binnenland	inland
buitenland	foreign (country)
couchette	couchette
dames	women
eerste hulp	first aid
eerste klas	first class
enkele reis	one-way (ticket)
geldwisselkantoor	foreign exchange
gevaar	danger
gevonden voorwerpen	lost/found
heren	men
ingang	entrance
inlichtingen	information
intercity/doorgaande trein	long-distance (train)
kruier	porter
ligrijtuig	couchette car
loket	ticket office
lorrie	baggage cart
naar	to
perron	platform
plaatsbewijs/kaartje	ticket
restauratie	dining car
retour	return (ticket)
roken	smoker
slaaprijtuig	sleeping car
spoor	track
spoorboekje	timetable
station	station
stationschef	stationmaster
stoptrein	local (train)
terugbetaling	refund
toeslag	supplement
trein	train
tweede klas	second class
uitgang	exit
verboden	forbidden
vertrek	departure
wachtkamer	waiting room
wagon	wagon
zitplaats	seat

English/Finnish

arrival	saapuminen
baggage	matkatavara
baggage cart	työntökärryt
baggage forwarding	lähtevä matkatavara
baggage locker	säilytyslokero
baggage pick-up	saapuva matkatavara
baggage store	matkatavarasäilö
couchette	lepopaikka
couchette car	leopvaunu
danger	vaara
departure	lähtö
dining car	ravintolavaunu
entrance	sisään
exit	ulos
first aid	ensiapu
first class	ensimmäinen luokka
forbidden	kielletty
foreign (country)	vieras (ulkomaan)
foreign exchange	valuutanvaihto
information	neuvonta
inland	kotimainen (sisämaan)
local (train)	paikallis (juna)
long-distance (train)	pikajuna
lost/found	löytötavara
men	miehille
one-way (ticket)	meno (lippu)
platform	laituri
porter	kantaja
refund	takaisinmaksu
reservation	varaus
return (ticket)	meno-paluu (lippu)
seat	istumapaikka
second class	toinen luokka
sleeping berth	makuupaikka
sleeping car	makuuvaunu
smoker	tupakoville
station	asema
supplement	lisämaksu
ticket	lippu
ticket office	lipputoimisto
timetable	aikataulu
to	-lle, jnkk suuntaan
track	raide
train	juna
wagon	vaunu
waiting room	odotushuone
women	naisille

Finnish/English

aikataulu	timetable
asema	station
ensiapu	first aid
ensimmäinen luokka	first class
istumapaikka	seat
juna	train
kantaja	porter
kielletty	forbidden
kotimainen (sisämaan)	inland
lähtevä matkatavara	baggage forwarding
lähtö	departure
laituri	platform
leopvaunu	couchette car
lepopaikka	couchette
lippu	ticket
lipputoimisto	ticket office
lisämaksu	supplement
löytötavara	lost/found
makuupaikka	sleeping berth
makuuvaunu	sleeping car
matkatavara	baggage
matkatavarasäilö	baggage store
meno (lippu)	one-way (ticket)
meno-paluu (lippu)	return (ticket)
miehille	men
naisille	women
neuvonta	information
odotushuone	waiting room
paikallis (juna)	local (train)
pikajuna	long-distance (train)
raide	track
ravintolavaunu	dining car
saapuminen	arrival
saapuva matkatavara	baggage pick-up
säilytyslokero	baggage locker
sisään	entrance
takaisinmaksu	refund
toinen luokka	second class
tupakoville	smoker
työntökärryt	baggage cart
ulos	exit
vaara	danger
valuutanvaihto	foreign exchange
varaus	reservation
vaunu	wagon
vieras (ulkomaan)	foreign (country)
-lle, jnnk suuntaan	to

English/French

arrival	arrivée
baggage	bagage
baggage cart	chariot, charette
baggage forwarding	enregistrement
baggage locker	consigne automatique
baggage pick-up	retrait de bagages
baggage store	consigne
couchette	couchette
couchette car	voiture-couchette
danger	danger
departure	départ
dining car	voiture-restaurant
entrance	entrée
exit	sortie
first aid	premiers soins
first class	première classe
forbidden	interdit, défendu
foreign (country)	(extérieur), étranger
foreign exchange	bureau de change
information	renseignements
inland	intérieur
local (train)	banlieue/régional
long-distance (train)	grandes lignes
lost/found	objets trouvés
men	hommes/messieurs
one-way (ticket)	simple/aller-simple
platform	quai
porter	porteur
refund	remboursement
reservation	réservation
return (ticket)	aller et retour
seat	place assise
second class	deuxième classe
sleeping berth	lit
sleeping car	wagon-lit/voiture-lit
smoker	fumeur
station	gare
supplement	supplément
ticket	billet
ticket office	guichet
timetable	horaire
to	vers
track	voie
train	train
wagon	voiture
waiting room	salle d'attente
women	dames

French/English

aller et retour	return (ticket)
arrivée	arrival
bagage	baggage
banlieue/régional	local/train
billet	ticket
bureau de change	foreign exchange
chariot, charette	baggage cart
consigne	baggage store
consigne automatique	baggage locker
couchette	couchette
dames	women
danger	danger
deuxième classe	second class
départ	departure
enregistrement	baggage forwarding
entrée	entrance
extérieur, étranger	foreign (country)
fumeur	smoker
gare	station
grande ligne	long-distance (train)
guichet	ticket office
hommes	men
horaire	timetable
interdit, défendu	forbidden
intérieur	inland
lit	sleeping berth
objets trouvés	lost/found
place assise	seat
porteur	porter
première classe	first class
premiers soins	first aid
quai	platform
remboursement	refund
renseignements	information
réservation	reservation
retrait de bagages	baggage pick-up
salle d'attente	waiting room
simple	one-way (ticket)
sortie	exit
supplément	supplement
train	train
vers	to
voie	track
voiture	wagon
voiture-couchette	couchette car
voiture-restaurant	dining car
wagon-lit	sleeping car

English/German

arrival	Ankunft
baggage	Gepäck
baggage cart	Gepäckwagen
baggage forwarding	Gepäckaufgabe
baggage locker	Schliessfach
baggage pick-up	Gepäckausgabe
baggage store	Gepäckaufbewahrung
couchette	Liegeplatz
couchette car	Liegewagen
danger	Gefahr
departure	Abfahrt
dining car	Speisewagen
entrance	Eingang
exit	Ausgang
first aid	erste Hilfe
first class	erste Klasse
forbidden	verboten, nicht
foreign (country)	Ausland
foreign exchange	Wechselstube
information	Auskunft
inland	binnen, Inland
local (train)	Nahverkehr
long-distance (train)	Fernverkehr
lost/found	Fundbüro
men	Herren
one-way (ticket)	einfache
platform	Bahnsteig
porter	Gepäckträger
refund	Erstattung
reservation	Reservierung
return (ticket)	Rückfahrkarte
seat	Platz
second class	zweite Klasse
sleeping car	Schlafwagen
sleeping berth	Bett
smoker	Raucher
station	Bahnhof
supplement	Zuschlag
ticket	Fahrkarte
ticket office	Schalter
timetable	Fahrplan
to	zu
track	Gleis
train	Zug
wagon	Wagen
waiting room	Wartesaal
women	Damen

German/English

Abfahrt	departure
Ankunft	arrival
Ausgang	exit
Auskunft	information
Ausland	foreign (country)
Bahnhof	station
Bahnsteig	platform
Bestellung	Reservation
Bett	sleeping berth
binnen	inland
Damen	women
einfache	one-way (ticket)
Eingang	entrance
Erstattung	refund
erste Hilfe	first aid
erste Klasse	first class
Fahrkarte	ticket
Fahrplan	timetable
Fernzug	long-distance (train)
Fundbüro	lost/found
Gefahr	danger
Gepäck	baggage
Gepäckabgabe	baggage pick-up
Gepäckaufbewahrung	baggage store
Gepäckaufnahme	baggage forwarding
Gepäckträger	porter
Gepäckwagen	baggage cart
Gleis	track
Herren	men
Liegeplatz	couchette
Liegewagen	couchette car
Nahverkehr	local (train)
Platz	seat
Raucher	smoker
Rückfahrkarte	return (ticket)
Schalter	ticket office
Schlafwagen	sleeping car
Schliessfach	baggage locker
Speisewagen	dining car
verboten, nicht	forbidden
Wagen	wagon
Wartesaal	waiting room
Wechselstube	foreign exchange
zu	to
Zug	train
Zuschlag	supplement
zweite Klasse	second class

English/Hungarian

arrival	érkezés
baggage	poggyász
baggage cart	poggyász kézikocsi
baggage forwarding	poggyászfelvétel
baggage locker	poggyászmegorzo automata
baggage pick-up	poggyászkaiadás
baggage store	poggyászmegorzo
couchette	kusett/fekvohely
couchette car	fekvohelyes kocsi
danger	veszély
departure	indulás
dining car	étkesokocsi
entrance	bejárat
exit	kijárat
first aid	elsosegély
first class	elso osztály
forbidden	tilos
foreign (country)	külföldi, nemzetközi
foreign exchange	valutaváltás
information	felvilágositás
inland	belföldi
local (train)	helyi
long-distance (train)	távolsági
lost/found	talált tárgyak
men	férfiak
one-way (ticket)	menetjegy (csak oda)
platform	peron
porter	hordár
refund	visszatérités
reservation	helybiztositás
return (ticket)	menettérti jegy
seat	ülohely
second class	másod osztály
sleeping berth	hálóhely
sleeping car	hálókocsi
smoker	dohányzó
station	állomás
supplement	pótdij
ticket	menetjegy
ticket office	pénztár
timetable	menetrend
to	-hoz
track	vágány
train	vonat
wagon	kocsi
waiting room	váróteremvonat
women	nok

Hungarian/English

állomás	station
bejárat	entrance
belföldi	inland
dohányzó	smoker
elso osztály	first class
elsosegély	first aid
érkezés	arrival
étkesokocsi	dining car
fekvohelyes kocsi	couchette car
felvilágositás	information
férfiak	men
hálóhely	sleeping berth
hálókocsi	sleeping car
helybiztositás	reservation
helyi	local (train)
hordár	porter
-hoz	to
indulás	departure
kijárat	exit
kocsi	wagon
külföldi, nemzetközi	foreign (country)
kusett/fekvohely	couchette
másod osztály	second class
menetjegy	ticket
menetjegy (csak oda)	one-way (ticket)
menetrend	timetable
menettérti jegy	return (ticket)
nok	women
pénztár	ticket office
peron	platform
poggyász	baggage
poggyász kézikocsi	baggage cart
poggyászfelvétel	baggage forwarding
poggyászkiadás	baggage pick-up
poggyászmegorzo	baggage store
poggyászmegorzo automata	baggage locker
pótdij	supplement
talált tárgyak	lost/found
távolsági	long-distance (train)
tilos	forbidden
ülohely	seat
vágány	track
valutaváltás	foreign exchange
váróterem	waiting room
veszély	danger
visszatérités	refund
vonat	train

English/Italian

arrival	arrivo
baggage	bagagli
baggage cart	carrello portabagagli
baggage forwarding	bagagli in partenza
baggage locker	custodia automatica
baggage pick-up	bagagli in arrivo
baggage store	deposito bagagli
couchette	cuccetta
couchette car	carrozza cuccette
danger	pericolo
departure	partenza
dining car	carrozza ristorante
entrance	entrata, ingresso
exit	uscita
first aid	pronto soccorso
first class	prima classe
forbidden	vietato
foreign (country)	estero
foreign exchange	cambio
information	informazioni
inland	interno
local (train)	locale
long-distance (train)	espresso/direttissimo
lost/found	oggetti rinvenuti
men	uomini, signori
one-way (ticket)	andata
platform	marciapiedi/binario
porter	portabagaglio
refund	rimborso
reservation	prenotazione
return (ticket)	andata e ritorno
seat	posto
second class	seconda classe
sleeping berth	letto
sleeping car	carrozza letto
smoker	fumatore
station	stazione
supplement	supplemento
ticket	biglietto
ticket office	biglietteria
timetable	orario
to	a
track	binario
train	treno
wagon	carrozza
waiting room	sala d'aspetto
women	donne, signore

Italian/English

a	to
andata	one-way (ticket)
andata e ritorno	return (ticket)
arrivo	arrival
bagagli	baggage
bagagli in arrivo	baggage pick-up
bagagli in partenza	baggage forwarding
biglietteria	ticket office
biglietto	ticket
binario	track
cambio	foreign exchange
carrello portabagagli	baggage cart
carrozza	wagon
carrozza cuccette	couchette car
carrozza letto	sleeping car
carrozza ristorante	dining car
cuccetta	couchette
custodia automatica	baggage locker
deposito bagagli	baggage store
donne, signore	women
entrata, ingresso	entrance
espresso/direttissimo	long-distance (train)
estero	foreign (country)
fumatore	smoker
informazioni	information
interno	inland
letto	sleeping berth
locale	local (train)
marciapiedi/binario	platform
oggetti rinvenuti	lost/found
orario	timetable
partenza	departure
pericolo	danger
portabagaglio	porter
posto	seat
prenotazione	reservation
prima classe	first class
pronto soccorso	first aid
rimborso	refund
sala d'aspetto	waiting room
seconda classe	second class
stazione	station
supplemento	supplement
treno	train
uomini, signori	men
uscita	exit
vietato	forbidden

English/Norwegian

arrival	ankomst
baggage	reisegods
baggage cart	bagasjekjerre
baggage forwarding	(reisegods)ekspedisjon
baggage locker	oppbevaringsboks
baggage pick-up	utlevering (av reisegods)
baggage store	(bagasje)oppbevaring
couchette	liggeplass
couchette car	liggevogn
danger	fare
departure	avgang
dining car	restaurantvogn
entrance	inngang
exit	utgang
first aid	førstehjelp
first class	første klasse
forbidden	forbudt
foreign (country)	utlandet
foreign exchange	vekslingskontor
information	opplysninger
inland	innenlands
local (train)	lokaltog
long-distance (train)	fjerntog
lost/found	hittegods
men	herrer, menn
one-way (ticket)	enkeltbillett
platform	perrong
porter	bærer
refund	tilbakebetaling
reservation	(plass)bestilling
return (ticket)	returbillett
seat	sitteplass
second class	andre/annen klasse
sleeping berth	køye
sleeping car	sovevogn
smoker	røykekupe
station	stasjon
supplement	tilleggsavgift
ticket	billett
ticket office	billettkontor
timetable	rutetabell
to	til
track	spor
train	tog
wagon	vogn
waiting room	ventesal
women	damer, kvinner

Norwegian/English

andre/annen klasse	second class
ankomst	arrival
avgang	departure
bagasjekjerre	baggage cart
(bagasje)oppbevaring	baggage store
billett	ticket
billettkontor	ticket office
bærer	porter
damer, kvinner	women
enkeltbillett	one-way (ticket)
fare	danger
fjerntog	long-distance (train)
forbudt	forbidden
første klasse	first class
førstehjelp	first aid
herrer, menn	men
hittegods	lost/found
innenlands	inland
inngang	entrance
køye	sleeping berth
liggeplass	couchette
liggevogn	couchette car
lokaltog	local (train)
oppbevaringsboks	baggage locker
opplysninger	information
perrong	platform
(plass)bestilling	reservation
reisegods	baggage
(reisegods)ekspedisjon	baggage forwarding
restaurantvogn	dining car
returbillett	return (ticket)
rutetabell	timetable
røykekupe	smoker
sitteplass	seat
sovevogn	sleeping car
spor	track
stasjon	station
til	to
tilbakebetaling	refund
tilleggsavgift	supplement
tog	train
utgang	exit
utlandet	foreign (country)
utlevering (av reisegods)	baggage pick-up
vekslingskontor	foreign exchange
ventesal	waiting room
vogn	wagon

English/Portuguese

arrival	chegada
baggage	bagagem
baggage cart	carrinho de bagagem
baggage forwarding	despacho de bagagens
baggage locker	depósito automático
baggage pick-up	levantamento de bagagens
baggage store	depósito de bagagens
couchette	beliche
couchette car	carruagem-beliches
danger	perigo
departure	partida
dining car	carruagem-restaurante
entrance	entrada
exit	saída
first aid	posto de socorros
first class	primeira classe
forbidden	proibido
foreign (country)	estrangeiro
foreign exchange	câmbio
information	informações
inland	nacional
local (train)	regional (suburbano)
long-distance (train)	rápido
lost/found	objectos achados
men	homens
one-way (ticket)	ida
platform	cais
porter	carregador
refund	reembolso
reservation	reserva
return (ticket)	volta
seat	lugar
second class	segunda classe
sleeping berth	cama
sleeping car	carruagem-camas
smoker	fumadores
station	estação
supplement	suplemento
ticket	bilhete
ticket office	bilheteira
timetable	horário
to	para
track	linha
train	comboio
wagon	carruagem
waiting room	sala de espera
women	senhoras

Portuguese/English

bagagem	baggage
beliche	couchette
bilhete	ticket
bilheteira	ticket office
cais	platform
cama	sleeping berth
câmbio	foreign exchange
carregador	porter
carrinho de bagagem	baggage cart
carruagem	wagon
carruagem-beliches	couchette car
carruagem-camas	sleeping car
carruagem-restaurante	dining car
chegada	arrival
comboio	train
depósito automático	baggage locker
depósito de bagagens	baggage store
despacho de bagagens	baggage forwarding
entrada	entrance
estação	station
estrangeiro	foreign (country)
fumadores	smoker
homens	men
horário	timetable
ida	one-way (ticket)
informações	information
levantamento de bagagens	baggage pick-up
linha	track
lugar	seat
nacional	inland
objectos achados	lost/found
para	to
partida	departure
perigo	danger
posto de socorros	first aid
primeira classe	first class
proibido	forbidden
rápido	long-distance (train)
reembolso	refund
regional (suburbano)	local (train)
reserva	reservation
saída	exit
sala de espera	waiting room
segunda classe	second class
senhoras	women
suplemento	supplement
volta	return (ticket)

English/Spanish

arrival	llegada
baggage	equipaje
baggage cart	carro
baggage forwarding	facturación
baggage locker	consigna automática
baggage pick-up	recogida
baggage store	depósito
couchette	litera
couchette car	coche litera
danger	peligro
departure	salida
dining car	coche comedor
entrance	entrada, acceso
exit	salida
first aid	primeros auxilios
first class	primera clase
forbidden	prohibido
foreign (country)	extranjero
foreign exchange	oficina de cambio
information	información
inland	nacional
local (train)	cercanias
long-distance (train)	largo recorrido
lost/found	objetos perdidos
men	caballeros
one-way (ticket)	ida
platform	andén
porter	mozo
refund	reembolso
reservation	reservación
return (ticket)	ida y vuelta
seat	asiento
second class	segunda clase
sleeping berth	cama
sleeping car	coche cama
smoker	fumador
station	estación
supplement	suplemento
ticket	billete
ticket office	taquilla
timetable	guía, horario
to	a
track	vía
train	tren
wagon	coche
waiting room	sala de espera
women	señoras

Spanish/English

a	to
andén	platform
asiento	seat
billete	ticket
caballeros	men
cama	sleeping berth
carro	baggage cart
cercanias	local (train)
coche	wagon
coche cama	sleeping car
coche comedor	dining car
coche litera	couchette car
consigna automática	baggage locker
depósito	baggage store
entrada, acceso	entrance
equipaje	baggage
estación	station
extranjero	foreign (country)
facturación	baggage forwarding
fumador	smoker
guía, horario	timetable
ida	one-way (ticket)
ida y vuelta	return (ticket)
información	information
largo recorrido	long-distance (train)
litera	couchette
llegada	arrival
mozo	porter
nacional	inland
objetos perdidos	lost/found
oficina de cambio	foreign exchange
peligro	danger
primera clase	first class
primeros auxilios	first aid
prohibido	forbidden
recogida	baggage pick-up
reembolso	refund
reservación	reservation
sala de espera	waiting room
salida	departure
salida	exit
segunda clase	second class
señoras	women
suplemento	supplement
taquilla	ticket office
tren	train
vía	track

English/Swedish

arrival	ankomst
baggage	bagage
baggage cart	bagagekärra
baggage forwarding	polletterat resgods
baggage locker	förvaringsbox
baggage pick-up	utlämning
baggage store	effektförvaring
couchette	liggplats
couchette car	liggplatsvagn
danger	fara
departure	avgång
dining car	restaurangvagn
entrance	ingång
exit	utgång
first aid	förstahjälpen
first class	första klass
forbidden	förbjuden
foreign (country)	utland
foreign exchange	växelkontor
information	upplysning
inland	inland
local (train)	lokaltåg
long-distance (train)	fjärrtåg
lost/found	hittegods
men	herrar
one-way (ticket)	enkel (biljett)
platform	perrong
porter	bärare
refund	återbetalning
reservation	beställning
return (ticket)	tur och retur (biljett)
seat	sittplats
second class	andra klass
sleeping berth	sovplats
sleeping car	sovvagn
smoker	rökare
station	station
supplement	tillägg
ticket	biljett
ticket office	biljettexpedition
timetable	tidtabell
to	till, mot
track	spår
train	tåg
wagon	vagn
waiting room	väntsal
women	damer

Swedish/English

andra klass	second class
ankomst	arrival
avgång	departure
bagage	baggage
bagagekärra	baggage cart
bärare	porter
beställning	reservation
biljett	ticket
biljettexpedition	ticket office
damer	women
effektförvaring	baggage store
enkel (biljett)	one-way (ticket)
fara	danger
fjärrtåg	long-distance (train)
förbjuden	forbidden
första klass	first class
förstahjälpen	first aid
förvaringsbox	baggage locker
herrar	men
hittegods	lost/found
ingång	entrance
inland	inland
liggplats	couchette
liggplatsvagn	couchette car
lokaltåg	local (train)
perrong	platform
polletterat resgods	baggage forwarding
restaurangvagn	dining car
rökare	smoker
sittplats	seat
sovplats	sleeping berth
sovvagn	sleeping car
spår	track
station	station
tidtabell	timetable
till, mot	to
tillägg	supplement
tur och retur (biljett)	return (ticket)
tåg	train
upplysning	information
utgång	exit
utlämning	baggage pick-up
utland	foreign (country)
vagn	wagon
väntsal	waiting room
växelkontor	foreign exchange
återbetalning	refund

Catalan/English

accès vies	to the track	lavabos	toilets
arribades	arrivals	llarg recorregut	long distance
bitllets	tickets	rodalies	local (train)
cap d'estació	station master	sortida	exit
	(emergencies)	sortides	departures
equipatges	baggage	trajecte llarg	long distance

English/Greek

arrival	άφιξη	men (W.C)	άνδρων
baggage	αποσκευων	one-way (ticket)	απλό εισιτήτιο
baggage forwarding	καταγραφή αποσκευων	platform	εξέδρα αποβάθρα
		porter	αχθοφόρος
baggage locker	ντουλάπι σκευοθήκη	refund	πληρωνω πίσω, επιστρέφω
baggage pick-up	παραλλαβή αποσκευων	return (ticket)	εισιτήτιο μεεεπισ– τροφή
baggage store	αποθήκευση αποσκευων	seat	θέση, κάθισμα
		second class	δεύτερης θέσης
couchette	κουκέτα	sleeping berth	κοιτωνίσκος
departure	αναχωριση	smoker	επιτρέπεται το
dining car	όχημα εστιατορίου		κάπνισμα
entrance	είσοδος	station	σιδηροδρομικός
exit	έξοδος		σταθμός
first aid	πρωτες βοήθειες	supplement	συμπλήρωμα
first class	πρωτης θέσης	ticket	εισιτήριο
foreign exchange	συνάλλαγμα	ticket office	γραφείο έκδοσης
information	πληροφορία		εισιτηρία
inland	εσωτερικού	timetable	πίνακας δρομολο–
local (train)	τοπικό (τραίνο)		γίων
long-distance (train)	υπεραστικό (τραίνο)	track	σιδηροδρομική γραμμή
lost/found	γραφείο απωλεσθεντων αντικειμένων	wagon	βαγόνι
		waiting room	αίθουσα αναμονής
		women (W.C)	γυναίκων

The Greek–English version was omitted since we assumed that those who can read Greek will not need the travel vocabulary. To ask for a direction, point at the Greek word opposite the word you need.

TRAVEL MANUAL

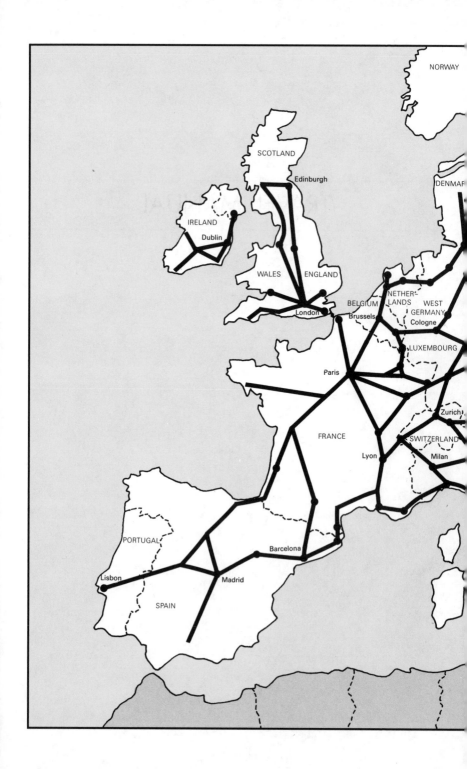

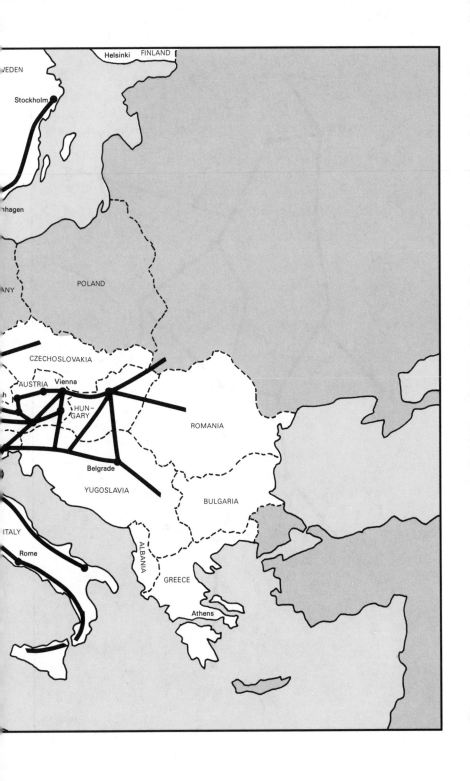

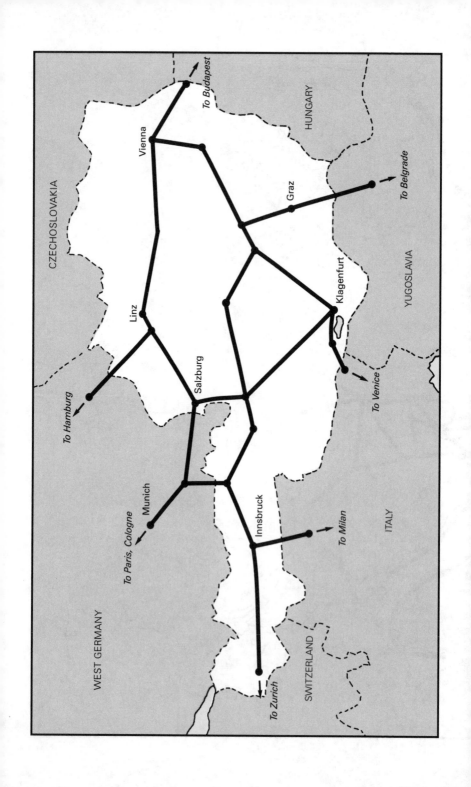

Austrian Federal Railways

Österreichische Bundesbahnen (ÖBB)

Austrians know how to make life pleasant. Thoughtful innovations like the *Bahn-Totalservice* and four-berth couchettes (instead of the usual crowded six) have shown that their traditional concern with comfort has survived, even on trains that until recently ambled at the comfortable speeds of olden times. In 1987 the ÖBB won approval of its ambitious program of renewal, *Die neue Bahn*, the new railway. With infusions of much money and improvements in technology, Austria has begun to revamp its system.

New engines and cars have been ordered, new tracks laid and old ones upgraded to raise the speed to 200 km/h on the main routes. The travel time between Vienna and Salzburg that has stood at 3 1/4 hours for decades will shrink to two hours. Meanwhile over thirty stations will be spruced up, and given better access and more services.

The regular interval system runs hourly trains from Vienna to Salzburg and Innsbruck. The best trains are the long-distance expresses that include several EuroCity trains which run through to Germany. The categories are express *(Expresszug,* marked *Ex* in timetables), fast *(Schnellzug, D)*, semi-fast *(Eilzug, E)* and local *(Regionalzug)*. The ÖBB also operates mountain rack railways and ships. With its extensive bus network it makes the remotest villages accessible by public transport. The VOR *(Verkehrsverbund Ost Region)* system integrates the five modes of Vienna city transit with main line trains in the area that spreads from St. Pölten in the west to the Hungarian border in the east, making all points accessible with a single ticket.

Information
You will find timetable leaflets *(Zugbegleiter)* on trains. Brochures and timetables are mostly in German. The information officers are multilingual, other staff less so. The stations are well marked with pictograms. In Vienna Südbahnhof and Westbahnhof, information officers, distinguishable by

their yellow cap bands, help out on the platforms; at smaller stations look for the man in the red cap, the *Fahrdienstleiter*.

Schedule changes

Train services may change on the following public holidays (for movable dates, see CALENDAR, page 54):

New Year	January 1
Epiphany	January 6
Good Friday	Movable date
Easter Monday	Movable date
Ascension	Movable date
Whit Monday	Movable date
Corpus Christi	Movable date
Assumption	August 15
National Holiday	October 26
All Saints	November 1
Immaculate Conception	December 8
Christmas	December 25-26

Fares

First class costs 50% more than second. Second-class fares in Austrian schillings (S) and US dollars:

Distance in km	100	200	400
Local prices, S	128	224	418
Eurailtariff, $	12	22	42

Supplements

Only first class of EuroCity trains requires a supplement of 40 S.

Reduced fares

Children under six travel free (two with each paying adult), aged six to fifteen pay half fare.

Short-distance returns *(Nahverkehrs-Rückfahrkarten)* for trips under 70 km and used within four days save 20%.

The **Kilometerbank** saves up to 35%. Up to six persons at a time may use the ticket on trips over 70 km. 1700 S buys 2000 km of travel.

Families, seniors, and holders of the one-year half-fare card may buy tickets with the appropriate ID card. Inquire at stations.

Go-as-you-please passes

Eurailpasses allow unlimited travel on trains, the Schneeberg and Schafberg rack railways, ÖBB ships on the Wolfgangsee and DDSG ships on the Danube; half fare on Bodensee ferries; reductions on most private railways and cable cars. **Inter-Rail Cards** allow unlimited travel on trains and half fare on buses and ships.

Network passes *(Bundes-Netzkarten)* allow unlimited travel on trains and half fare on Danube and Bodensee ships. They include the EuroCity supplement.

	1st class	2nd class
One month, S	4650	3100
One year, S	37200	24800

Flexipasses, including the *Rabbit Card, Rabbit Card Junior*, and *Regional-Netzkarten*, allow unlimited travel over the entire rail network or a region on four days chosen during a ten-day period. The *Rabbit Card* (and *Rabbit Card Junior* for youths under 26) allow unlimited travel on trains and include the EuroCity supplement. Identification with photo has to be shown when used. *Regional-Netzkar-*

ten are valid on trains in one of 18 regions; they do not include the EuroCity supplement.

	1st class	2nd class
Rabbit Card, S	1290	890
Rabbit Card Junior, S	690	490
Regional-Netzkarte, S	500	400

Tickets

Tickets for less than 70 km are valid on the day of purchase without stopover, over 70 km for four days, return tickets for two months with unlimited stopovers.

Reservations

Seats on most fast trains are reservable for 30 S. Reserve from six months to three hours before departure.

Baggage

Forwarding inland costs 40 S a piece, up to 50 kg (110 lbs), and in international traffic 90 S a piece, up to 30 kg (66 lbs). House-to-house delivery costs 140 S for two pieces.

Storage costs 10 S a day. Lockers use ten-schilling coins and cost 10 to 30 S a day, depending on size.

The *Bahn-Totalservice*

This innovation brought back the forgotten leisure of comfortable house-to-house travel in style. Order your ticket and a *Bahn-Servicepass* by phone, receive them by mail and pay later at the station. On departure day you and your baggage are driven to the station where a porter takes the suitcase to your seat. Then, a complimentary newspaper and a drink in the dining car. The ticket includes baggage insurance and discounts on hotels, casinos, sightseeing, and telephone card. The service costs 180 S for the first person, 150 S for the next or for the same arrangement on return. You can ask for it in Vienna, Linz, Salzburg, Innsbruck, Graz, and Klagenfurt. Phone 1700 in any city.

Meals

Most long-distance trains carry dining cars with full table service. Buffet cars with table or self-service offer a smaller selection of meals. The menus may not be exciting but the fare is good and solid, and the bill never shocks. Vending carts (mini-bars) are on most trains except short-distance locals.

Austrian station restaurants have a long-standing reputation for the quality of their food. For a picnic meal on wheels you can shop at the stations in Vienna where well-stocked delicatessens offer cold cuts, fresh bread, fruit, wine and beer; they are open for long hours, even on Sundays. In smaller towns go to nearby shops for the same; they close early but you can always rely on the station kiosks for good sandwiches.

Inquire about the *Casinos Austria Gourmet Express,* special excursions with dinner and—on New Year's Eve—dance.

Night travel

Inland sleepers and couchettes run only between Vienna and Bregenz.

Couchettes with second-class tickets in four-berth compartments cost 220 S, in six-berth compartments

160 S. Reserve up to two months in advance and at least five hours before departure.

Sleeping car berths may be reserved three months in advance. They vary in price, depending on route.

	Vienna-Bregenz	Vienna Venice	International
Single	–	–	1640
Special	700	1130	–
Double	590	680	710
Triple (T3)	–	–	470

Other services

Ship/train/bus trips along the Danube are offered during the summer with combined tickets (Kombi-Karte).

Car rental (Auto am Bahnhof) may be arranged at travel agencies and stations, or ask the conductors aboard train at least two hours before arrival to have a car ready at the destination.

Bicycle rental (Fahrrad am Bahnhof) is offered at over 130 stations from April through October. Return the bicycle at any station. The cost is 40 S a day. Bring ID with photo.

Telephones (Zugtelefon) are on most main line trains. You can make local or long distance (intercontinental) calls. Buy telephone cards (Telefon-Wertkarten) at station kiosks, from the conductor or dining car staff. Office compartments on first class are reservable for 150 S.

Assistance

Handicapped: Write or phone the station of departure three days in advance and give itinerary to have assistance where needed along the route.

The railway staff will help with getting on and off or changing trains. Station facilities in the older buildings are limited but improving.

Medical, family and social aid: The Bahnhofsmission usually provides a nursery where babies can be changed and fed, a place to sit for elderly or handicapped passengers, and a nurse who can give first aid or call a doctor. If your money is lost, the staff will call a welfare office, arrange phone calls to relatives, and meanwhile give you a meal and a place to wait.

Emergency: The nearest help on trains is the conductor, at stations the station master. The duty office is called Fahrdienstleitung.

Salzburg

Tourist information

Find information and accommodation service at the railway station, Hauptbahnhof (daily 8:00–19:00), airport and in the city center (Mozartplatz 5). Phone 84 75 68 or write to Fremdenverkehrsbetriebe, Auerspergstrasse 7, A-5020 Salzburg.

City transit

Buses, trolleybuses (Obus), and the Bergheim tram are included in the transit system. Find information and tickets at the bus stop opposite Hauptbahnhof or in the transit office (Mon–Fri 7:30–18:00, Sat 7:30–12:00, Griesgasse 21).

Tourist passes for 24 hours of unlimited travel (24-Stunden-Netzkarte) cost less than four single tickets.

Sign before first use. You may buy a batch of five transferable passes (Umweltkarte) for less than two singles. Personal **weekly passes** (Wochenkarte) cost seven singles. Single tickets bought in advance save about 20%. Tourist passes and tickets are sold by tobacconists, longer term passes at transit and tourist offices.

Validate passes and tickets in punch clocks aboard buses and trolleybuses.

Taxis
Tel. 8111

Post, telephone, telegraph
Permanent service in the post office at Hauptbahnhof.

Help in emergencies
Police: Tel. 133
Ambulance: Tel. 144
Medical clinic on 24-hour duty: Tel. 79 603, 72 338.
Pharmacy on 24-hour duty: Addresses posted in pharmacy windows.
Lost & found: Police. Alpenstrasse 90. Regular office hours. Tel. 29 511 ext. 2330.

Airport
Salzburg Airport. City bus No.77 runs from Hauptbahnhof; travel time is 16 minutes.

Rail connections
All trains use Hauptbahnhof.
1 to 2 hours: Linz, Munich, Innsbruck
3 to 4 hours: Klagenfurt, Vienna
Overnight: Brussels, Hamburg, Cologne, Paris, Rotterdam, Zurich

Vienna (Wien)

Tourist information
Information and accommodation services are at the railway stations (Südbahnhof and Westbahnhof; see next pages for working hours), airport (daily 9:00–23:00), and in the Opernpassage, underground at Opernring and Kärntnerstrasse (daily 9:00–19:00). Phone 43 16 08 or write to Vienna Tourist Board, A-1095 Wien.

City transit
The system integrates buses, trams, rapid transit (Schnellbahn, Stadtbahn, U-Bahn), regional and main line trains in and around the urban area. Find information, maps, and tickets at the railway stations under the green VOR sign and at these major U-Bahn stations: Karlsplatz, Mon–Fri 7:00–18:00, Sat–Sun 8:30–16:00; Stephansplatz, Mon – Fri 8:00 – 18:00, Sat–Sun 8:30–16:00; Praterstern, Zentrum Kagran, Mon–Fri 10:00–18:00.

Tourist passes for unlimited travel for 24 or 72 hours (24-Stunden-Wien, 72-Stunden-Wien) cost the same as two or five single fares, respectively. They are transferable. The eight-day pass (8-Tage-Umwelt-Streifen-Netzkarte) may be used by several persons together: each of the eight strips on the card is a tourist pass for one person for one day (validate one strip for each person at first use); the cost is the same as 11 singles. **Weekly passes** (Wochenkarte) cost the same as six singles; a photo is required. **Multiride tickets** *(Streifenkarte)* save 20% over single tickets.

Passes and tickets are sold at transit and railway stations, 72-hour passes also at tourist information offices. Singles are sold by drivers or automats aboard buses and trams.

Validate passes and tickets in punch clocks marked *Entwerter* at stations and aboard buses and trams near door.

Taxis:
Tel. 3130, 4369, 6282, 9101.

Post, telephone, telegraph
Permanent service in the railway stations and at Fleischmarkt 19.

Help in emergencies
Police: Tel. 133
Ambulance: Tel. 144
Medical and dental clinic (24 hrs): Tel. 5500
Pharmacy on 24-hour duty: Addresses posted in pharmacy windows.
Lost & found: Wasagasse 22, Mon–Fri 8:00–13:00.
Tel. 316 61 10

Airport
Wien-Schwechat Airport. Schnellbahn trains run hourly from Wien-Nord station and Wien-Mitte/Landstrasse (City Air Terminal); travel times are 30 and 27 minutes. Airport buses run hourly from Südbahnhof and Westbahnhof (travel times are 20 and 35 minutes), and every 20 minutes from the City Air Terminal (travel time is 20 minutes).

Rail connections
The west station (Westbahnhof) handles all traffic to the west of the country, Germany, and Switzerland. From the south station (Südbahnhof) trains leave to the south, Italy, Yugoslavia, Czechoslovakia and Poland, as well as the EuroCity *Lehár* to Budapest. Other Budapest trains use Westbahnhof. Three minor stations (Franz Josef, Mitte, Nord) handle local traffic and some trains to Czechoslovakia and Poland.

The two main stations are connected by tram No.18.

2 to 3 hours: Budapest by EC-*Lehár*, Graz (Südbf)
3 to 4 hours: Budapest, Salzburg (Westbf)
4 to 6 hours: Munich, Innsbruck (Westbf)
Overnight: Basel (Westbf), Belgrade, Bologna, Florence (Südbf), Hamburg, Cologne (Westbf), Milan (Südbf), Paris (Westbf), Rome, Venice (Südbf), Zurich (Westbf).

Station plans
Salzburg Hauptbahnhof: pp 264–5
Vienna/Wien Südbahnhof: pp 274–5
Vienna/Wien Westbahnhof: pp 276–7

Belgian National Railways

Nationale Maatschappij der Belgische Spoorwegen (NMBS)
Société Nationale des Chemins de fer belges (SNCB)

Belgium seems to have as many trains as some other countries cars. You don't need a timetable in Brussels: in half an hour there will be a train to any destination. Then, in little over an hour, you can be on the sandy beach in Ostend or walk in an Ardennes forest. The railway busily markets its services at good discounts (two-thirds of Belgians travel regularly at reduced fares). It tempts with suggestions to get away for a day to the coast or the mountains with cheap return tickets. The all-in-one city and country tourist pass makes travel simple as well as inexpensive.

The short distances don't require more than simple and functional equipment, and until a few years ago the commuter-type cars were a bit lackluster. However, the new generation of rolling stock has been designed with flair, adding a look and feel of luxury to efficiency, comfortable enough for longer trips than is possible within the borders.

The domestic system consists of two overlapping networks, the Inter-City (IC) and InterRegio (IR) routes. The latter, together with local feeder lines (L), serve all areas outside the major cities. On the main lines there are fast electric trains; branch lines are served mostly by railcars. Connections are close and frequent.

Some of the finest international expresses have run from Brussels for over a century. Many of the great north-south transcontinental routes have their northern terminal here. Continuing the tradition, Belgium is host to EuroCity trains (successors to TEEs) to Amsterdam, Cologne, Paris, and Zurich.

One famous international express disappeared some years ago. The legendary *Night Ferry* with all-first-class sleeping cars was once the most comfortable connection to London. But there will be a better way in 1993 when the Channel Tunnel opens. Instead of overnight, the journey will take a mere three hours with the *TGV Nord* which will also connect to Paris

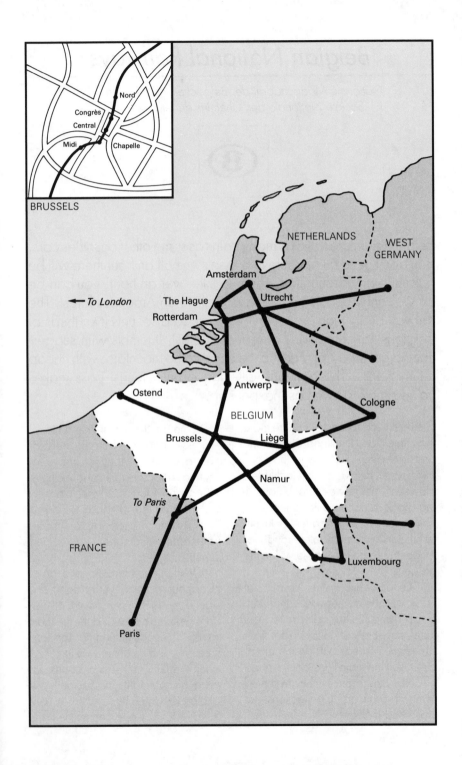

and Amsterdam. The Brussels TGV station will soon be built next to Zuid/Midi.

Information

The timetable *(Spoorboekje/ Indicateur)* contains a 23-page English section that explains the schedules, fares and supplements in detail. Other printed material is mostly in Flemish and French. Most staff who deal with passengers at stations speak English but some French is useful when dealing with conductors. Stations are well marked with pictograms. Train schedules, including track numbers, are displayed on large posters. Electronic indicators are on every platform.

Timetables and indicator boards may list unfamiliar names of cities. Here are the Flemish and French versions:

Flemish	*French*
Aarlen	Arlon
Antwerpen	Anvers
Bergen	Mons
Brugge	Bruges
Brussel	Bruxelles
Dendermonde	Termont
Doornik	Tournai
Gent	Gand
Ieper	Ypres
Kortrijk	Courtrai
Leuven	Louvain
Luik	Liège
Mechelen	Malines
Namen	Namur

Schedule changes

Train services may change on the following public holidays (for movable dates see CALENDAR, page 54):

New Year	January 1
Easter Monday	Movable date
May 1, Ascension	Movable date
Whit Monday	Movable date
National Day	July 21
Assumption	August 15
All Saints	November 1
Armistice Day	November 11
Christmas	December 25

When traveling between Belgium and Britain remember that Britain keeps Western European Time, one hour earlier, and changes to summer time and back on different dates from Belgium.

Fares

First class costs 50% more than second. Second-class fares in Belgian francs (BF) and US dollars:

Distance in km	*100*	*200*
Local prices, BF	285	555
Eurailtariff, $	9	19

Supplements

On first class of EuroCity trains the supplement is 380 BF.

Reduced fares

Children under the age of six (up to four children with each adult) travel free in Belgium (under four on international routes); those aged six to twelve pay half fare.

Return tickets on weekends and to selected destinations are reduced by 40%. Weekend travel must begin between Friday and Sunday noon, and end between Saturday and Monday noon. Same-day return tickets are valid from any city to the seaside or the Ardennes and back during the holiday period (mid-June to mid-September). Two to six people traveling together with return tickets pay the **collective fare** (*Meermans-tarief/Tarif multi*), a reduction of 60%. The maximum fare is for 150 km on one trip.

Reduction card (*Reduktie-kaart/ Carte de réduction*) allows you to buy half-fare tickets; it costs 500 BF for one month.

Benelux-Weekend tickets to the Netherlands or Luxembourg offer reductions of 25% to one or two passengers, and 50% to others in a group up to six. Valid between Thursday 16:00 and Monday 24:00.

Go-as-you-please passes

Eurailpasses, Inter-Rail, and **Benelux-Tourrail Cards** allow unlimited travel on trains.

B-Tourrail, the national tourist pass, allows unlimited travel on trains on five days chosen during a 17-day period. Mark the day each time before starting travel. Children between four and twelve pay half of the adult price.

Class	1st class	2nd class
Age 6 to 25, BF	1950	1300
Above 25, BF	2550	1700

The **TTB card** is similar to the *B-Tourrail* but adds unlimited travel on public transport (bus, metro, tram) in any city.

Class	1st class	2nd class
Age 6 to 25, BF	2350	1700
Above 25, BF	3050	2200

Network passes (*Gewoon abon-nement/Abonnement ordinaire*) allow unlimited train travel. Order four days in advance at any station.

Class	1st class	2nd class
16 days, BF	4580	3050
1 month, BF	8170	5450

Tickets

Single tickets are valid for one day (if you buy in advance, state the day of use). Return tickets are valid for three days. One stopover is allowed; the ticket has to be endorsed at the departure or stopover station.

Reservations

Seats are not reservable inland. International passengers have first claim on seats. Reservation is obligatory on first class of EuroCity trains with the fee included in the supplement. Reserve from two months to 24 hours before departure.

Baggage

Forwarding costs 260 BF a piece, up to 30 kg (66 lbs). Hand in baggage at least two hours before departure. Pickup and delivery service is available in 25 cities. Storage costs 30 BF a day. Lockers use five-franc coins and cost 15 BF a day.

Meals

Main line trains may carry buffet cars during meal times, others are catered by mini-bars. Dining cars are only in international traffic. The station restaurants are not cheap, but they're good.

Night travel

There are no inland services, but the Belgian railways handle couchette cars and Wagons-Lits sleepers on international routes. Couchettes cost 480 BF in six-berth compartments, 640 BF in four-berth, and may be reserved from two months in advance until a day before departure.

Sleeping car berths are reservable from three months in advance (two months to France and Switzerland) until a day before departure.

	Local prices	Eurailtariff
	BF	$
Single	4850	146
Special	3460	104
Double	2080	63
Triple (T3)	1390	42

Other services

Car rental (Train+Auto) is available at ten stations.

Bicycles (Train+Vélo) may be rented at 61 stations and returned at any of 87. The charge is reduced for train ticket holders to 100 BF a day; tandems cost 250 BF. Ask for a free tour map.

Assistance

Handicapped: The station staff will assist if you phone the information office in advance. Arriving at the station, contact a sous-chef de gare who will make arrangements. Wheelchairs are available; many stations have raised platforms, others use mobile ramps.

Emergencies: Contact a sous-chef de gare or a policeman.

Brussels

Tourist information

The national organization has a desk in the airport baggage claim area (summer: daily 7:30–20:30; winter: daily 8:00–20:30). Other services are near Centraalstation. The national tourist office (summer: daily 9:00–21:00; winter: 9:00–19:00) is at Grasmarkt 61 (rue du Marché aux Herbes); the city tourist office (9:00–18:00, closed on Sundays in winter) is in the city hall (Stadhuis/Hôtel de Ville) on Grand'Place. Phone 513 89 40 or write to Tourist Information Brussel, Stadhuis, Grote Markt, B–1000 Brussel.

City transit

The network includes buses, premetro (underground trams), metro, and trains in the city. Find information and maps at Porte de Namur, Rogier and Zuid/Midi metro stations. Tel. 515 30 64.

The **tourist pass** for 24 hours of unlimited travel costs less than four single fares. Buy it at tourist offices, metro and railway stations. **Weekly or monthly passes** may be bought at any station if you have a carte de validation with photo; get it at Porte de Namur metro station. Weekly passes cost the same as nine singles, monthlies as 30 singles. **Multiride** cards for five trips are sold by bus drivers, for ten trips at metro stations and news kiosks. **Single tickets** are sold by drivers. Validate passes and tickets in punch clocks at stations and aboard buses and trams.

Taxis
Tel. 242 22 22, 512 31 23, 268 13 13

Post, telegraph
Mon–Sat 8:00–20:00 at Zuid/Midi station.

Telephone
Daily 8:00–20:00 at Kaiserinlaan 17 (blvd. de L'Impératrice), next to Centraalstation.

Help in emergencies
Police: Tel. 906
Ambulance: Tel. 479 18 18, 648 80 80
Physician: Tel. 479 18 18, 648 80 80
Dentist: Tel. 426 10 26 (nights), 428 58 88 (weekends)
Pharmacy on 24-hour duty: Tel. 648 80 0
Lost & found:
Transit: 15, av. de la Toison d'Or. Tel. 512 17 90.

Other places: Police, Grand'Place. Tel. 517 96 11.

Airport
Brussels National Airport (Zaventem). See details on page 282.

Rail connections
The three main stations lie along the north-south line. Long distance trains stop at both north (Noordstation, Gare du Nord) and south (Zuidstation, Gare du Midi). For example, trains from France stop first at Zuid/Midi, then cross the city to end at Noord. Not all trains stop at Centraalstation. Only trains to Namur-Luxembourg stop at Quartier Léopold station.

The stations are connected by frequent trains, metro, and premetro.
Under 1 hour: Antwerp, Namur
1 to 2 hours: Liège, Ostend, Rotterdam
2 to 3 hours: Paris, Luxembourg, Cologne, Amsterdam
4 to 5 hours: Strasbourg, Frankfurt
Over 5 hours: London via Ostend-Dover (5 hours by jetfoil, 7 3/4 hours by ship)
Overnight: Bologna, Hamburg, Copenhagen, London, Marseille, Milan, Munich, Salzburg, Vienna, Zurich

Danish State Railways

Danske Statsbaner (DSB)

DSB

The Danish railway should be called seaway, trains spend so much time on water. While bridges connect most of the large islands, DSB ferries still have to carry entire trains between the Jylland peninsula, Fyn, and Sjaelland, and to Sweden and Germany. They cope with any weather and keep the trains running on time. The boat rides are a welcome treat for the bored passenger who is free to stroll and enjoy the sea air once the train is secured aboard.

The Kalundborg-Århus crossing leaves three hours for dinner, but main line speed doesn't allow a leisurely lunch: the Storebaelt is crossed in little over an hour.

The DSB is putting an end to some of this seafaring in 1993 when it opens the fixed link between Sjaelland and Fyn. A 9-km bridge and a 6-km undersea tunnel will allow trains to cross the Great Belt without wetting their wheels—and shorten travel between Copenhagen and the cities of Jylland by one hour.

Meanwhile the future has arrived in the shape of the IC/3. It seems that the *lyntoget,* or lightning-trains, introduced not so long ago, weren't fast enough at 140 km/h. They are being replaced by this new generation of InterCity trains with a speed of 200 km/h, to be raised to 230. However, in a small country speed is less important than comfort. The IC/3 features heating, lighting, and communication systems that are slightly ahead of the state-of-the-art, and such considerate additions as wheelchair-accessible toilets and platform-to-train elevators. IC/3 may be the rolling stock of choice to form faster EuroCity trains between Copenhagen and Hamburg.

DSB continues to sell itself to the business traveler with reservable office compartments, conference rooms, and train telephones, but doesn't neglect vacationing families. On weekend trains children may be sent out to play—in a special section, with attendants to keep them happy.

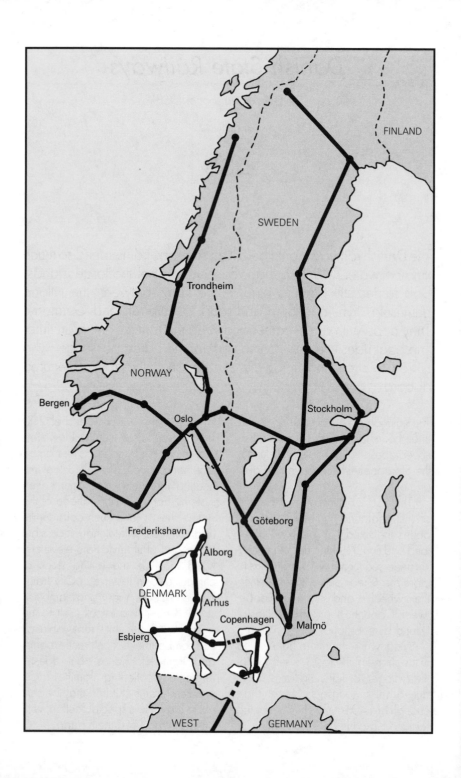

The railway's capital district (hovedstadområdet) covers half of the island of Sjaelland, where Copenhagen lies on the northeast coast, with a dense high-frequency commuter network. Much of the area is served by the S-tog system which is, in fact, Copenhagen's metro, crossing the city underground and extending to suburbs. Conventional local trains (regionaltoget) serve the smaller towns as does a large bus network. The DSB finds time to think up attractive novelties such as the 'quiet compartment' (stillekupé), IC-Salons for first-class passengers, and the Inter-Rail Center in Copenhagen.

Information

Most of the printed material is only in Danish but the staff, even outside information offices, are fluent in English. Finding one's way without asking is easy: pictograms and clear, coordinated signs make the busiest stations easy to cope with.

Schedule changes

Train services may change on the following public holidays (for movable dates see CALENDAR, page 54):

New Year	January 1
Maundy Thursday	Movable date
Good Friday	Movable date
Easter Monday	Movable date
Store Bededag=Prayer Day	Movable date (fourth Friday after Easter)
Ascension	Movable date
Whit Monday	Movable date
Constitution Day	June 5
Christmas	December 25-26

Fares

First class costs 50% more than second. Low fares (see REDUCED FARES) are 25% less. Fares are calculated by zones. Approximate second-class fares in Danish crowns (Dkr) and US dollars:

Distance in km	100	200	400
Local prices, Dkr	58	122	175
Eurailtariff, $	9	19	21

Supplements

There are no supplements in inland service.

Reduced fares

Regular fares apply Friday through Monday between May 1 and October 31, on Fridays and Sundays between November 1 and April 30; and Easter and Christmas holiday periods. Other days are low-fare days. Days count from 4:00 to 4:00. Many reductions don't apply in the Copenhagen area (hovedstads-området) and on Århus commuter services.

On **low-fare days** (billigdage), travel on second class costs 25% less.

Children under four travel free, four to eleven pay half fare. **Child's reduction** (børnerabat) allows a paying child to take one adult free if traveling at least 13 zones, on second class, on low-fare days.

Multiride ticket (10-turslippekort) is valid for ten trips on the same route. Validate before each trip in punch clock at the station.

Seniors over 65 with ID-card (65-billet, 5 Dkr, with photo) travel at low fare, or half fare on low-fare days).

Youths between 12 and 25, and with ID-card (*DSB-Ungdomskort*, 210 Dkr a year, with photo) may buy low-fare tickets.

Group tickets (*Gruppebillet*) for at least three persons give 20–50% reduction, depending on the number of people.

Monthly route pass (*Månadskort*) for frequent travel on a set route varies in price with distance, about 860 Dkr for 100 km, 1525 Dkr for 200 km.

Go-as-you-please passes

Eurailpasses allow unlimited travel on trains, ferries in Danish waters and to Sweden and Germany; fare discounts of 20% on DFDS ships sailing between Esbjerg and Britain or the Faeroe Islands, and between Copenhagen and Oslo.

Inter-Rail Cards and **Nordturist Tickets** allow unlimited travel on trains and DSB ferries.

Network pass (*DSB-Danmarkskort*) costs 1990 Dkr for a month.

Tickets

Single tickets are valid only on the day of issue or as dated, return tickets for two months. One stopover is allowed each way, but the ticket must be validated, before your journey is resumed, in the red or yellow punch clock at the station. If you return on a regular-fare day with a low-fare ticket, the difference is payable.

Reservations

Reservation is obligatory only when crossing the Storebaelt at Nyborg-Korsør or Århus-Kalundborg. It costs 25 Dkr on *lyntog* and 15 Dkr on InterCity trains. Reservations on trains to Germany cost 36 Dkr. Reserve from two months before departure.

Baggage

Forwarding costs 25 Dkr a piece, up to 50 kg (110 lbs). Hand in baggage at least 15 minutes before departure.

Storage costs 10 or 15 Dkr a day, depending on size of luggage. Lockers use tokens; buy them at the luggage store or in machines by the lockers. Machines take five- and ten-krone coins.

Meals

On *lyntog* and InterCity trains, buffets and trolleys serve sandwiches and drinks, also full meals on trays. Aboard the ferries, restaurants with table service are open during meal times, self-service cafeterias at all hours.

Don't miss the great smorgasbord (*Det store kolde bord*) in the Bistro of Copenhagen H station! All major stations have restaurants, although the others are less lavish. DSB kiosks sell sandwiches, sausages, and soups.

Duty-free shops on international ferries have good prices on spirits and wines. They also sell chocolates, cigarettes, cheeses and whole sides of smoked salmon. Tickets must be shown when shopping.

Night travel

Couchettes cost 60 Dkr in five-berth compartments, 70 Dkr on trains to Sweden and Norway, 111 Dkr to other countries. Reserve from two months before departure.

Sleeping car berths in singles are reservable with first-class tickets, in doubles with second class, from three months before departure. Prices vary with destination.

Local prices in Dkr.

	Inland	Scand.	Other
Single	300	495	867
Special	-	-	620
Double	160	162	372
Triple (T3)	-	108	248

Eurailtariff in US$

	Inland	Scand.	Other
Single	47	81	146
Special	-	-	105
Double	25	26	63
Triple (T3)	-	18	42

On the ferry between Kalundborg and Århus, berths in sleeping cabins may be reserved. Sheets, blanket, and pillow are supplied.

Other services

First-class service center: First-class passengers can get tickets, reservations of seats, conference compartments or *lyntog* salons, rent cars, reserve hotel rooms and theatre tickets in special offices in Copenhagen, Odense, Århus, Aalborg, and Esbjerg.

Quiet compartments *(Stillekupé)* run on InterCity trains. Passengers who prefer reading to talking can reserve seats in a second-class non-smoking compartment.

Telephone calls may be made from any *lyntog* and new InterCity trains. The minimum charge for 3-minute inland calls is 10 Dkr.

Children's playrooms: On train ferries between Århus and Kalundborg.
Bicycle rental: In the summer at several stations (not Copenhagen).
Car rental: Rent a car at any major station, return at other stations.

Assistance

Handicapped: Wheelchairs are provided at all stations. Some new InterCity trains have special compartments, toilets, and elevators to enter. Folding wheelchairs may be taken into compartments, others must be forwarded as baggage, free of charge. Passengers should phone in advance to arrange for help.

Passengers with allergies may reserve InterCity compartments with non-allergenic furnishings.

Emergencies: Contact the train information office or police.

Copenhagen

Tourist information

Find information at the main office (May through September: Mon–Fri 9:00–18:00, Sat 9:00–14:00, Sun 9:00–13:00; October through April: Mon–Fri 9:00–17:00, Sat 9:00–12:00), adjacent to Tivoli Gardens, follow signs from the railway station. Phone 33 11 13 25 or write to Danmarks Turistråd, H.C. Andersens Blvd 22, DK-1553 Copenhagen.

City transit

The system includes buses and rapid transit *(S-tog)* underground trains. Find information, timetable, and map at the railway and rapid transit stations and HT transit offices.

The **Copenhagen Card** (*Køben-havnerkortet*) for unlimited travel and admission to 36 museums and sights costs 80 Dkr for one day, 140 Dkr for two, 180 Dkr for three. Buy it at tourist offices and hotels, sign before use. **Tourist passes** for 24 hours of unlimited travel in the greater urban area cost the same as five single fares; they are sold at *S-tog* stations. **Multiride cards** (*rabatkort*) for ten trips save 25% over singles; sold at stations and transit offices. Single tickets are sold aboard buses and at stations. Children from five to twelve pay half fare. Validate tickets in punch clocks aboard buses and on *S-tog* platforms. They are valid for one hour with transfers.

Taxis

Tel. 31 35 35 35. Tip is included in the fare.

Post office

Mon–Fri 8:00–22:00, Sat 9:00–16:00, Sun 10:00–17:00 in the railway station.

Telegraph office

Daily 9:00–22:00 at Købmagergade 37.

Telephone

Mon–Fri 8:00–22:00, Sat 9:00–16:00, Sun 10:00–17:00 in the railway station.

Station plan
Copenhagen - København pp 214-215

Help in emergencies

Police, ambulance: Tel. 000
Physician: Tel. 0041
Dentist (clinic): *Tandlaegevagt*, Oslo Plads 14. Daily 20:00–22:00, Sat–Sun also 10:00–12:00.
Pharmacy on 24-hour duty: Steno Apotek, Vesterbrogade 6 (opposite railway station).
Tel. 33 14 82 66.
Lost & found: Police: Carl Jacobsensvej 30.
Tel. 31 16 14 06. Mon–Fri 10:00–15:00 (Thu 10:00–17:00). Transit: City Hall, Radhuspladsen.
Tel. 33 14 74 48. Mon–Fri 6:00–18:00, Sat 10:00–14:00.

Airport

Copenhagen Kastrup Airport. Airport buses run from the railway station every 20 minutes; travel time is 30 minutes.

Rail connections

All trains use the main station.
3 to 5 hours: Fredericia, Göteborg, Esbjerg, Århus
5 to 6 hours: Hamburg, Ålborg
Overnight: Amsterdam, Brussels, Frankfurt, Cologne, Oslo, Paris, Rotterdam, Stockholm, Utrecht

Boat connection

Catamaran service from Havnegade ferry terminal. Access by bus No. 28 or No. 41 from the railway station.
Under 1 hour: Malmö

Finnish State Railways

Valtionrautatiet (VR)

Far north from the land of mañana Finnish trains depart right at the scheduled moment and run very smoothly. VR offers not only reliable transportation but comfortable travel, well above the average European level. Low fares and the high standard of service make train travel in Finland one of the best values in Europe. Comfort stems partly from the broad-gauge track: cars are wider and more spacious than in standard systems. It is also democratically distributed: the only difference between classes is in walking space. Seating is two and two abreast on second, two and one on first class.

The rolling stock is mostly new, the best of it being the recently introduced InterCity cars (marked on the outside CX for first class, EX for second, and RX for restaurant car). They combine the latest technology with roomy luxury. Adjustable seats that flip up for easier access have stereo earphone jacks in the armrests, individual air inlets and reading lights built into the overhead luggage rack. Next to the automatic doors on the outside of the wagons, instead of route boards, there are electronic displays showing the route, departure and arrival times at major stops along the route. In each car you find a mix of compartments and open seating. This generation of cars includes new diners with matching comfort and space.

The top trains are the InterCity trains (*InterCity-juna*, marked IC in timetables) and special expresses (*erikoispikajuna*, EP), all with first- and second-class accommodation, and dining or buffet cars. Fast trains (*pikajuna*, P), regionals (*R-juna*), and locals (*henkilöjuna*) sometimes carry only second-class cars. Railcars (*kiskoauto, sähkomoottorijuna*) are second class with limited luggage space.

Information

A timetable of train, bus, boat, and plane schedules, and information in

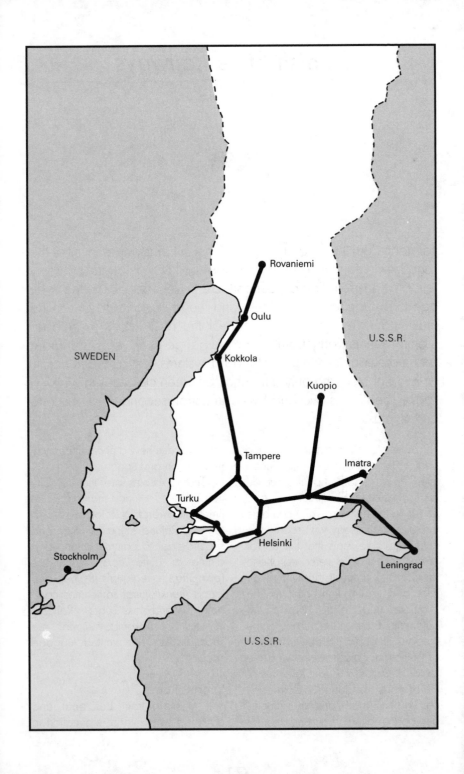

English, is available at Finnish tourist and Finnair offices. The regular timetable includes an English section with essential details.

Most railway staff know some English; at major stations they are fluently trilingual (Finnish, Swedish, English). Announcements are made in several languages aboard main line trains that tourists may take.

Schedule changes

Train services may change on the following public holidays (for movable dates see CALENDAR, page 54):

New Year	January 1
Epiphany	nearest Saturday to January 6
Good Friday	Movable date
Easter Monday	Movable date
May Day	May 1
Mothers' Day	the second Sunday in May
Ascension	Movable date
Midsummer or Finnish Flag Day	nearest Saturday to June 24
All Saints	nearest Saturday to November 1
Independence Day	December 6
Christmas	December 24–26

Finland is on Eastern European Time. When traveling to Sweden remember that it is on Central European Time, one hour earlier.

Fares

First class costs 50% more than second. Second-class fares in Finnish marks (FIM) and US dollars:

Distance in km	100	200	400
Local prices, FIM	34	61	111
Eurailtariff, $	–	15	28

Supplements

Supplements which include seat reservations are payable on InterCity trains, 50 FIM on first class (includes a light meal), 25 FIM on second class.

Reduced fares

Children under four travel free, four to twelve pay half fare.

Families or groups of at least three persons traveling together get 20% reduction. Tickets are valid for one month.

Return tickets cost about 5% less than regular fare, depending on distance. Valid for one month above 75 km. One stopover is allowed each way (tickets must be endorsed).

Seniors over 65 pay half fare with an ID-card (65-kortti) with photo, sold at stations for 50 FIM without a time limit on validity.

The **low-fare card** (VR-alennuskortti) is good for a reduction of 30% except at peak times. The card with photo costs 150 FIM and is valid for one year.

Go-as-you-please passes

Eurailpasses allow unlimited travel on trains and on Silja Line ferries between Helsinki or Turku and Stockholm.

Inter-Rail Cards and **Nordturist Tickets** allow unlimited travel on trains and half fare on ferries.

The **Finnrailpass** (Lomalippu), the national tourist pass, allows unlimited travel on trains and some inland ferries. InterCity supplements are payable. Buy it in Finland at stations and travel agencies, and in the US from Holiday Tours of America, New York; Scantours, Santa Monica; and Travel Service Ray K. Jones, Seattle.

Class	1st class	2nd class
8 days	600 FIM/$135	400 FIM/$90
15 days	900 FIM/$218	600FIM/$145
22 days	1125 FIM/$272	750FIM/$181

Tickets

One-way tickets for trips under 75 km are valid on the day of issue, return tickets for three days. Tickets for over 75 km are valid for one month. One stopover is allowed; tickets must be endorsed at the station before resuming travel.

Reservations

Reservation is obligatory on special expresses (EP) and costs 15 FIM and InterCity trains, where the fee is included in the supplement. On other trains reservation is optional at 10 FIM. Reserve from one year before to departure time.

You may make reservations for trains outside Finland but at a higher fee and with the additional cost of the telex order.

Baggage

Forwarding costs 15 FIM for each 30 kg (66 lbs). Storage costs 3 FIM a day. Lockers use one- and five-markka coins, and cost daily 3 FIM for regular, 10 FIM for large sizes.

Meals

InterCity trains and special expresses carry both full-service dining cars and self-service cafeterias, often in the same car. The first-class fare on InterCity trains includes breakfast in the morning or, at other times, snacks served at seats. Regular expresses have self-service cafeterias. Groups may order special catering.

Snack bars and kiosks at stations stock a variety of hearty Finnish meat pies, sandwiches and cakes. The restaurants are good. The "Eliel" in Helsinki, named after the station's architect, the elder Saarinen, has an authentic interior, which attracts students of Art Deco.

Night travel

Instead of couchettes, you find more comfortable and inexpensive sleeping cars. Breakfast trays may be ordered in advance. Berths in triple (tourist) compartments are available with second-class tickets, doubles and singles with first-class ticket or pass. Sleepers are reservable a year in advance and must be paid for at the latest 48 hours before departure. At Easter, Midsummer, and Christmas pay a week before departure.

Class	Local price	Eurailtariff
	FIM	US$
Single	150*	39
Double	75	20
Triple	50	13

* For single occupancy two first-class fares and supplement for two berths are charged.

Couchette and sleeping car reservations on trains outside Finland may be made here but at a higher fee and with the additional cost of the telex order.

Other services

Telephones are available on InterCity trains.

Car rentals are on offer at major stations.

Assistance

Handicapped: Platform officers help at stations. Wheelchairs are available. All trains have reserved seats for ill or handicapped passengers. For arrangements write to Helsinki Station, Kaivokatu 1–2–5, SF-00100 Helsinki 10, or phone 707 34 22.

Emergencies: Contact the station master or one of the platform officers (*Vahtimestari*) or the police (*Poliisi*).

Helsinki

Tourist information

The Travel Center (*Matkakeskus*), next to the railway station, has information and accommodation services (May 16–September 15: Mon–Fri 9:00–21:00, Sat 9:00–19:00, Sun 10:00–18:00; September 16–May 15: Mon–Fri 9:00–18:00). The city office is at Pohjoisesplanadi 19 (May 16–September 15: Mon–Fri 8:30–18:00, Sat 8:30–13:00; September 16–May 15: Mon 8:30–16:30, Tue–Fri 8:30–16:00). Phone 169 3757 or write to Helsinki City Tourist Office, Pohjoisesplanadi 19, SF-00100 Helsinki.

City transit

The transport system integrates buses, trams, trains, and metro in Helsinki, Espoo, and Vanta. Find information at tourist offices and metro stations.

The **Helsinki Card** is good for unlimited travel, free sightseeing trips and museum admissions, discounts on ferries, in restaurants, and entertainments. Buy it at tourist offices, the railway station, airport, and ferry terminals, travel agencies, and many hotels: 65 FIM for one day, 85 FIM for two, 105 FIM for three; for children (4–11) 35 FIM, 45 FIM, and 55 FIM. **Tourist tickets** (*matkailijalippu*) for unlimited travel cost the same as six single fares for 24 hours, 12 singles for three days, 20 singles for five days. Sold at tourist and transit offices, and on trams. **Multiride tickets** for ten trips save 20% over singles for adults, 80% for children.

Post office

Mon–Fri 9:00–17:00 (winter: Mon 9:00–18:00) at Mannerheimintie 11, next to the railway station.

Telephone, telegraph

Daily 7:00–23:00 at Mannerheimintie 11B, next to the railway station.

Help in emergencies

Police: Tel. 002
Ambulance: Tel. 006
Physician: Tel. 008

Dentist: Tel. 736 166
Pharmacy on 24-hour duty: Yliopiston. Mannerheimintie 5.
Lost & found: Police. Mon–Fri 8:00–16:15. Päijänteentie 12A. Tel. 1891.

Airport
Helsinki-Vantaa Airport. Buses (Finnair or No. 615) run every 15–30 minutes from the railway station; travel time is 25–30 minutes.

Rail connections
All trains use Rautatieasema.
2–3 hours: Tampere, Turku

3–5 hours: Imatra, Kokkola, Kuopio, Leningrad
Overnight: Oulu, Rovaniemi, Joensuu, Moscow

Boat connections
Boats dock in the South Harbor (Eteläsatama), Silja Line at Olympia, Viking Line at Katajanokka terminals.
Overnight: Stockholm*, Travemünde**

---

* Day and night crossings also from Turku.
** With Silja Finnjet, 22 hours June 10 to August 14, 38 hours at other times.

Station plan
Helsinki Rautatieasema pp 224-225

French National Railways

Société Nationale des Chemins de fer français (SNCF)

A railway of superlatives: the world's fastest trains run in the country with Europe's most extensive network of tracks. A few years ago the SNCF also ran some of the most luxurious cars, but since then other countries have raised the quality of their rolling stock. But the SNCF won't fall behind, it'll continue to work hard and get a car-obsessed nation off the roads and onto the rails. The distances between major cities are greater than in most countries, so long non-stop runs and the excellent technical condition of the railway allow trains to reach their destinations in conveniently short travel times at impressively high speeds.

For many years the TEEs on the Paris-Bordeaux route averaged 144 km/h (90 mph) on a four-hour run. That became past glory in 1983 when the TGV service started between Paris and Lyon, halving the previous travel time at 275 km/h (172 mph). The TGV *Atlantique* passed that in 1989, running at 300 km/h (187 mph). It also holds the world record at 482.4 km/h (301 mph).

On the main lines the regular trains consist mostly of *Corail* cars. These were introduced some years ago, but their comfort matches newer rolling stock in other countries. Soundproof-ing, air-conditioning, automatic doors, spacious seating are standard.

The *démocratisation de la vitesse*, to share speed and comfort more equitably among passengers, is nearly complete. But budget passengers are still excluded from three trains, the last all-first-class TEEs. (Why call them Trans-Europe if they only run in France?) All other trains, including TGVs, have two-class accommodations.

The bleak side of the SNCF empire are the transversal routes. In France everything has always centered on Paris, including the railway. Paris passengers ride fast and convenient

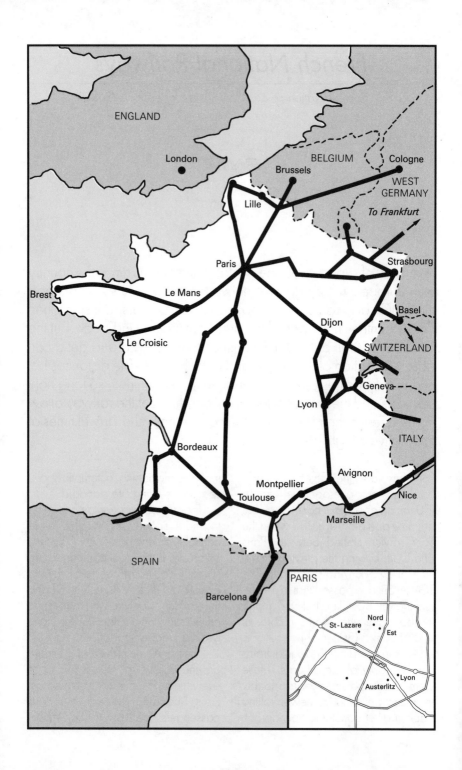

rapides, while those shuttling in the provinces get the old cars and awkward schedules. A sign of change is the Lille-Lyon TGV which connects the two cities directly, skirting Paris. Between other places it is often faster to go to Paris and change trains than trying to travel directly.

The only other cause for complaint that passengers sometimes raise is the attitude of some of the staff. Travelers may dispute which is the most infuriating bureaucracy in Europe. But having faced the Napoleonic disdain of a French station clerk you easily spot the winner. You must be prepared to insist if he tells you that the train you want doesn't exist. A second check on the computer often proves he is wrong.

Information

Overseas SNCF offices have schedules and fares, not only for France but all of Europe (see TRAVELCRAFT IN PLANNING, page 12). At stations *agents d'accueil* (information officers) with orange bands on caps and sleeves, help with problems, answer questions in several languages. In the information office you'll find a slew of leaflets explaining everything and timetable extracts covering all routes. Some knowledge of French is useful on rural trains and even at Paris stations—railway strikes *(la grève)* are not announced in other languages.

Schedule changes

Train services may change, and reduced fares not apply, on the following public holidays (for movable dates see CALENDAR, page 54):

New Year	January 1
Easter Monday	Movable date
May 1, Ascension	Movable date
Whit Monday	Movable date
Bastille Day	July 14
Assumption	August 15
All Saints	November 1
Armistice Day	November 11
Christmas	December 25

Fares

First class costs 50% more than second. Second-class fares in French francs (F) and US dollars:

Distance in km	100	200	300
Local prices, F	58	106	190
Eurailtariff, $	11	20	39

Supplements

On first-class TEEs, EuroCity trains and some selected *rapides* the supplement varies with distance and type of train. Your only guide is the official timetable that lists the trains and amounts. Expect to pay 13 to 32 F more on second class, 32 to 80 F more on first.

On the TGV *Sud-Est,* a supplement is payable only at peak times. The amount from Paris to Lyon varies between 45 and 77 F on second class, fixed at 77 F on first; to Marseille the range is 61 to 93 F on second, 93 F on first class.

On the TGV *Atlantique,* you need a RESA 300 supplement that varies with the time of arrival or departure in Paris. The regular amounts are 29 F on second and 37 F on first class; at peak times the supplement rises to 61 to 77 F on second, 101 to 107 F on first class. The supplement between provincial towns is 13 F.

Reduced fares

Fares are discounted only on 'blue days' in the railway's calendar, not at peak times before holidays or during some weekends.

Children under four travel free, four to eleven pay about 35% less. The *Carte Kiwi* for children up to sixteen allows them and up to four persons traveling with them to buy tickets at half price. It costs 350 F for one year.

Seniors over 60 and **youths** between 12 and 26 may travel for half fare with ID-cards: *Carte Vermeil*, costs 125 F, *Carte Jeune* 160 F for one year.

Couples traveling together with a *Carte Couple* pay half fare for the second person.

Go-as-you-please passes

Eurailpasses allow unlimited travel on SNCF trains, the Digne-Nice train of the Chemins de Fer de la Provence, and Irish Ferries boats between France and Ireland.

Inter-Rail Cards are valid for free travel on trains, half fare on Europabuses, and a 30–50% reduction on Channel ferries and ferries to Corsica.

The **BritFrance Railpass** is valid for free travel on trains and crossing the Channel to Britain by hovercraft.

France-Vacances is the national flexipass that allows unlimited travel on trains on days chosen in a longer period. It includes free airport transfer in Paris, one day of unlimited travel on Paris city transit, sightseeing tours, museum admissions, and car rental and hotel discounts. It is sold to non-residents only, both overseas and in France. Children from four to twelve pay half price by the French tariff, slightly above that overseas.

Class	1st class	2nd class
4 days in 15	880 F	660 F
9 days in 1 month	1650 F	1130 F
4 days in 15	$149	$99
9 days in 1 month	$249	$175

Network or route passes (*modulopass*) for unlimited travel on designated routes or the entire system, for one month or more come in a variety. Inquire at stations.

Tickets

Tickets may be bought two months in advance. They must be validated before boarding in orange punch clocks (*composteurs*) at access to trains. Validate again after stop overs and on return trips. If you miss the train after validation, the ticket office will annul the stamp. Unused tickets may be returned for refund up to two months after expiry.

Reservations

Seat reservation is obligatory on some trains so marked in the timetable, optional on others but recommended in busy periods. The charge is 13 F, included in supplements.

Reserve before noon on trains leaving between 17:00 and 24:00; by 20:00 for trains leaving between midnight and 17:00 the next day. Reservations may be made 6 months in advance by mail, 2 months in person, and 9 days by phone.

On the TGV *Sud-Est*, reserve seats when buying tickets. Failing that, you can do it up to a few minutes before departure at an automat marked *TGV Réservation rapide*. The machine issues reservations for the first TGV with available seats leaving within 90 minutes but without choice of window or aisle or smoking/non-smoking section. Reservation is free.

On the TGV *Atlantique*, you need the *RESA 300* supplement with your ticket. This includes reservation.

Baggage

Forwarding costs 45 F each for up to three pieces of 30 kg (66 lbs), bicycles 68 F if wrapped, 90 F if not. Baggage may be sent to any destination, even if you reach it by bus or ship. Send it at least 30 minutes in advance; or it may go on a later train.

Pickup and delivery may be ordered by calling the station's baggage office. The charge is 45 F for each service and piece.

Storage costs 12 F a day. Lockers cost 5–10 F a day, depending on size, electronic lockers 20 F for 72 hours. You'll need ten-, five-, one- or half-franc coins. Note: If you use an electronic locker that needs a code instead of a key, do NOT accept help or you may lose your belongings to a kind stranger who has read the magic number!

Meals

The French take food seriously. The scarcity of delicatessens in sta-

tions discourages frivolous picnicking. Stock up elsewhere on cheeses, patés, fresh bread and better quality wine.

Besides kiosks selling the usual dry *sandwich au jambon*, a large station may have a *relais gastronomique* or *buffet de la gare*. This is not a buffet, but a culinary citadel that guards the fine style of more opulent days at above-average prices. The brasseries are reliable for decent food at economical prices.

There are few dining cars but those left on EuroCity and TEE trains maintain the tradition with expert staff and linen napkins. The self-service *Gril-Express* offer a selection of hot main courses and cold plates at all hours. More and more trains—*Corail* and *Turbotrain*—serve meals at seats but in a manner more civilized than on planes: not all at once, but course after course. Order meals when you reserve your seat. On TGVs full meals are served at seats in first class, cold tray meals in second; there is also a bar serving hot and cold snacks. Lesser routes are catered only by minibars.

Night travel

Couchette cars have four berths in a compartment in first class, six in second. Either costs 72 F inland, 77 F in international service. Reserve from two months to two hours before departure, not later than 20:00.

Sleepers are more expensive than in international service. Reserve from three months to two hours before departure and not later than 18:00.

	Local prices	Eurailtariff
	F	$
Single	801	157
Special	572	110
Double	344	66
Triple (T3)	229	43

Some trains carry *Cabine 8* compartments with eight reclining couches (four in a stack), a cramped arrangement available for the regular seat reservation fee.

Other services

Bicycle rental *(Train+Vélo)*: Available at 280 stations for 40 F a day, less for longer periods.

Car rental *(Train+Auto)*: May be rented at over 220 stations and returned to any station in the region.

Hotels *(Train+Hôtel)*: Reserve a hotel room when reserving seats on the train. Many excursions include discounts on overnight stays.

Children *(Jeune Voyageur Service)*: Children four to fourteen may travel alone, accompanied on the train by hostesses.

Assistance

Handicapped: Most large stations have special toilets, and elevators or ramps for boarding; many trains have special sections for wheelchairs. On arrival handicapped passengers should contact the *Bureau d'accueil* (welcome office) for assistance. For advance information and arrangements contact an overseas SNCF office or your station of departure.

Medical, family, and social aid: Contact *SOS voyageurs* at stations.

This organization provides help, sometimes medical aid, and a resting place for mothers with infants, elderly or ill passengers, or anyone in trouble.

Emergencies: Contact an *agent d'accueil* (with an orange band on his cap and sleeve) at platform entrances or in the *Bureau d'accueil*. At night look for the duty officer in the station master's or in the telegraph office.

Lyon

Tourist information

Information and accommodation services are in *Centre d'Echanges* at Perrache station (Mon–Sat 9:00–12:30/14:00–18:00). Phone 78 42 25 75 or write to Office du Tourisme de Lyon-Communauté, Place Bellecour, F-69002 Lyon.

City transit

The network combines bus, trolleybus, metro, and funicular. Find information at Perrache and Part-Dieu metro stations, and in Place de la République.

Tourist passes *(Ticket-Liberté)* cost the same as eight single fares for two days, 12 singles for three days; they are sold at transit kiosks. Buy **single tickets** or *carnets* of six from bus drivers and automats; they are valid for one hour with three transfers. Validate passes and tickets in punch clocks on buses and at metro stations.

Taxis

Tel. 78 28 23 23

Post, telegraph, telephone
Mon–Fri 8:00–19:00, Sat 8:00–12:00 in Place Antonin Poncet.

Help in emergencies
Police: Tel. 17
Ambulance: Tel. 18 and 78 83 51 51
Physician on 24-hour duty: Tel. 78 95 05 05
Lost & found: 5, rue Bichat. Tel. 78 42 43 82

Airport
Lyon-Satolas Airport. Airport buses run from *Centre d'Echanges* at Perrache station; travel time is 35–45 minutes.

Rail connections
Perrache and the new station at Part-Dieu lie on the same line and most trains stop at both, except some TGVs going to the south. Check timetable for station of departure. The stations are connected by frequent trains.
1 to 2 hours: Avignon, Dijon, Geneva, Paris
2 to 3 hours: Marseille
5 to 6 hours: Milan, Strasbourg
Overnight: Barcelona (change at Cerbère/Port Bou)

Marseille

Tourist information
Offices are at the railway station (daily 8:00–20:00, winter Mon–Fri 9:00–12:30/14:00–18:30) and near the Old Port (daily 8:00–21:00, winter Mon–Fri 9:00–18:30). Phone 91 54 91 11 or write to Office de Tourisme, 4, la Canebière, F-13001 Marseille.

City transit
Buses, metro, and a tram comprise the system. Find information and maps at metro stations and transit kiosks.

The only **tourist pass** for unlimited travel is the one-month coupon mensuel for the price of 30 single fares. Tickets bought in advance in sixes save about 30%. Buy them at transit kiosks and automats at metro and tram stops. Validate tickets in punch clocks and keep the accompanying talon till all tickets are used up. Tickets are good for 70 minutes with transfers.

Taxis
Tel. 91 66 68 10, 91 49 91 00

Post, telegraph, telephone
Permanent service at place de l'Hôtel des Postes (Colbert metro stop).

Help in emergencies
Police: Tel. 17
Ambulance: Tel. 18
Physician on 24-hour duty: Tel. 91 52 91 52
Pharmacy on 24-hour duty: Tel. 91 52 91 52
Lost & found: Commissariat Central, 2, rue Antoine Becker. Tel. 91 91 90 40

Airport
Marseille-Province Airport. Airport buses run every 15 minutes from the station; travel time is 30 minutes.

Rail connections

All trains use Gare St-Charles.
1 to 2 hours: Montpellier
2 to 3 hours: Lyon, Nice
4 to 5 hours: Paris, Toulouse
Overnight: Brussels, Strasbourg, Venice

Paris

Tourist information

There are information desks at both airports, offices with information and accommodation services at all railway stations (see following pages for working hours), and at 127, Champs-Elysées (daily 9:00–20:00). Phone 47 23 61 72 or write to Office de Tourisme de Paris, 127 av. des Champs-Elysées, F-75008 Paris.

City transit

The urban area network includes buses, metro, and RER (rapid transit) lines, extending into the suburbs with SNCF commuter trains. Phone 43 46 14 14 for information in English. Maps are available at RATP kiosks at larger métro and RER stations.

Bus and RER fares vary with distance. The following cost comparisons are based on fares for the central zones.

There are several **tourist passes**. The Paris Sésame passes are valid on all lines except SNCF trains, and offer discounts on sightseeing tours. They cost the same as 12 single fares for

two days, 18 for four, 30 for seven; buy them at airports and stations, tourist offices, and some metro stations.

With a *Carte Orange* (photo needed) buy a yellow coupon for a week (valid Mon–Fri) for the cost of ten singles; an orange one for a month costs 34 singles; both cover suburban trains. Sold at stations and RATP kiosks.

Formule 1 cards for one day cost the same as four singles; sold at metro stations. **Carnets** of ten tickets save about 40% over singles. First-class metro tickets cost 44% more.

Passes come with magnetic cards to open the electronic turnstiles at metro and RER stations. Tickets are validated automatically when inserted in the turnstiles and are needed at the end of the trip to exit.

Taxis

Tel. 47 39 47 39, 42 02 42 02, 47 30 23 23, 42 70 41 41
Check the phone book for numbers of nearby stands.

Post, telegraph, telephone

Daily 8:00–19:00 for postal services, all hours for telephone and telegraph, at 52, rue du Louvre.

Help in emergencies

Police: Tel. 17
Physician on 24-hour duty:
Tel. 47 07 77 77, 45 33 99 17
Pharmacy on 24-hour duty:
84, Champs-Elysées.
Tel. 45 62 02 41

Lost & found:
36, rue des Morillons.
Tel. 48 28 32 36.

Airports
Roissy-Charles-de-Gaulle Airport, Orly Airport. See details on pages 289.

Rail connections
There are four international stations in Paris (Gare St-Lazare has only a few boat trains to Britain via Dieppe and Le Havre).

Trains to the south and southwest (Bordeaux, Toulouse, also Spain and Portugal) use Gare d'Austerlitz. Northern connections to Belgium and the Netherlands, northern Germany, and Scandinavia run from the Gare du Nord. The Gare de l'Est is the terminal for trains to Germany, Switzerland, and Austria. Gare de Lyon handles regular trains to the south-east of France and to Italy, and high-speed TGV trains to the south-east, the Alps, and Switzerland (Bern, Geneva, Lausanne).

Stations are connected by metro but may require transfer. Direct connections are provided by SNCF interstation buses.

(Departure stations in parentheses)
1 to 2 hours: Lille (Nord), Lyon (Lyon)
2 to 3 hours: Brussels (Nord)
3 to 4 hours: Bern, Geneva, Lausanne (Lyon), Strasbourg (Est)
4 to 5 hours: Basel (Est), Bordeaux (Austerlitz), Marseille (Lyon), Rotterdam (Nord)
5 to 6 hours: Amsterdam, London by hovercraft (Nord), Zurich (Est)
Over 6 hours: London by ship (Nord)

Overnight: Barcelona, Madrid, Toulouse (Austerlitz), Frankfurt, Salzburg (Est), Bologna, Milan, Venice (Lyon), Hamburg, Copenhagen, Cologne (Nord)

Strasbourg

Tourist information
Three offices provide information and accommodation services (daily 8:00–19:00 during the summer). In winter the offices at the railway station and Pont d'Europe are open Mon–Fri 9:00–12:30/13:45–18:00; on Place Gutenberg Mon–Sat 8:45–12:15/13:45–19:00.

Phone 88 32 57 07 or write to Office du Tourisme, 10, Place Gutenberg, F-67000 Strasbourg.

City transit
For information and tickets, see the transit office at the railway station or on Place Broglie. Buy **carnets** of five tickets, saving 30% on singles, from transit offices or automats. Single tickets are sold aboard buses.

Taxis
Tel. 88 36 13 13, 88 75 19 19, 88 78 05 65.

Post, telephone, telegraph
Late service at avenue de la Marseillaise.

Help in emergencies
Police: Tel. 17

Ambulance, physician, dentist:
Tel. 88 33 33 33
Pharmacy on 24-hour duty:
Tel. 88 36 09 93
Lost & found: Police Mon–Thu
9:00–12:00/14:00–18:00, Fri
9:00–12:00. 11, rue de la Nuée-
Bleue. Tel. 88 32 99 08.

Airport
Strasbourg-Entzheim Airport. Airport
buses from Grand Hotel and outside
railway station leave according to
flight schedule; inquire at tourist office; travel time is 25 minutes.

Rail connections
All trains use the main station.
1 to 2 hours: Basel, Metz
2 to 3 hours: Frankfurt, Luxembourg
3 to 4 hours: Paris
4 to 5 hours: Brussels, Lyon, Munich
Overnight: Marseille, Milan, Venice,
Zurich

German Federal Railway

Deutsche Bundesbahn (DB)

Germany's passenger service scores highly on any scale of evaluation. Other railways may pride themselves on some outstanding features but the Bundesbahn keeps consistently high standards in all aspects of its enormous and busy operation. Italian dining cars may endear themselves to gourmets but the DB serves good food *and* runs on time; French TEEs may move faster but the German InterCity trains offer speed and comfort on both classes at less cost.

In the InterCity (IC) network four routes connect 47 cities, most of these with hourly trains—soon to be half-hourly—in both directions. Between Hamburg in the north and Munich in the south the routes intersect at Dortmund, Hannover, Cologne, Mannheim and Würzburg; trains arrive at neighboring platforms at the same time for easy and quick transfer. IC trains carry both first- and second-class cars, with air-conditioning on first- and much of second class, and full-service dining cars. They feature public phones, route announcements in several languages and efficient multilingual staff. They are clean and comfortable.

Continuing to improve both speed and comfort, the DB has two new achievements. The first is the success of its high-speed train, the ICE, or *InterCity Experimental*, as it was called during its development. It has passed the test, setting a world rail record at 406 km/h (since overtaken by the French). No longer experimental, it will enter service as the *InterCity Express*, integrated in the regular-interval IC system and loping along at a mere 250 km/h.

Comfort has increased even away from the main lines. The *InterRegio* (IR) is to IC what IC was to the trains of the '60s—these luxurious new cars seem to have been designed for the 2000s. The 18 IR routes with two-hourly trains will complement the IC network and replace the *D-Zug* express trains.

The special long-distance expresses (*Fern-Express*, FD) run the length of the country to tourist areas, the Alps, Lake Constance (the

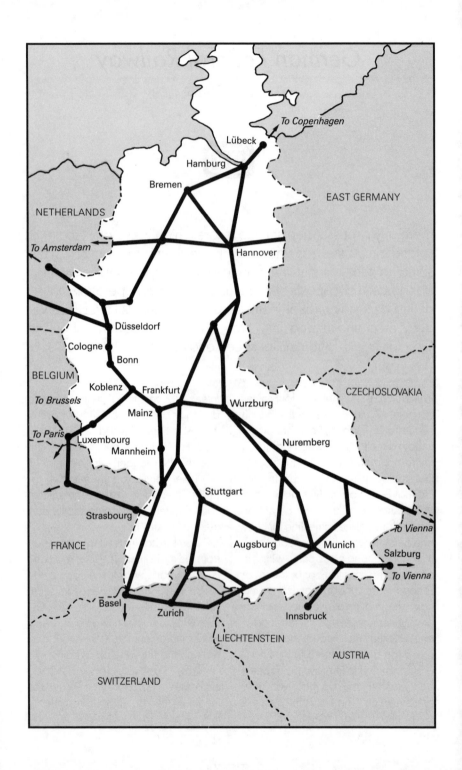

Bodensee), and beyond borders to Paris, Vienna, and Klagenfurt. Regular international expresses and inland fast trains (*Schnellzüge*, D) and slow regionals (*Eilzüge*, E) fill the gaps.

Train tickets and passes let you sail on DB's own ships on Lake Constance and aboard Köln-Düsseldorfer ships on the Rhine. KD offers a leisurely alternative to trains on the spectacular section of the river between Cologne and Mainz. DB also operates an extensive network of buses. On scenic routes, like the Romantic Road between Frankfurt and Munich, you may prefer the slower bus to the train.

Surprisingly for a vast government enterprise, prone to bureaucratic callousness, the Bundesbahn upholds the private-sector principle that the customer comes first. Clients are called *Fahrgäste*, traveling guests, and treated with personal care and hospitality.

Information

German tourist offices overseas and stations stock brochures with details on rail travel in several languages.

At each station large posters display the local schedule. Electronic displays and platform indicators show imminent arrivals and departures. Aboard IC, trains leaflets list the schedule and all connections.

In major stations information officers, distinguishable by yellow capbands, help to find trains. The information office can give more details about further connections and fares. Railway staff along the busier routes speak English.

Schedule changes

Train services may change on the following public holidays (for movable dates see CALENDAR, page 54):

New Year	January 1
Epiphany	January 6
Good Friday	Movable date
Easter Monday	Movable date
May Day	May 1
Ascension	Movable date
Whit Monday	Movable date
German Unity Day	June 17
Corpus Christi	Movable date
Assumption	Movable date
All Saints	November 1
Repentance Day	November 21
Christmas	December 25–26

Fares

First class costs 50% more than second. Second-class fares in German marks (DM) and US dollars:

Distance in km	100	200	400
Local prices, DM	19	41	82
Eurailtariff, $	14	29	51

Supplements

The supplement for travel on EuroCity and InterCity trains is 6 DM (7 DM if paid on the train). On InterRegio, D and FD trains pay only on trips under 50 km: 3 DM (4 DM if paid on the train).

Reduced fares

Children under four travel free, four to twelve pay half fare.

Savers are fixed-price return tickets. The *Sparpreis* sets the maximum fare to correspond to 446 km for longer trips. It is valid for return in one month. The *Super-Sparpreis* costs the same as the fare for 299 km and is valid for ten days. You cannot travel with it on certain days (see calendar at a station). The EC or IC supplement doubles on Fridays and Sundays.

Class	1st class	2nd class
Sparpreis, DM	270	180
Super-Sparpreis, DM	180	120

You may combine these with **companion fares** (*Mitfahrer-Fahrpreis*) when two or more persons travel together. They apply for distances over 203 km. The first person pays full fare (or saver), the others each pay half. Return must be the same day on trips under 101 km, or within one month over that distance.

Rail & Fly-Tickets are fixed-price return tickets between airports and any German city, valid for return in two months. The listed fares are for one person. Two to five additional persons traveling together each pay half fare, children a flat rate of 10 DM.

Class	1st class	2nd class
Under 251 km, DM	106	70
Over 252 km, DM	157	106

Families, seniors, and **youths** pay half fare with ID-cards valid for one year. Inquire at stations.

Go-as-you-please passes

Eurailpasses allow unlimited travel on trains, DB buses, Europabuses on the Castle Road (Mannheim-Nürnberg) and the Romantic Road (Wiesbaden-Munich), Köln-Düsseldorfer day ships on the Rhine (supplement payable on hydrofoils) and Mosel, and ferries to Denmark; half fare on DB ships on the Bodensee and on TT-Saga ferries to Sweden (Lübeck-Malmö).

Inter-Rail Cards allow unlimited travel on trains and half fare on buses.

The **GermanRail Pass** or DB-Tourist Card *(DB-Tourist Karte)* is sold only to visitors. It allows unlimited travel on trains, DB and German Touring buses, Köln-Düsseldorfer day ships on the Main, Mosel, and Rhine. All supplements are included in the price. Buy it in Germany at major stations and airports, and overseas at German railway offices.

Local price in DM	1st class	2nd class
4 days	260	175
9 days	390	260
16 days	530	355

Overseas price in US$	1st class	2nd class
4 days	135	90
9 days	202	135
16 days	285	190

GermanRail Junior Passes for youths between 12 and 26 are valid only on second class and cost about 60% of the adult second-class passes. Children pay half of the adult price.

The **Tramper-Monats-Ticket** for youths under 23 (students till 27) allows one month of unlimited travel on trains (second class), including supplements and taking a bicycle, and DB buses. It costs 234 DM.

Touring cards *(Tourenkarte)* allow unlimited travel on trains (second class) and buses in an approximately 100-km area on ten days chosen during a period of 21 days. They may be bought only with a ticket (minimum distance 250 km) or pass used to reach the area. D and FD supplements are included, EC and IC are not. They cost 47 DM for one, 64 DM for two, 79 DM for a family.

A **monthly pass** *(Monatsnetzkarte)* is a good investment if you plan to explore Germany thoroughly. One month of unlimited travel on trains, DB buses and most regional buses costs 1257 DM on first, 838 DM on second class. It includes supplements and free forwarding of one piece of baggage. Inquire about other passes for part of the network or a district, for a week, month or quarter-year.

Tickets

One-way and return tickets for less than 100 km are valid for one day. For longer trips, one-way tickets are valid for four days, return tickets for a month. Stopovers are allowed.

Reservations

Reservation is optional on FD and D expresses for 3.50 DM. On EuroCity and InterCity trains the supplements include reservations. Reserve from two months to one day before departure.

Baggage

Forwarding costs 9.50 DM a piece, up to 30 kg (66 lbs); first get a Gepäckkarte, or luggage card, at the ticket window. House-to-house ser-vice costs 6.20 DM each for pickup and delivery.

Storage costs 1–2 DM a day, depending on size. Lockers use one-mark pieces (change machines take two-, five- and ten-mark coins).

Baggage to and from airports *(Rail & Fly-Gepäckservice)*

Forward baggage directly to the Frankfurt and Düsseldorf airports from many stations (inquire there). Send before 17:30 on weekdays, 12:00 on weekends, to pick up after 6:00 next morning. If sent further in advance, it will be stored free for five days. Lufthansa passengers departing from Frankfurt or Düsseldorf may have their baggage taken directly to the plane if they check in at stations in Augsburg, Bonn, Cologne, Koblenz, Munich, Nuremberg or Würzburg. The cost is 15 DM.

Baggage may be forwarded to any destination in Germany directly from Frankfurt or Düsseldorf airports for 9.50 DM.

Meals

All IC trains carry dining cars which are always open for full meals or snacks. *Bord Restaurant* cars also have a bar/lounge section. The new Inter-Regio trains carry *Bistro Café* cars serving light meals and drinks. Tables in dining cars are reserved for diners at meal times, other times you may use the place as a lounge. The food is good, the menu lists a selection of agreeable wines, service is smooth, and the prices are not above those charged on solid ground.

Couchette and sleeping car attendants stock snacks and drinks for the evening and can serve full breakfasts. On some international trains catering may be limited to mini-bars.

All stations have several restaurants, reliably good and never too expensive. The best are the DSG's Inter-City Restaurants in some of the largest stations; they look plush and serve fine food, yet the prices are in the medium range. Major stations have several delicatessens, bakeries, and fruit shops. The DSG delicatessens stay open late, and also on Sundays, selling absolutely everything you may need for a picnic.

Night travel

Couchettes are all second class. Reservations may be made from two months until two hours before departure. The price is 23 DM in a six-berth, 31 DM in a four-berth compartment.

Sleeping car berths cost less than in international service and are reservable three months in advance. Some new cars have showers.

	Local price	Eurail tariff
	DM	US$
Single	207	121
Special	148	86
Double	89	52
Triple (T3)	59	34

Local transit

Most cities have integrated systems which combine main line trains through the area, rapid transit (S-Bahn) run by DB, trams, buses, and U-Bahn. Tickets and passes are valid on all modes of transport.

Other services

Car rental *(Rail & Road)*: Available at most stations and at a discount with train ticket. Conductors on IC trains can order cars about two hours before arrival.

Bicycles *(Fahrrad am Bahnhof)* may be rented at 270 stations and returned at any station. Cost is 5 DM a day with train ticket, 10 DM without. **Telephones** *(Zugtelefon)* are on all IC and IR trains. Have five-mark coins ready for overseas calls.

Assistance

Handicapped: All major stations have special toilets, telephones, elevators or ramp entrances for wheelchairs. Personal assistance is given by railway staff, police, Red Cross or *Bahnhofsmission*. If possible, write or phone in advance and give the time of departure, route, and type of assistance required.

Family or social aid: Mothers with babies, and elderly, ill or moneyless passengers are helped by the *Bahnhofsmission*. Its shelters have a nursery, sickroom, and first-aid facilities. **First aid and medical help:** Contact the Red Cross *(Deutsches Rotes Kreuz)*.

Emergencies: Contact a platform supervisor *(Bahnsteigaufsichtsbeamter)*, an information officer, or police *(Bahnpolizei)*.

The Lufthansa Airport Express

Flight LH 1005 skims along the Rhine at altitude zero, presenting Lufthansa passengers with a view of the most magnificent scenery in Germany. It is one of four daily 'flights' that combine the best of air and rail travel. The train passes lush vineyards and romantic castles on the shores of the busy river while complimentary meals and drinks are served at seats or in the lounge car. There are newspapers, magazines, a pay phone, and service by Lufthansa stewards and stewardesses.

The Airport Express is a pleasant alternative to flying the 250-km distance between Frankfurt and Düsseldorf; it offers direct access to both central Bonn and Cologne—and something beautiful to look at while getting there. The trains run between Frankfurt and Düsseldorf airport stations, stopping in Bonn, Cologne, Cologne-Deutz, and Düsseldorf central stations, with convenient transfer to main line trains. Travel time is 2 hours 40 minutes. Since the Airport Express is operated by Lufthansa, it may be taken only with an airline ticket (specify it when reserving your flight). Baggage is checked through to your destination. Allow 55 minutes for transfer between plane and train at the airport.

Frankfurt

Tourist information

Offices for information and accommodation are at the railway station, Hauptbahnhof (Mon–Sat 8:00–21:00, Sun 9:30–20:00) and in the Hauptwache-Passage. Phone 212 88 49 or write to Frankfurter Verkehrsverein, Gutleutstrasse 7–9, D-6000 Frankfurt/M.

City transit

Buses, trams, rapid transit (S-Bahn, U-Bahn), and regular trains are integrated in the system that reaches the airport, Mainz, and Wiesbaden. For information, maps, and English brochures see FVV transit offices at Hauptbahnhof and rapid transit stations.

The one-day **tourist pass** *(24 Stunden Frankfurt)* for unlimited travel in the urban zone, including the airport, costs less than four single fares. **Weekly and monthly passes** are sold at FVV offices for the same cost as 9 and 34 singles (get a *Kundenkarte* first). **Return tickets** at any time cost as much as two off-peak tickets (cheaper than singles during rush hour). Tickets and day passes are sold by blue automats at S-Bahn and U-Bahn stations. Instructions are given in English. The machines usually give change; if not, the display *"Bitte abgezählt zahlen"* asks for exact amount. Tickets need not be validated (do not buy day pass until ready to use). Single tickets are also sold by bus drivers. Validate advance and return tickets in punch clock at stations and aboard trams.

Taxis
Tel. 25 00 01, 23 00 01

Post, telephone, telegraph
Permanent service at Hauptbahnhof and airport.

Help in emergencies
Police: Tel. 110
Ambulance: Tel. 112
Physician, dentist, pharmacy: Inquire from Police, tel. 110

Lost & found: Fundbüro, Mainzer Landstrasse 323. Tel. 265 56 45

Airport

Frankfurt/Main Airport. See details on page 283. To send baggage directly to airplane, see page 111.

Rail connections

All trains use Hauptbahnhof.
Under 1 hour: Mainz, Mannheim
1 to 2 hours: Karlsruhe, Koblenz, Würzburg
2 to 3 hours: Basel, Cologne*, Nürnberg, Strasbourg, Stuttgart
3 to 4 hours: Munich
4 to 5 hours: Brussels, Hamburg, Luxembourg, Utrecht, Zurich
5 to 6 hours: Amsterdam, Lausanne, Rotterdam, Salzburg
Overnight: Milan, Paris, Vienna

Hamburg

Tourist information

Offices for information and accommodation are at the main railway station, Hauptbahnhof (daily 7:00–21:00), downtown in the Hanse-Viertel, in the harbor, and at the airport. Phone 30 05 10 or write to Hamburg Tourist Board, Burchardstrasse 14, D-2000 Hamburg.

City transit

Three rapid transit rail networks, buses, and harbor ferries are combined in the integrated system. Information at HVV transit offices in Hauptbahnhof and major U- and S-bahn stations.

---

* Lufthansa Airport Express; see page 112

Tourist passes are good for unlimited travel by one adult and up to three children under 12. **Day cards** *(Tageskarte)* cost less than four single fares; they may be bought in advance for multiple days of your choice. **Family/group tickets** *(Familien/Gruppenkarte)* may be used by four adults and three children at the cost of less than six singles. Day passes are valid after 9:00 on weekdays and all hours at weekends. The **three-day pass** *(3-Tage-Karte)* is valid any time for 72 hours after purchase, and costs the same as nine singles. **Passes for a week or a month,** costing the same as nine or 36 singles, are sold at transport offices. Other passes and single tickets are sold by automats at stations and bus drivers. Validate in punch clocks aboard buses and at station entrances at first use.

Taxis

Tel. 44 10 11, 21 12 11.
For handicapped, tel. 410 54 58

Help in emergencies

Police: Tel. 110
Ambulance: Tel. 112
Physician: Tel. 22 80 22
Dentist: Tel. 468 32 60
Pharmacy on 24-hour duty:
Tel. 22 80 22
Lost & found: Mon, Thu 8:00–15:30, Tue–Wed, Fri 8:00–12:00. Bäckerbreitergang 73. Tel. 35 18 51

Airport

Hamburg-Fuhlsbüttel Airport. City bus No. 110 runs every 10 minutes from Ohlsdorf U/S-Bahn station (on lines

U1, S1), airport bus from the main railway station every 30 minutes; travel time is 30 minutes.

Rail connections

All trains use Hauptbahnhof. Many also touch Altona and Dammtor.

Under 1 hour: Lübeck, Bremen
1 to 2 hours: Hannover
3 to 4 hours: Berlin, Dortmund, Düsseldorf, Cologne
4 to 5 hours: Frankfurt
5 to 6 hours: Amsterdam, Copenhagen
Overnight: Basel, Brussels, Göteborg, Munich, Paris, Salzburg, Stockholm, Vienna, Zurich

Cologne

Tourist information

The office for information and accommodation is a short walk from the railway station, Hauptbahnhof (daily 8:00–22:30, Sun from 9:00; winter Mon–Sat 8:00–21:00, Sun 9:30–19:00). Phone 2211 or write to Verkehrsamt der Stadt Köln, Unter Fettenhennen 19, D-5000 Köln.

City transit

The KVB system includes buses, trams, and U-Bahn. Find information at U-Bahn stations.

The **tourist pass** for 24 hours of unlimited travel costs the equivalent of four single fares; buy it at ticket offices and validate at first use. Buy **single tickets** from automats at U-Bahn stations or bus or tram drivers. Validate tickets in punch clocks at U-Bahn stations and aboard buses and trams.

Taxis
Tel. 2882

Post, telegraph, telephone
Daily 7:00–22:00 in Hauptbahnhof.

Help in emergencies
Police: Tel. 110
Ambulance: Tel. 112
Physician: Tel. 72 07 72
Pharmacy on 24-hour duty: Tel. 1 15 00
Lost & found: Fundstelle, Herkulesstrasse. Mon–Fri 7:30–16:00 with lunch break. Tel. 221 63 12

Airport

Cologne-Bonn Airport. City bus No. 170 runs every 20 minutes from the bus terminal at the railway station; travel time is 25 minutes.

To send baggage directly to airplane, see page 111.

Rail connections

All trains use Hauptbahnhof. The Lufthansa Airport Express also stops at Deutz.

Under 1 hour: Aachen, Bonn, Düsseldorf*, Koblenz
1 to 2 hours: Dortmund
2 to 3 hours: Amsterdam, Brussels, Frankfurt*, Trier, Utrecht
3 to 4 hours: Rotterdam
4 to 6 hours: Basel, Munich, Paris, Strasbourg
Overnight: Bologna, Milan, Salzburg, Vienna

---

* Lufthansa Airport Express; see page 112.

Munich

Tourist information

Offices with information and accommodation are at the main railway station, Hauptbahnhof (daily 8:00–23:00), the airport (Mon–Sat 8:30–22:00, Sun 13:00–21:00), and Rathaus (Town Hall) (Mon–Fri 9:00–17:00). Phone 2 39 11 or write to Fremdenverkehrsamt München, Postfach, D-8000 München 1.

City transit

Buses, trams, U-Bahn, S-Bahn, and main line trains are integrated in the transit network. Find information at the tourist office or at the MVV transit office in the Starnberger Bahnhof (adjacent to Hauptbahnhof) and S-Bahn and U-Bahn stations.

The **tourist pass** for 24 hours of unlimited travel costs the same as three single fares (or five, if including suburbs). Buy it from automats at S-Bahn and U-Bahn stations and tourist offices, and sign it before first use. Buy **single tickets** from automats and tram or bus drivers; validate in punch clock.

Taxis

Tel. 2 16 11

Post, telegraph, telephone

Permanent service at Bahnhofplatz 1, opposite Hauptbahnhof.

Help in emergencies

Police: Tel. 110
Ambulance: Tel. 1 92 22
Physician: Tel. 55 86 61
Dentist: Goethestrasse 70. Tel. 5 16 01
Pharmacy on 24-hour duty: Tel. 59 44 75
Lost & found: Daily 8:30–2:00. Ruppertstrasse 19. Tel. 2331.

Airport

Munich-Riem Airport. Airport buses run from main railway station; travel time is 20-30 minutes.

To send baggage directly to airplane, see page 111.

Rail connections

All trains use Hauptbahnhof.
1 to 2 hours: Innsbruck, Nuremberg, Salzburg
2 to 3 hours: Stuttgart, Würzburg
3 to 4 hours: Frankfurt
4 to 5 hours: Strasbourg, Vienna, Zurich
Overnight: Bologna, Hamburg, Cologne, Milan, Paris, Rome, Utrecht, Venice

British Rail (BR)

At one time we feared that rail travel's cradle would be its grave as well. British Rail's revenues were down, expenses up, the government unsympathetic, and trains cut in the name of rationalization. But BR rallied and regained its passengers from air and road competition. Its pride, the InterCity service, has been one of the few passenger systems in Europe—in the world!—to turn a profit.

InterCity's numerous staff pamper passengers with personal service, especially on Pullmans which have been attracting business travelers. The cars are new and comfortable. British cars generally have a lot of space. Instead of airline-type seating (economical and unfortunately prevalent), BR has kept the traditional pattern of facing seats with tables between them. The tables are large enough for full-sized settings at meals with lots of elbow room. When not set with linen and china, they become work desks.

The InterCity sleeper trains have spacious single and double compartments, excellent service (morning tea in bed), and first-class lounge cars open all night for drinks and snacks, something that the Continentals should look into.

Air-conditioning and double-glazed windows—as unBritish as they are—have become standard. However, foreigners may find it a bit too British that cars built in the era of 300-km/h trains still do not have inside door handles: you have to lower the window and, sleet or snow, open the door from the outside.

Speed is limited by the many curves on the tracks, some laid 150 years ago, with no room to straighten them out. The station-to-station performance of the so-called high-speed trains (HST in the timetable) is around 90 mph, not the 125 implied by the *InterCity 125* logo on engines. The highest speed thought to be technically feasible and commercially sufficient in Great Britain will be 140 mph or 225 km/h.

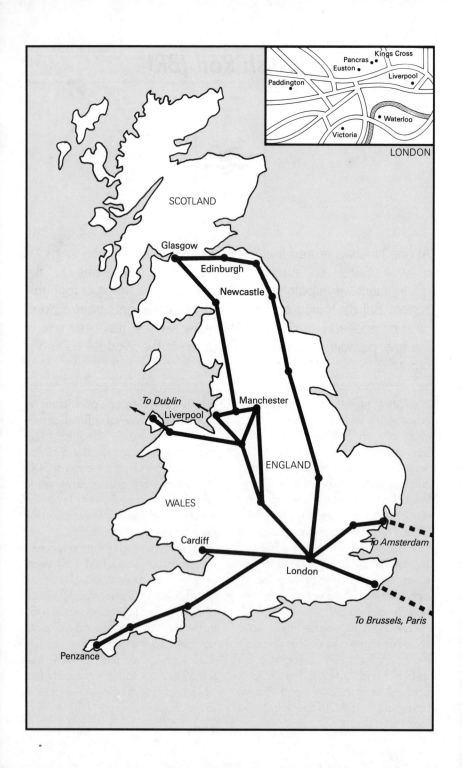

BR succeeds despite the constant tinkering by marketing wizards obsessed with 'brand image'. They thought 'second-class' sounded too second-class, and called it *economy*, then *standard*. They segregated full-fare passengers in *Silver Standard* cars, creating a third class (below standard?) for those traveling at low fare. They invented cute but meaningless names, like *White Saver*, *Blue Saver*, and *AwayBreak* (only *Cheap Day Return* tells you what it is). Luckily, the confusion doesn't extend to the more sensible train and station staff.

Information

Transatlantic visitors may have difficulties with the spoken language but a profusion of brochures explains everything. Station facilities are clearly signposted. Indicator boards and TV monitors list departures.

Schedule changes

Trains do not run on Christmas Day and Boxing Day (December 25–26) in Britain and Northern Ireland, nor on New Year's Day (January 1) in Scotland. Schedules differ on weekdays and on Sundays. Amended weekday or Sunday schedules may apply on the following public holidays (for movable dates see CALENDAR, page 54):

New Year	January 1
in Scotland also	January 2
St. Patrick's Day	March 17 (only in Northern Ireland)
Good Friday	Movable date
Easter Monday	Movable date (not in Scotland)
May Day	Movable date
Battle of the Boyne	July 12 (only in Northern Ireland)

Britain keeps Western European Time. When traveling to Belgium or France, remember that they run one hour later and change to summer time and back on different dates.

Fares

First class costs about 50% more than *standard* (second class). Fares are not calculated by distance. Approximate standard fares in pounds (£) and as priced at overseas BritRail offices in US dollars:

Distance in km	100	200	400
Local prices, £	8	18	36
Overseas, $	15	34	65

Supplements

None.

Reduced fares

Children under five travel free, five to sixteen pay half fare.

Savers are reduced return tickets for travel outside peak hours (not 6:00–9:30 on weekdays) and not on first class; return must be within one month. *White Savers* are valid any day, *Blue Savers* are not valid Fridays all year and Saturdays in July–August. The reductions vary between 20% and 50%; sometimes there is no difference between the two.

Cheap day returns are half-fare tickets for one-day trips in and out of London; not valid during weekday morning peak times.

Railcards for further reductions cost £15 for a year. They are good for 33–50% discount on standard class fares, saver and cheap day return tickets. Inquire at stations about railcards for families, seniors (over 60), youths (16 to 24), and disabled. Railcards for use in a limited area include the *Cornish Railcard* for Cornwall and the *Network Card* for London and the southeast.

Go-as-you-please passes

Eurailpasses are not valid in Britain and Northern Ireland.

Inter-Rail Cards allow unlimited travel on trains and half fare on ferries.

BritFrance Railpass is valid for free travel on trains and crossing the Channel to France by hovercraft.

BritRail Pass, the national tourist pass for non-residents, allows unlimited travel on trains. There are passes for consecutive days (from eight days to one month) and flexipasses with the choice of four days of travel in eight days or eight in fifteen. You can only buy them overseas; you receive a coupon which you exchange for the pass in Britain (at Gatwick or Heathrow airports or any one of 76 offices). Validate the pass at a BR ticket office before first use. Prices in US dollars:

Class	1st class	Standard
4 days in 8	229	159
8 days	285	190
8 days in 15	329	229
15 days	409	285
22 days	499	359
1 month	589	415

The pass for youths between 16 and 25 is issued only for standard class for 15% less than the adult standard pass. The pass for seniors over 60 is issued only for first class for 15% less than the adult first-class pass. Children between five and fifteen pay half price on either class.

All-Line Rovers allow unlimited travel on trains and Sealink ferries to the Isle of Wight.

Class	1st class	Standard
7 days, £	225	125
14 days, £	340	215

There are also nine **Regional Rovers** for seven or fourteen days of travel in an area. Prices for seven days range from £19 (Heart of England) to £44 (Scotland). **Local Rovers** cover small districts.

Children and holders of Railcards (Young Persons, Senior Citizens, Disabled) may buy *Rovers* for 34% less.

Tickets

Single tickets are valid for three days, except in the London area where they must be used on the date marked; if you buy them in advance, specify the day of use. Ordinary return tickets are valid for three months, savers for one month.

Reservations

Main line trains are reservable for £2 on first, £1 on *standard* class, free on *Silver Standard* and on trains with obligatory reservations. Reserve 24 hours before departure.

Baggage

You cannot forward except with the *Red Star* parcel service. Take extra baggage to the guard's van and collect it after the journey. Reserve space for bicycles on InterCity and some cross-country trains for £3, free on other trains. Storage costs £1.50 to £3 a day, depending on size of luggage and station (Victoria costs more than Euston).

Meals

InterCity trains carry full-service restaurant cars or buffets. On Pullmans, in first-class carriages, meals are served at seats. Trolleys cater on most cross-country services and some longer commuter runs into London.

In station restaurants, buffets and pubs, quality doesn't necessarily follow price: a decent restaurant meal can be had at a reasonable price, hamburgers at the ubiquitous outlets are terrible and costly.

Railway-type sandwiches are sold at station kiosks. Large stations have liquor stores. Shop for provisions elsewhere.

Night travel

Unquestionably the best deal in Europe. The new air-conditioned sleeping cars are considered the quietest and smoothest. Attendant service is old-fashioned, i.e., friendly and thoughtful. Morning tea or coffee and biscuits, served in compartments, are complimentary.

First-class ticket holders may reserve single sleepers, *standard* class a berth in a double, for £18. Reservations are held for three days and you have to claim your berth 30 minutes before departure.

Assistance

Handicapped: Larger stations have ramps and other facilities for wheelchairs. Most InterCity cars have wide doors and handrails; call in advance to secure space for wheelchair. For personal assistance at stations contact the office of the Area Manager. **Emergencies:** Contact the office of the Area Manager.

London

Tourist information

There are Tourist Information Centres at Victoria Station (Easter through October: daily 9:00–20:30; November through Easter: Mon–Sat 9:00–19:00, Sun 9:00–17:00), Heathrow Airport Terminals 1,2,3 tube station (daily 9:00–18:00), Harrods and Selfridges stores, and at the Tower's West Gate. Accommodation services are at Heathrow and Victoria. Phone 730 3488 or write to London Tourist Board, 26 Grosvenor Gardens, London SW1.

City transit

The Underground, known as the tube, buses, and regular trains cover all of London and its environs. The tube runs from 5:30 to midnight. Night buses run about hourly, all passing through Trafalgar Square.

Find information and maps in London Transport Travel Information Centres at Victoria, Euston, King's Cross stations, Heathrow Airport, Piccadilly and Oxford Circus tube stations. Phone 222 1234.

Travelcards for unlimited travel by tube, bus, Docklands Light Railway, and regular trains (BR Network SouthEast) are priced by zone; visitors travel mostly in Zones 1 and 2. A **Seven-Day 2-Zone Travelcard** costs about the same as nine single fares, a **Monthly** about 35. Take a passport photo to a tube station for a free Photocard, then buy Travelcards or bus passes at tube stations and many newsstands.

The **One-Day Travelcard** is valid in all zones (including Heathrow Airport) after 9:30 on weekdays, anytime on weekends; it costs little over the price of a five-zone single. The **Visitor Travelcard** includes discounts for sightseeing and some museums; however it's not 'the only way to get about in London' as advertised, just the most expensive: costing nearly three times as much as a Travelcard, which you can pick up on arrival.

Red Bus Rovers are valid for one day of unlimited travel on red buses for the price of less than four singles. Single tickets, priced according to distance, are sold aboard buses and at tube stations.

Bus tickets are valid for one ride. Tube line tickets are transferable, provided that you stay within stations; keep the ticket till the end of the trip and hand it to the guard when leaving the station.

Taxis
Tel. 272 3030, 286 1125, 286 4848, 286 6010

Post office
Mon–Fri 8:00–20:00, Sun 10:00–17:00 at 24–28 William IV Street, near Trafalgar Square.

Telephone
7:45–19:45 in BTI at Heathrow Airport Terminal 4.

Help in emergencies:
Police, ambulance: Tel. 999
Medical help, clinic: Hospital casualty departments
Pharmacy on 24-hr duty: Bliss, 50–56 Willesden Lane, Kilburn, NW6. Tel. 624 8000
Lost and found: Any police station or London Transport, 200 Baker Street, Mon–Fri 9:30–14:00

Airports
Gatwick and Heathrow Airports. See details on pages 285 and 286.

Rail connections
Victoria Station is still the European terminal with trains to Dover and Folkestone, connecting to boats for Brussels and Paris; this will change when the Channel Tunnel is in service. Liverpool Street Station handles boat trains to Harwich, connecting to ferries for the Netherlands. Trains to the west of Scotland and for Ireland leave from Euston Station.

All London stations are connected by tube.

1 to 2 hours: York (King's Cross)
2 to 3 hours: Liverpool, Manchester (Euston)
4 to 5 hours: Edinburgh (King's Cross), Glasgow (Euston), Penzance (Paddington)
5 to 6 hours: Brussels by jetfoil, Paris by hovercraft (Victoria)

7 to 8 hours: Brussels, Paris by ship (Victoria)
Over 9 hours: Dublin via Holyhead (Euston)
Overnight: Amsterdam via Harwich-Hook of Holland (Liverpool Street), Brussels via Dover-Ostend (Victoria), Dublin via Liverpool (Euston)

Station plans
London Euston: pp 230-231
London Liverpool: pp 232-233
London Victoria: pp 234-235

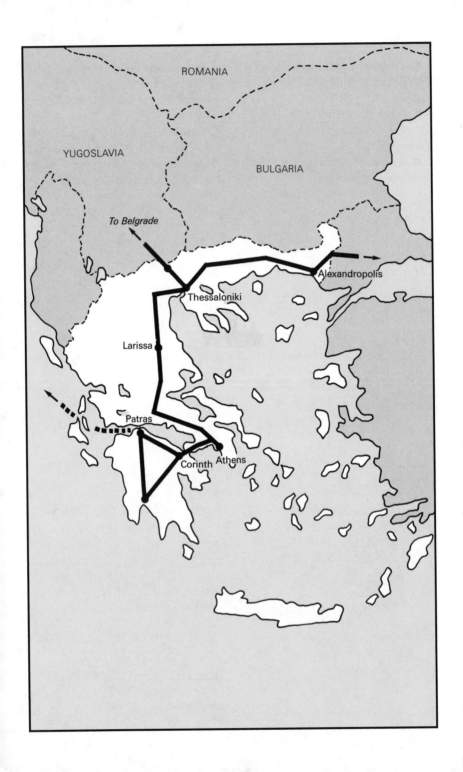

Greek Railways Organization

Organismos Siderodromon Ellados (OSE)

The few trains, in this country of sea and mountains, are slow but comfortable, and the fares are among the lowest in Europe. There are two rail networks: the standard-gauge system runs from Athens north to Thessaloniki and beyond, with international services to Belgrade, Sofia, and Istanbul; the southern section is a meter-gauge line starting from Athens and circling the Peloponnese Peninsula. The Athens terminals of the networks are next to each other.

Future developments, projected between now and 1997, will see new sections in the northern network for eventual 200 km/h speeds, and improvements on the Athens-Patras line for better service to the Patras-Brindisi ferry to Italy.

International trains run on the northern section as expresses. But the designation does not imply higher speed: express means a long-distance train with more comfort than the local but not faster; a supplement is charged and reservation may be obligatory.

Information

The official timetable includes an explanation in French.

Major routes and fares are listed in the *Greek Travel Pages,* available at the offices of the Greek National Tourist Organization. At larger stations the train information offices have multilingual staff and brochures in English.

Schedule changes

Services may change on the following public holidays (for movable dates, see CALENDAR, page 54):

New Year	January 1
Epiphany	January 6
St. John	January 7
National Holiday	March 25
Good Friday	Movable date
Easter Monday	Movable date
St. Constantine & St. Helen	May 21
Assumption	August 15
St. Dimitrios	October 26
National Holiday	October 28
Blessed Mary	November 21
St. Catherine	November 25
Christmas	December 25–26

Greece is on Eastern European Time. When traveling to Italy or Yugoslavia, remember that they are on Central European Time, one hour earlier.

Fares

First class costs 50% more than second. Second-class fares in Greek drachmas (drs) and US dollars:

Distance in km	100	200	400
Local prices, drs	300	650	1250
Eurailtariff, $	6	10	22

Supplements

The express supplement is 240 drs up to 350 km and 470 drs over that. On other designated trains the charge is 150 drs under 350 km and 240 drs above.

Reduced fares

Children under four travel free, four to twelve pay half fare.

Students registered in Greece pay half fare with ID-card.

Seniors over 60 may take five trips for a fixed total price of 6000 drs on first and 4000 drs on second class.

Return tickets are 20% cheaper than two singles.

Go-as-you-please passes

Eurailpasses allow unlimited travel on trains and on ferries of the Hellenic Mediterranean Lines between Patras and Brindisi (Italy).

Inter-Rail Cards allow unlimited travel on trains and half fare on Hellenic Mediterranean Lines ferries to Italy.

The **Greek Tourist Card** allows unlimited travel on trains (second class) and buses operated by the railways. It is issued for up to five passengers traveling together and sold at major railway stations in Europe. Prices in drachmas:

	10 days	20 days	30 days
1 person	6000	9000	12000
2 persons	10000	16000	22000
3 persons	13000	21000	29000
4 persons	15000	25000	34000
5 persons	17000	27000	37000

Tickets

One-way tickets are valid only on the day for which issued, return tickets for one month. Stopovers are allowed.

Reservations

Reservation is obligatory on some express trains, without a fee. Reserve from one month before to departure time.

Baggage

Forwarding costs 60 drs for every 10 kg (22 lbs) for every 100 km. Storage costs 60 drs a day.

Meals

Dining cars are carried only on international expresses. On other trains snacks and drinks are sold from trolleys.

Night travel

Sleeping cars and couchettes run only in the northern section.

Couchettes are second-class, reservable one month before and up to departure time for 520 drs.

Sleeping car berths can be

reserved one month before and up to departure time.

| Single | 3500 drs | Double | 1400 drs |
| Special | 2320 drs | Triple | 700 drs |

Assistance
Handicapped: There are no facilities. Railway staff or porters give personal help.
Emergencies: Contact the station post of the Tourist Police.

Athíne (Athens)

Tourist information
Find information at the Tourist Police post at the railway station (daily 7:00–24:00), and in national offices at the airport and at Karagiorgi Servias 2, near Syntagma (Mon–Fri 8:00–14:00/14:30–20:00, Sat 8:00–14:00). Phone 3222-545 or write to National Tourist Organization of Greece, Amerikis 2, 105 64 Athens.

City transit
Buses, trolley buses, and metro run about 6:00–24:00, depending on route (every 10 minutes to Piraeus). Find information at EAS (bus), HLPAP (trolley), and HSAP (metro) offices.

Monthly passes for unlimited travel cost the same as 35 single fares. They are issued for the calendar month between the 27th of one month to the 5th of the next, at transit offices; a photograph is required. **Booklets of ten** tickets are sold at metro stations and transit offices, singles are sold at metro stations and aboard buses.

Validate tickets in punch clocks on buses and in the turnstiles in metro stations. Pay exact fare on buses.

Taxis
Tel. 3237–942, 6718–191

Post office
Mon–Fri 7:40–20:30 at Eolou 100.

Telephone, telegraph
Permanent service at Patisíon 85.

Help in emergencies
Police: Tel. 100
Tourist Police: Tel. 171
Ambulance: Tel. 166
Clinic with 24-hour service: K.A.T. Leoforos Mesogion. Tel. 770–1211.
Pharmacy on 24-hour duty: Tel. 171
Lost & found: Alexandras 17.

Airport
Athens-Hellinikon Airport. City buses run from near Zappion, in the city, to the East and West Terminals; travel time is 20–30 minutes.

Rail connections
International trains to the north leave from Larísis station. The terminal for the separate network covering the Peloponnese peninsula is adjacent.
Under 1 hour: Piraeus (Omonia)
4 to 5 hours: Lárisa (Larísis) Patras (Peloponnísou)
Overnight: Thessaloniki (Larísis)

Boat connection
Overnight: Brindisi (from Patras)

Station plan Athens/Athíne Larísis: pp194–5

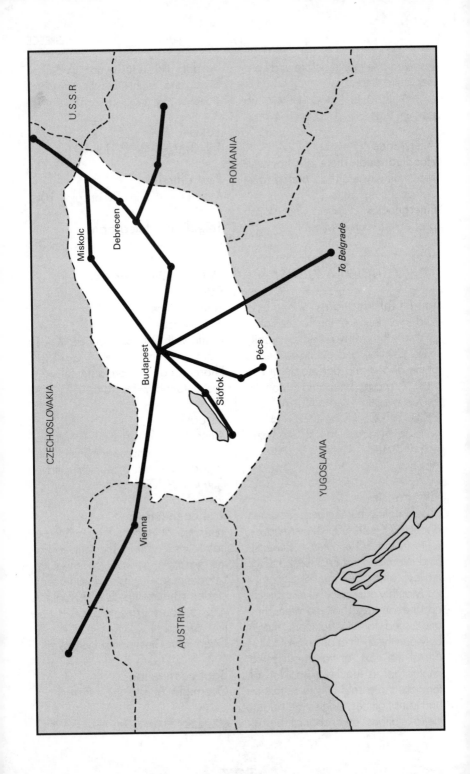

Hungarian State Railways

Magyar Államvasutak (MÁV)

In 1989 Hungary joined the Eurailpass community, the first country from the socialist bloc to do so. The move demonstrated the country's interest in improving communications to the West. Although some international trains, like the remnants of the *Orient Express*, have always run, Hungary did not have convenient connections with the rest of Europe after the Second World War. Only recently, in 1987, did it double the number of trains from Vienna to four a day with the introduction of the *Arrabona* and daily service by the *Lehár*. In 1988 the *Lehár* became the first EuroCity train to run east of Vienna, joined in 1989 by the EC-*Franz Liszt* to Dortmund, soon to be followed by the *Béla Bartók* to Stuttgart.

MÁV has to reserve its best rolling stock for international services at the expense of inland traffic. It's the irony of market economy that the very good railway cars that Hungary has manufactured for sixty years, establishing a reputation on three continents, are all exported: the Hungarian railways cannot afford to buy them. Consequently, the cars in inland service are either old or built for one function: to get you there, but not necessarily to make you enjoy the process.

With more conscientious effort than money, MÁV runs a comprehensive system. Up to twelve departures a day assure nearly hourly service on the main lines. These are served mostly by fast trains *(gyorsvonat)*. Branch lines have much fewer and slower passenger trains *(személyvonat)* which sometimes turn out to be railcars with only second-class seating.

Information
The timetable contains an English section. Leaflets with schedules are on board international trains. Schedules are posted at stations (yellow for departures, white for arrivals). Staff dealing with international tickets and reservations are multilingual. At smaller stations English-speakers are scarce; try the local tourist office.

Schedule changes

Train services may change on the following public holidays (for movable dates, see CALENDAR, page 54):

New Year	January 1
National Holiday	March 15
Easter Monday	Movable date
Liberation Day	April 4
May Day	May 1
Constitution Day	August 20
Christmas	December 25–26

Fares and supplements

Two different tariffs apply on international trains. Tickets sold in Hungary for travel to socialist countries come under the inland tariff. Tickets for travel to Austria and Yugoslavia, or sold by agencies outside Hungary, are priced according to the *CIV* tariff. Eurailtariff prices are converted from *CIV* fares. The supplement for fast trains is included in the price. First class costs 50% more than second. Second-class fares in Hungarian forints (Ft) and US dollars:

Distance in km	100	200	400
Inland trains, Ft	68	128	206
Inland fast trains, Ft	108	188	286
CIV tariff, Ft	358	653	1046
Eurailtariff, $	11	15	24

The supplement for Comfort Car (*komfort kocsi*) is 100 Ft (see OTHER SERVICES).

Reduced fares

Children under four travel free (two per paying adult), aged four to ten pay half fare.

Adults with two children under 18 get a 20% reduction.

Seniors (men above 60, women above 55) and **young people** under 26 get 20% reductions.

Multiride tickets *(füzetjegy)* contain ten tickets at 20% reduction. Mark date of use and have it endorsed at station before boarding.

Balaton reduction *(Balatoni kedvezmény)* is 20% on trips between resorts on the Lake Balaton. Available only June 1 to August 31.

A **promotional discount** of 30% applies on all tickets for the *Lehár* trains between Budapest and Vienna.

Go-as-you-please passes

Eurailpasses and **Inter-Rail Cards** allow unlimited travel on trains.

Tourist passes *(turista bérletek)* allow unlimited travel on MÁV trains and 20% reduction on GySEV trains.

	1st class	2nd class
7 days, Ft	1560	1040
10 days, Ft	2340	1560

Balaton passes *(Balatoni bérletek)* allow unlimited travel on trains (second class) along the northern or southern shore of Lake Balaton (each pass is valid only on one shore). They cost 260 Ft for seven days and 390 Ft for ten days. You may travel first class by paying the difference for the distance traveled.

Tickets

Travel must begin on the day of issue or the stamped date if bought in advance. Tickets for trips under 200 km are valid for one day, under 400 km for two days, over 400 km for three days. Return tickets under 100 km are valid for one day, over 100 km for one month.

Reservations

Reservation is obligatory on some international expresses, optional on fast trains, for 16 Ft. Reserve from two months before to departure time.

Baggage

Forwarding costs for each 20 kg (44 lbs) 25 Ft up to 100 km, 41 Ft to 200 km, 73 Ft to 400 km.

Storage costs 10–20 Ft a day, depending on size. Lockers take ten-forint pieces.

Meals

Dining cars with full table service run only on international trains between Budapest and Vienna where they provide a relatively expensive introduction to Hungarian cuisine. Land prices are far lower.

On inland main lines self-service buffet cars (bisztró) serve sandwiches, sausages, cakes, coffee, and drinks. Lesser trains are catered for by vendors.

Night travel

There are no couchette or sleeper trains.

Other services

The **Comfort Car** (komfort kocsi) is a first-class car where hostesses serve breakfast or snacks and drinks at seats. Magazines, newspapers, and video entertainment are offered. When reserving (for 100 Ft), you may order secretarial services and a taxi waiting at your destination. Comfort cars run between Budapest and Vienna on the EC-Lehár, and irregularly on a few inland routes. Reserve in advance or on board if a seat is available.

Bicycles (kerékpárok) may be rented at several stations, mostly in touristic areas, for 70 Ft for one day, 110 Ft for two days, 140 for three days, 70 Ft for subsequent days. Bicycles may be reserved from any station.

Nostalgic trains (nosztalgiavonat) with steam or diesel traction will be appreciated by rail fans. They are not kept in museums but run in scheduled service at regular fares. Check the summer timetable.

Steam engine driving (gözmoz-donyvezetés) is offered on certain nostalgic trains. Passengers may take over for a fee of about US$ 25, and receive an honorary engine driver's certificate.

Assistance

Handicapped: There are no facilities at stations. Special cars are available only for groups of at least ten travelers. Porters may give personal assistance. Inquire in advance at information offices.

Emergencies: The responsible duty officer (ügyeletes tiszt) is in the station master's office. Because of language difficulties, it's best to contact the international information office at the station.

Budapest

Tourist information

Find offices for information and accommodation at railway stations (see working hours there). Room reservations may be made at all hours at *IBUSZ*, Petöfi tér 3. Tel. 1185-707. The information center downtown is at Sütö u. 2, near the Deák tér metro station (daily 8:00–20:00). Phone 1179–800 or write to Tourinform, Sütö u. 2. H-1052 Budapest.

City transit

Buses, trolleybuses, trams, metro, cogwheel trains, and suburban electric trains are integrated. Find information and maps at BKV offices in major metro stations (Felszabadulás tér, Keleti, Moszkva tér).

The **tourist pass** for 24 hours of unlimited travel *(napijegy)* costs the same as eight single fares; sold at metro stations. **Passes** for a calendar month cost the same as 60 singles; a photo card is required. Since single tickets are not valid for transfer, a simple trip may require two or three; so the passes really cost about as much as two trips a day. **Single tickets** (different for bus and tram/metro) must be bought in advance at stations, kiosks, tobacconists, etc., and validated in punch clocks aboard vehicles and at metro station entrances.

Taxis

Tel. 1222–222, 1666–666, 1555–000

Post, telegraph

Permanent service in the offices at Keleti and Nyugati railway stations.

Telephone

Mon–Fri 7:00–21:00, Sat 7:00–20:00, Sun 8:00–13:00 at Petöfi Sándor u. 17.

Help in emergencies

Police: Tel. 07
Ambulance: Tel. 04
Pharmacies on 24-hour duty: Alkotás u. 1/b (at Déli station). Ring bell at night. For other addresses, phone 04.
Lost & found: Engels tér 5. Tel. 1174-961. Public transit: Akácfa u. 18. Tel. 1226–613.

Airport

Budapest-Ferihegy Airport. Airport buses run every half hour from Engels tér; travel time 30–40 minutes. City bus No.93 (black number from Terminal 1, red number from Terminal 2) connects to the metro going downtown.

Rail connections

Information, tickets, reservations, and Eurail Aid are available Mon–Fri 9:00–18:00, Sat 9:00–13:00 at the MÁV Passenger Service *(Közönség-szolgálat)*, Népköztársaság útja 35. Tel. 1228–049.

Of the three major stations, the southern (Déli) is the terminal for trains to the resorts along Lake Balaton, and for the EuroCity *Lehár* to Vienna. The eastern (Keleti) station has the western connections, like all Vienna trains (except the *Lehár*). The western (Nyugati) station handles mostly commuter traffic and international trains from the east. All stations are connected by metro.

1 to 2 hours: Siófok/Lake Balaton (Déli)
2 to 3 hours: Debrecen, Miskolc (Keleti), Vienna (Déli)
3 to 4 hours: Pécs, Vienna (Keleti)

Station plans
Budapest Déli pályaudvar: pp 208–9
Budapest Keleti pályaudvar: pp 210–1

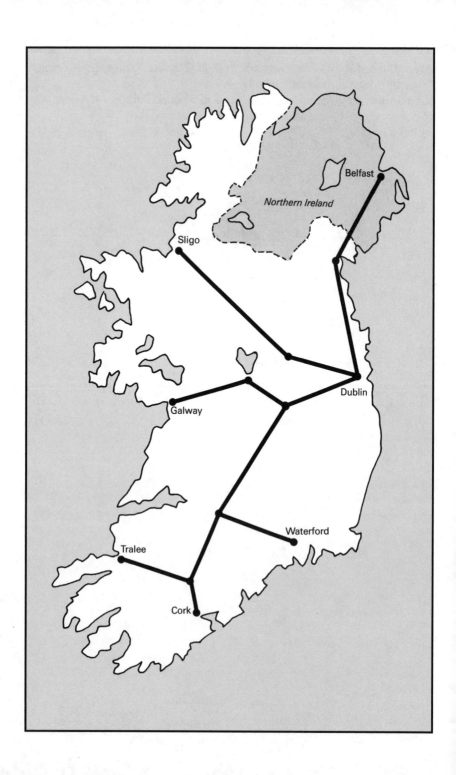

Irish Rail

Iarnród Éireann (IE)

The entire intercity train timetable fits on a single foldout sheet—the book of bus schedules is more substantial. The thinly spread transport system has only a few main train lines. Perhaps because of the reliance on road travel, the railways were secondary in the state-owned transport company, the CIE. Irish Rail have only recently started running their own affairs, but since then they have considerably perked up the intercity service.

The new rolling stock is based on the British Mark III design but built in Ireland. The cars are air-conditioned, double-glazed, carpeted, and feature automatic doors (don't wait for them, press the lighted button!) and—unfortunately—seats facing in one direction, making rail travel as anti-social as flying. They are comfortable, though, and more spacious than their British cousins since the gauge here is about a foot wider. On lesser routes you'll still find rolling stock from the '60s, some in shabby state, which are also open saloon types but with seats facing each other in groups of four.

The new equipment is good for up to 144 km/h (90 mph) but the size of the country, and the temperament of its citizens, demand less.

There are no speed categories, such as express. Most of the accommodation is *standard* (second class). *Superstandard* (first class) runs only on a few routes (to Belfast, Cork, Limerick, Waterford). The distinction between classes consists of added head rests and at-seat catering on first class.

Information

Advance information is available from tourist offices and travel agencies. At stations, the information office and the station master's staff will help, on trains the conductor.

Schedule changes

There is no rail service on New Year's Day (January 1) and Christmas Day (December 25).

Different train schedules are in effect on weekdays and on Sundays. Train services may change on the following public holidays (for movable dates, see CALENDAR, page 54):

St. Patrick's Day	March 17
Good Friday	Movable date
Easter Monday	Movable date
Whit Monday	Movable date
August Holiday	first Monday in August
Hallowe'en	November 1
St. Stephen's Day	December 26

Ireland is on Western European Time like Britain.

Fares

For *superstandard* (first class), see **Supplements,** below. *Standard* (second-class) fares in Irish pounds (IR£) and US dollars:

Distance in km	100	200	400
Local prices, IR£	10.50	21.00	29.50
Eurailtariff, $	11	20	35

Supplements

The supplement for superstandard (first-class) accommodation is IR£4.50 under 210 km and IR£6.50 above. The supplement must be paid for each journey, i.e., twice if the trip includes a change of trains.

Reduced fares

Children under five travel free, five to sixteen pay half fare to a maximum of IR£9.

Youths from 16 to 26 get 45%–55% reductions with a *Fair Card* which costs IR£8.

Students from 16 to 32 with identification pay half fare.

Return tickets for the weekend cost little over a single fare.

Families, including parents and up to four children under sixteen, may travel together for a flat fare of IR£21.

Go-as-you-please passes

Eurailpasses allow unlimited travel on trains and Irish Ferries boats between Rosslare or Cork and Le Havre or Cherbourg.

Inter-Rail Cards allow unlimited travel on trains and half fare on ferries to Britain and the Continent.

Rambler Tickets allow unlimited travel on trains and/or buses. Days of travel must be within two weeks of date of issue for eight-day tickets, within 30 days for 15-day tickets. Families (parents and at least one child) and groups of at least six pay 8–15% less.

	Train or bus	Train and bus
8 days in 14		
Adult	52.00	66.00
Child	26.00	33.00
15 days in 30		
Adult	77.00	95.00
Child	38.50	47.50

Tickets

Single and ordinary return tickets are valid from the day for which issued to three months, other return tickets during the specified period (one, four, or eight days, weekend, one month). Stopovers are allowed only on the return journey.

Reservations

Reservation is optional on main line trains for IR£1 on *standard* class and included in the supplement on *superstandard*. Reserve from three months to one hour; (3 $^1/_2$ hours by phone) before departure.

Baggage

Forwarding costs IR£6.60 for the first 10 kg (22 lbs) and 66p for each additional 10 kg, plus 25% VAT.

Storage charge is 80p a day.

Meals

Self-service buffet and bar cars run on main lines, but not on all trains. On lesser routes, between meal times, and on Sundays the service consists of snack bar or vending trolley catering. *Superstandard* passengers may order meals at their seats.

Station restaurants, cafeterias and bars tend to close early.

Night travel

There are no sleeping cars or couchettes.

Other services

Car rental is arranged by the booking office at the departure station. Ask as far in advance as possible.

Assistance

Handicapped: No special facilities are available. Contact the station master's office on the day of travel for help by the staff.

Emergencies: Contact station staff or conductor.

Dublin

Tourist information

The Tourist Information Centre is at 14 Upper O'Connell Street (January through October: Mon–Sat 9.00–17.00; November and December: Mon–Fri 9:00–17:00, Sat 9:00–13:00). Phone 747 733 or write to Bord Failte, P.O.Box 273, Dublin 8.

City transit

Find information, tickets, and passes at Dublin Bus, 59 Upper O'Connell Street.

Bus passes for one day of unlimited travel cost the same as 3–4 singles, for one week about the same as ten singles. Passes that include rapid transit (DART) cost about a tenth more. **Single tickets** (not valid for transfer) vary with distance. Tickets and passes are valid from purchase; just show them to the bus driver.

Taxis

Tel. 783 333, 772 222, 557 777, 761 111

Post, telegraph, telephone

Mon–Sat 8:00–20:00, Sun 10:30–18:30 at the General Post Office on O'Connell Street.

Help in emergencies

Police: Tel. 999
Ambulance: Tel. 999
Physician: See the Golden Pages telephone directory
Dentist on 24-hour duty: Dr. Goode,

24 Lower Baggot Street. Tel. 766 760

Pharmacies on late duty:
Tel. 338 803, 730 427, 973 977, 907 179.

Lost & found: Police stations or public transit (Mon–Fri 9:00–17:30), 98 Marlborough Street. Tel. 720 000.

Airport

Dublin Airport. Buses run from Busaras bus terminal, Store Street; travel time is 20–25 minutes.

Rail connections

The station for international connections is Connolly. Trains to Cork, the southwest and Galway use Heuston.

The stations are connected by the DART feeder bus No.90.

1 to 2 hours: Athlone (Heuston), Belfast (Connolly)

2 to 3 hours: Cork (Heuston), Galway (Heuston)

3 to 4 hours: Sligo (Connolly), Westport (Heuston), Tralee (Heuston)

Boat connections

There are two departure points for ferries to Britain. From Connolly Station DART trains run to Dun Laoghaire, buses to Dublin Ferryport. Buses to Dun Laoghaire also run from Heuston.

9 to 10 hours: Liverpool, London

Overnight: London

Station plan
Dublin Connolly: pp 216–7

Italian State Railways

Ferrovie Italiane dello Stato (FS)

Italy is a land of confusion and compassion. Italians sympathize with you if your travel plans have just fallen apart and cheerfully admit that nothing works as it should. This response may add to your frustration when you want practical help. The railway reflects the contrasts of the country. The beautiful trains may run late or not run at all if there is a strike. However, the staff are always genuinely sorry and apologetic while nothing is done. After a few days in the country, when you have absorbed some Mediterranean attitudes, you'll appreciate the general kindness and ignore the problems.

Still, train travel in Italy can be enjoyable. You can relax over an excellent meal in an elegant dining car as a reward for patience. And, when it makes the effort, the railway delivers comfort and speed. To the unpampered North American, even the previous-generation *gran confort* cars verge on science fiction: whisper-quiet ride, futuristic decor, pushbutton conveniences inside and the advanced technology of the special suspension underneath.

The best train, the *MiRo*, runs non-stop between Milan and Rome in four hours. This is the ETR 450, Italy's first move toward high speed. The regular-interval InterCity system now provides hourly trains between Milan and Rome, two-hourly on the Turin-Venice main line. All the first-class Trans-Europ-Expresses have been replaced by EuroCity and InterCity trains, currently twenty and more to come.

Your first choices are InterCity and *rapidi*. The less exalted categories, the *espressi*, *direttissimi*, and *diretti* are fast or semi-fast in name only.

The tariff policy is feudal. The low basic fare buys only slow second class in old cars and no services (not even toilet paper). To ride in comfort the charge is steep: an 80% increase for first class and supplements charged by distance. A 200-km trip, that costs L.9800 on second class, runs to L.22,540—more than twice as much—on a first-class *rapido*.

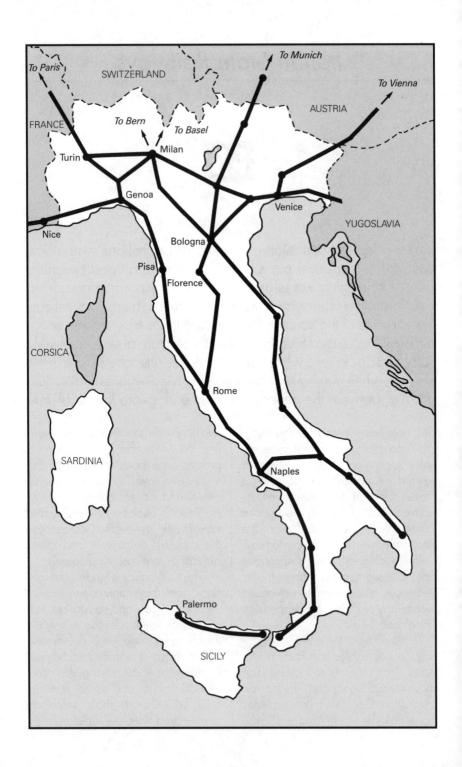

Italian stations merit special mention. Many are justly admired as examples of the finest in both the classic nineteenth- and modern twentieth-century railway architecture. All are veritable cities within the city. At the *albergo diurno* (day inn) one can eat, drink, bathe or shower, get a haircut and manicure, buy socks, or sleep. A great place to rejuvenate after a slow ride.

Information
The overseas offices of CIT Tours supply information as well as sell passes and tickets, and make reservations.

The information offices in stations are often mobbed. A good alternative is the CIT office, staffed by multilingual guides.

Schedule changes
Train services may change on the following public holidays (for movable dates, see CALENDAR, page 54):

New Year	January 1
Easter Monday	Movable date
Liberation Day	April 25
Labor Day	May 1
Assumption	August 15
Conception	December 8
Christmas	December 25-26

Feast days of patron saints may affect local transit in Florence and Genoa (June 24), Naples (September 19), Bologna (October 4), Milan (December 7).

Fares
First class costs 80% more than second. Eurailtariff prices include supplements. Second-class fares in Italian lira (L.) and US dollars:

Distances in km	100	200	400
Local prices, L.	4900	9800	19500
Eurailtariff, $	6	· 15	28

Supplements
InterCity supplements are charged by distance. In Italian lire:

	100 km	200 km	400 km
1st class	3000	6000	11900
2nd class	1800	3500	7000
EC, IC	1400	2800	5500
Rapidi, speciali	2500	4900	9800

Reduced fares
Children under four travel free, four to twelve pay half fare.

Seniors (men over 65, women over 60) may travel for about 30% less with *Carta d'Argento* (L.10,000 for one year).

Youths from 12 to 26 may travel for about 30% less with *Carta Verde* (L.10,000 for one year).

Families of at least three members traveling together pay 30% less with *Carta Famiglia* (L.10,000 for one year).

Return tickets *(andata e ritorno)* save about 15% on trips at least 250 km each way.

The **kilometerbank** *(Biglietto chilometrico)* for 3000 km total distance costs L.254,000/$200 in first class, L.150,000/$115 in second class.

Go-as-you-please passes
Eurailpasses allow unlimited travel on trains and on the ferries of Adriatica di Navigazione and Hellenic

Mediterranean Lines from Brindisi to Greece (pay high-season supplement from June 1 to September 30).

Inter-Rail Cards allow unlimited travel on trains and half fare on ferries.

The **BTLC** *(Biglietto Turistico di Libera Circolazione)*, the national tourist pass, allows unlimited travel on trains, including supplements. Obligatory reservations must be made but the charge is included. The pass is sold in Italy and abroad by FS and CIT offices and travel agents to non-residents. Children pay half price.

Local prices in L.	*1st class*	*2nd class*
8 days	L.207,000	L.140,000
15 days	L.250,000	L.168,000
21 days	L.300,000	L.197,000
30 days	L.362,000	L.242,000

Overseas in US$	*1st class*	*2nd class*
8 days	$160	$106
15 days	$196	$126
21 days	$230	$148
30 days	$280	$180

Italy Flexi Railcard is a pass for unlimited travel on days selected from a longer period. As its big brother, the Eurail Flexipass, it lessens the cost and extends the life of the pass—and your vacation.

Children between four and twelve pay half fare.

Local prices	*1st class*	*2nd class*
4 days in 9	L.153,000	L.104,000
8 days in 21	L.225,000	L.148,000
12 days in 30	L.283,000	L.188,000

Overseas	*1st class*	*2nd class*
4 days in 9	$112	$ 76
8 days in 21	$164	$108
12 days in 30	$206	$136

Tickets

Tickets for less than 250 km are valid for one day. One day may be added for each additional 200 km, up to six days. Stopovers are allowed. Return tickets are valid from three to six days, according to distance; discount returns for one day under 50 km, above that, for three days.

Reservations

Reservation is obligatory on some InterCity trains, optional on others, for L.4000. Reserve from two months to five hours before departure. Some smaller stations cannot make reservations on trains originating elsewhere.

Baggage

Forwarding to the final destination or any stop along the route costs for each 25 kg (55 lbs) L.19,600 to 100 km, L.21,600 to 300 km, L.23,600 to 500 km. Note that baggage forwarded to Italy has to be cleared by customs during official hours (not nights or weekends). Inquire at station about delivery and pickup in large cities and resorts.

Meals

The station is the place to eat. The luxury restaurant may open only for lunch, but there are always several others serving good food around the clock. Some station restaurants pack box lunches. Most bars will sell you sandwiches, pizzas, cold cuts, cheeses, and wine to take out. There are food shops near every station; however, these tend to close early.

The *rapidi* have excellent dining cars. The prices are commensurate with the gourmet menu and elegant service: expect to pay as much as in a better restaurant. Second-class passengers may sit in the dining car only for meals, first-class passengers at any time. Self-service buffets are classless. Ordinary trains have very ordinary trolleys.

Night travel

Couchettes are first and second class with four or six berths in a compartment. Travel first class! Second class is crowded, uncomfortable and not always clean. Definitely low-budget travel for L.16,800 or US$14 in Eurailtariff. Couchettes are reservable from two months till five hours before departure.

Sleeping car prices vary with distance:

	Local price L	Eurailtariff $
Single	120,000–163,000	93–127
Special	82,300–111,900	64–86
Double	57,800–78,600	52–60
Triple	49,000–66,600	38–52

Other services

Travel agency: CIT handles tickets, reservations, hotel, baggage delivery, ship and airline tickets. It also provides interpreter-guides at stations. **Car rental** (*Treno+Auto*): Rented cars reservable before departure.

Train telephone: InterCity trains have pay phones.

Assistance

Handicapped: Wheelchairs are provided and may be taken to destination. To arrange assistance in advance, fill out a form at the ticket office.

Emergencies: Contact the information office or CIT for an English-speaking official. If you speak Italian, contact the station master (*Capo Stazione*).

Bologna

Tourist information

Offices for information and accommodation are at the railway station, Centrale (Mon–Sat 9:00–19:00, Sun 9:00–13:00) and 23 Strada Maggiore. Phone 23 96 60 or write to APT, 23 Strada Maggiore, I–40100 Bologna.

City transit

Find information at the bus stop outside Centrale.

Tourist passes for one day (*biglietto giornaliero*) cost less than four single fares, passes for up to ten users (*tesserino dieci*) less than 10 singles. Buy them at transport offices. Buy **single tickets** from automats aboard buses or in advance at tobacconists. Validate advance purchase tickets in punch clocks aboard buses.

Taxis

Tel. 37 27 27, 53 41 41

Post office

Mon–Sat 8:00–21:00, Sun 8:00–14:00 in Piazza Minghetti.

Telephone, telegraph

Permanent service at Piazza VIII Agosto and Via Fossalta.

Help in emergencies

Police: Tel. 113
Ambulance: Tel. 33 33 33
Physician: Tel. 33 33 33
Pharmacy on 24-hour duty: Inquire at 33 33 33
Lost & found: 18 Via Solferino.

Airport

Bologna-Guglielmo Marconi Airport. City buses run from outside the railway station; travel time is 30–35 minutes.

Rail connections

All trains use Centrale.
1 to 2 hours: Florence, Milan, Padua, Venice, Verona
3 to 4 hours: Rome
Overnight: Brussels, Frankfurt, Cologne, Luxembourg, Munich, Paris, Strasbourg, Vienna

Milan (Milano)

Tourist information

Offices for information and accommodation are at the Centrale station, (Mon–Sat 9:00–12:30/14:15–18:00) and at Via Marconi 1 (Duomo metro station). Phone 80 96 62 or write to Ufficio di Informazione e di Accoglienza Turistica, Via Marconi 1, I-20123 Milano.

City transit

Metropolitana (metro), trams, and buses serve the city. Find information at ATM transit office in Centrale (Mon–Sat 8:00–20:00) and at the Centrale FS and Duomo metro stations.

The **tourist pass** (biglietto turistico) for one day of unlimited travel costs the same as four single fares; buy it at transport offices in Centrale FS and Duomo metro stations. **Single tickets** are sold in tobacconists and by automats in metro stations. They are valid for 75 minutes with transfer.

Taxis

Tel. 5353, 6767, 8585

Post, telegraph

Mon–Fri 8:15–19:40, Sat 8:15–17:40 at Piazza Cordusio 1. Permanent telegraph service.

Telephone

Daily 7:00–00:45 at Via Cordusio 1.

Help in emergencies

Police: Tel. 112
Ambulance: Tel. 113
Physician: Tel. 113
Pharmacy on 24-hour duty: In Centrale. Tel. 669 07 35
Lost & found: Via Unione. Tel. 87 08 21

Airports

Milano-Linate Airport. Airport buses run from Centrale and Piazza Garibaldi stations, city bus No. 73 from Piazza S. Babila, every 20 minutes; travel time is 40 minutes.

Milano-Malpensa Airport. Airport buses run every 20 minutes from Centrale station; travel time is 50 minutes.

Rail connections

Most trains use Centrale. The only exceptions are a few trains to the north from Piazza Garibaldi and the Italia Express going through Lambrate.

All stations are connected by metro No. 2 (green line).

1 to 2 hours: Bologna, Genoa, Turin, Verona

2 to 3 hours: Florence, Venice

3 to 4 hours: Lausanne, Rome, Zurich

5 to 6 hours: Basel, Lyon

Overnight: Brussels, Frankfurt, Cologne, Luxembourg, Marseille, Munich, Paris, Strasbourg, Vienna

Rome (Roma)

Tourist information

Information and accommodation services are at the main railway station, Termini (daily 9:00–13:00/15:00–20:00) and at Via Parigi 5. Phone 46 37 48 or write to Ente Provinciale per il Turismo di Roma, Via Parigi 5, I-Roma.

City transit

All buses, trams, metro, and main line trains in the city are integrated. Find information at ATAC booth at bus stop outside Termini.

Tourist pass for seven days of unlimited travel *(giro turistico)* costs the equivalent of 14 single fares. The **day pass** *(B.I.G.)* costs the equivalent of four singles. Passes are sold at ATAC offices. **Single tickets** are sold by automats aboard buses and trams and at tobacconists and bars. **Blocks** of ten tickets *(blocco)*, for savings of 15% over singles, are sold at the ATAC pavillion in front of Termini and some bars and kiosks.

Transfer between metro lines at Termini. There is no transfer on buses or trams. Validate ticket in punch clock when boarding.

Taxis

Tel. 3570, 3875, 4994, 8433.

Post, telegraph

Mon–Sat 8:00–19:30, Sun 8:00–12:30 in Termini.

Telephone

Permanent service in Termini.

Help in emergencies

Police: Tel. 113
Physician: Tel. 475 67 41
Pharmacy: Daily 7:00–23:30 in Termini. For 24-hour service see addresses posted in pharmacy windows.
Lost & found: City: Via Bettoni 1. Tel. 581 60 40. Transit: ATAC, Via Volturno 65. Tel. 4 69 51

Airport

Roma Leonardo da Vinci Airport. See details on page 292.

Rail connections

Most trains use Termini. Some night trains to Genoa leave from Ostiense, some through night trains (Milan-Rome-Naples) stop at Tiburtina. Check timetable.

2 to 3 hours: Naples, Florence
3 to 4 hours: Bologna, Milan
5 to 6 hours: Venice
Overnight: Basel, Lausanne, Munich, Vienna, Zurich

Venice (Venezia)

Tourist information

Find information at the railway station (daily 8:00–20:00) and Piazza San Marco. Phone 522 63 56 or write to Azienda di Promozione Turistica, Venezia.

City transit

Transportation is by ship (vaporetto) in Venezia proper; buses run in Mestre and Lido.

Find information, tickets, and map at vaporetto stop (fermata) outside the railway station or ACTV transit office in Piazzale Roma.

Tourist passes cost the same as five single fares for one day, ten singles for three. Buy them at vaporetto stops and ACTV offices; validate in punch clock at first use. **Single tickets** are also sold by automats at stops. Validate in punch clock before boarding.

Taxis

Water: Tel. 71 69 22.
Road (from Piazzale Roma):
Tel. 523 77 74

Post, telegraph, telephone

Daily 8:00–21:30 in Piazzale Roma.

Help in emergencies

Police: Tel. 112
Ambulance: Tel. 113 or 523 00 00
Physician (hospital): Tel. 529 41 11
Pharmacy on 24-hour duty: Inquire at tel. 113

Airport

Marco Polo Airport. Motorboats run from Piazza San Marco (travel time is 45 minutes), buses from Piazzale Roma (travel time is 25–35 minutes).

Rail connections

Trains ending in Venice arrive in Santa Lucia station. Other trains may stop only at Mestre on the mainland and sections continue to Santa Lucia. Check the timetable for stations and through-cars.

The stations are connected by frequent trains.
1 to 2 hours: Verona, Bologna
2 to 3 hours: Florence, Milan, Trieste
5 hours: Rome
Overnight: Frankfurt, Munich, Paris, Vienna

Station plans
Bologna – Stazione Centrale: pp 200–1
Milan – Stazione Centrale: pp 246–7
Rome – Stazione di Termini: pp 260–1
Venice – Santa Lucia: pp 272–3

Luxembourg National Railways

Société Nationale de Chemins de Fer Luxembourgeois (CFL)

The smallest national railway in Europe has only about 350 km (220 miles) of tracks—the longest distance is 90 km—but there are 64 stations. Together with the bus network and ships on the Mosel, it can take you to any corner of the country. And any excursion will be worth it: Luxembourg is the finest argument that small is beautiful.

Inland routes are served mostly by railcars with limited luggage space, some with only second-class seating. You can travel on the international expresses between Luxembourg stations but remember that long-distance passengers have first claim on seats. Luxembourg is the starting point for many transatlantic travelers arriving by Icelandair and a waystation on the route from the northwest to Italy.

Information

At Railtour, the travel center, staff are at least trilingual in French, German, and English. The fourth language that you may hear in announcements is the native language, Lëtzebuergesch.

Printed material is mostly in French.

Schedule changes

Services may change on the public holidays (for movable dates, see CALENDAR page 54):

New Year	January 1
Shrove Monday	Movable date
Easter Monday	Movable date
May Day	May 1
Ascension	Movable date
Whit Monday	Movable date
National Day	June 23
Assumption	August 15
Christmas	December 25-26

Fares

First class costs 50% more than second. Second-class fare in Luxembourg francs is 300 LF for 100 km.

Supplements

No supplements are charged for travel in Luxembourg. Pay EuroCity and French *rapide* supplements from the border before boarding.

Reduced fares

Children under four travel free, four to twelve pay half fare.

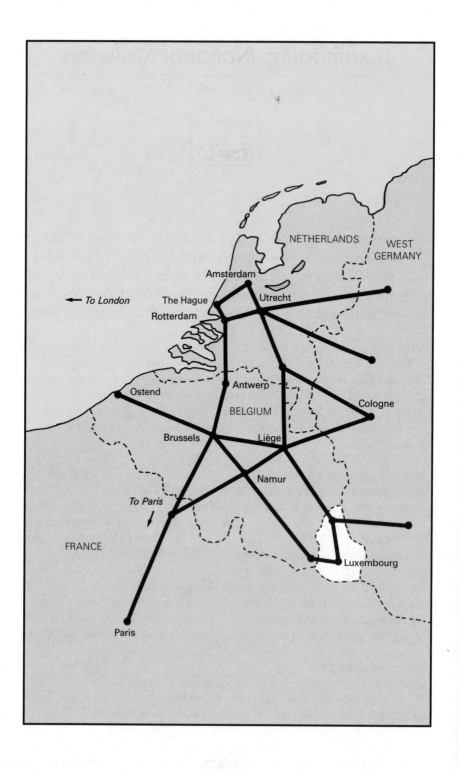

Seniors above 65 may travel at half fare with proof of age.

Weekend return tickets are valid between Friday 16:00 and Monday morning; return from any station. The reduction is 50%.

Groups of five may travel on second class at 60% reduction, more than five at 70%.

Go-as-you-please passes

Eurailpasses, Inter-Rail Card, Benelux-Tourrail Cards allow unlimited travel on trains.

Network passes allow unlimited travel on trains (second class) and CFL and RGTR buses. The one-day pass (billet réseau) costs 217 LF, the five-day pass (abonnement réseau de 5 jours) 658 LF, the monthly pass (abonnement réseau mensuel) 1748 LF.

Tickets

Tickets, except weekend returns, are valid for one day. Stopovers are allowed.

Reservations

Seats are not reservable inland. International passengers have first claim on seats. Reservation is possible on international trains for 70 LF. Additional reservations on connecting trains are free. Reserve from two months to 24 hours before departure. If you stay less than 24 hours, reserve by mail: write to Railtour, Gare Centrale, Luxembourg.

Baggage

Forwarding costs 22 LF for each 25 kg (55 lbs). Storage costs 60 LF for the first two days, then 20 LF daily. Lockers use five- and ten-franc coins.

Meals

Only international trains have meal services. Buy provisions near Luxembourg Gare Centrale in rue de Strasbourg and avenue de la Gare.

Night travel

Couchette and sleeping cars run only in international service.

Assistance

Handicapped: Write in advance for arrangements Railtour, Gare Centrale, Luxembourg, or phone 49 24 24. At stations the information officer or duty officer will assist.

Emergencies: Contact the information officer or the duty officer (chef de surveillance).

Luxembourg

Tourist information

Find information and maps at the office in the Luxair building, next to the railway station (daily 9:00–19:30, winter 9:00–12:00/14:00–18:00, closed Sundays), at the airport (daily 10:00–18:30), and in Place d'Armes. Phone 228 09 or write to Office National du Tourisme, P.O.B. 1001, L-1010 Luxembourg.

City transit

Ask for information in the tourist offices. Bus tickets in batches of 10 save about 30% on singles; sold at railway stations, banks and some shops. Bus drivers sell singles. Baggage taken on city buses costs an extra ticket.

Taxis

Tel. 48 22 33

Post, telephone, telegraph

Daily 6:00–22:00 in Place de la Gare, opposite station.

Help in emergencies

Police, ambulance, physician, pharmacy, dentist: Tel. 012.

Lost & found: Police, rue Glesener. Tel. 40 94 01.

Airport

Luxembourg Findel Airport. See details on page 288.

Rail connections

All trains use Gare Centrale.

Under 1 hour: Metz
1 to 2 hours: Namur
2 to 3 hours: Brussels, Liège, Strasbourg
3 to 4 hours: Paris, Basel
Overnight: Bologna, Milan

Station plan
Luxembourg Gare Centrale: pp 236–7

The Netherlands Railways

Nederlandse Spoorwegen (NS)

One can seldom travel more than 150 km across the Netherlands without running into a border or the sea coast. The moderate distances ease the burden of fares, high for most visitors who earn less than the citizens of this prosperous country. The Dutch do not complain about the price: the excellent service would be sound value even without the generous discounts for regular users. Half-hourly trains connect over 40 cities in the InterCity system. Hourly trains to Brussels extend the network into Belgium; as many as 20 trains a day—on two routes—connect to the German network at Cologne.

The smaller towns are served by *stop-treins* which, predictably, stop everywhere and convey passengers to the main lines. Because of the frequency of trains, and the short times spent on them, there is no need for elaborate passenger services on board. No meals, except refreshments, and of course no sleepers.

The Netherlands have long been an important cornerstone of the European rail network and there is a large amount of international traffic. Rotterdam and Hook of Holland are the bridgehead to Britain for trains from Copenhagen, Munich and Berlin. Amsterdam has been the terminal for many of the great long-distance ex-

presses, the now-extinct *Rheingold*, the *Flandres-Riviera*, the *Britannia*, and others. No wonder that the idea of the Trans-Europ-Express was conceived by a president of the NS: his company has been host to many of the finest international trains for over a century.

Information

The NS publishes a useful brochure, "Touring Holland by Rail", which gives details about tourist passes, reduced fares and excursions. It is distributed by Dutch tourist bureaus and KLM airline offices.

At stations timetables are displayed on large posters near entrances and on every platform. As well, most

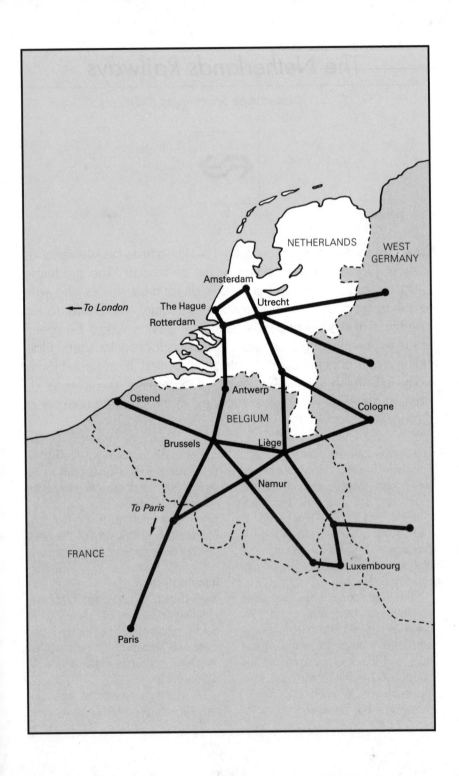

platforms have electronic display boards overhead indicating the time and direction of the next departure. Information officers help out on the Euro-City platforms in major stations. Most staff speak English.

Note that most stations are through-stations where trains may enter or leave at either end. There may be two trains on the same track, departing at different times in different directions. To find the right train, check the letter beside the track number (for example, *Spoor* 2a or 2b) which indicates the appropriate platform section.

Schedule changes

Train services and local transit may change on the following public holidays (for movable dates, see CALENDAR, page 54):

New Year	January 1
Good Friday	Movable date
Easter Monday	Movable date
Queen's Birthday	April 30
Liberation Day	May 5. Every fifth year, next in 1990 and 1995
Ascension	Movable date
Whit Monday	Movable date
Christmas	December 25–26

Fares

First class costs 50% more than second. Second-class fares in Dutch gulden (*f*) and US dollars:

Distance in km	100	200
Local prices, *f*	20.50	33.00
Eurailtariff, $	12	22

Supplements

No supplements are charged on inland trains. The EuroCity supplement on trains going beyond the border is payable before boarding.

Reduced fares

Children under four travel free, four to eleven pay a flat fare of *f* 1 if traveling with an adult (max. three children with an adult) or, if traveling alone, pay 40% of the fare.

Return tickets for one day (*Dagretour*) are reduced by about 10%.

Evening returns (*Avondretour*) for travel after 18:00 cost a single fare plus *f* 5.

Weekend returns (*Weekendretour*) for one-way travel on Saturday, Sunday for return, cost a single fare plus *f* 2.50.

Seniors (over 60) get reductions with *60+Seniorenkaart*, **families** with *NS-Gezinskaart*. Inquire at stations.

Go-as-you-please passes

Eurailpasses, Inter-Rail, and Benelux-Tourrail Cards allow unlimited travel on trains.

Network passes for unlimited travel come in a wide variety. The one-day pass (*Dagkaart*) costs as much as the fare for 380 km, a distance one cannot travel in a day. The three- and seven-day and month passes (*Netkaart*) offer savings. Week and month passes need an ID-card (*NS-Stamkaart*) with photo, available at stations. With the *Stad-Streekabonnement* you can add unlimited travel on intercity buses and public transport in all Dutch cities.

	1st class	2nd class	*
1 day, ƒ	78.75	53.00	5.35
3 days, ƒ	118.50	79.50	10.00
7 days, ƒ	167.50	115.50	20.15
1 month, ƒ	616.00	419.00	65.75

* Bus and city transit supplement

The **youth's network pass** (*Jeugdmaandnetkaart*) for those under 18 allows unlimited second class travel for a month. It costs ƒ 335. Add public transit for ƒ 65.75.

Family passes are valid on four days chosen during a period of ten; available only in June through August. The *Gezinstoer* costs ƒ 200 for first, ƒ 160 for second class; the *Gezinstoer-Plus* adds the use of all public transit at ƒ 240 for first, ƒ 200 for second class.

The **teenager pass** (*Tienertoerkaart*) for under-18s is valid for second class on four days during a period of ten; sold in June through August, and in the fall, Christmas, and Easter school vacations. It costs ƒ 44, or ƒ 55 with public transit.

The **group pass** (*Meer Man's Kaart*) is for a couple, family, or group of up to six persons traveling together. The pass allows one day of unlimited travel (not before 9:00, Mon–Fri).

	1st class	2nd class
2 persons, ƒ	110	74
3 persons, ƒ	135	93
4 persons, ƒ	152	104
5 persons, ƒ	175	115
6 persons, ƒ	192	126

Tickets

Single and return tickets are valid on the day of issue.

Reservations

Seats are not reservable inland. International passengers have first claim on seats. Reservation is obligatory on EuroCity trains for ƒ 11, optional on other international trains and costs ƒ 4. Reserve from two months ahead to departure time.

Baggage

Forwarding on international trains only costs ƒ 15 a piece, up to 30 kg (66 lbs). Storage costs ƒ 1.25 a day. Lockers use 25-cent coins.

Meals

InterCity trains carry mini-bars selling snacks and drinks. Only the international expresses have dining cars.

Station restaurants have a moderate selection of full meals during the day. Since the restaurants also serve as waiting rooms, drinks and snacks are available at all hours even after the kitchens are closed.

Night travel

Only international trains have services.

Couchettes are reservable from two months till one day before departure. They cost ƒ 27 in six-berth, ƒ 36 in four-berth compartments. First-class four-berth couchettes run on the Amsterdam-Paris route and cost ƒ 27.

Sleeping car berths are reservable from three months till one day before departure.

Single, ƒ	269
Special, ƒ	192
Double, ƒ	115
Triple, ƒ	77

Other services

Bicycles *(Fiets en spoor)* may be rented at 83 stations.

Assistance

Handicapped: Most stations have ramps or elevators, trains have widened doorways and special space inside for wheelchairs. To request assistance in advance, phone 30/33 12 53 before 13:00 a day before departure (Friday for travel during the weekend or Monday).

Emergency: Contact a platform supervisor *(Perronopziehter)* in red cap, railway police, or the station master *(Stationschef)*.

Amsterdam

Tourist information

Find information and accommodation at VVV offices outside Centraalstation (July–August: daily 9:00–23:00; Easter to June and September: as in July–August except Sun till 21:00; October to Easter: Mon–Fri 9:00–18:00, Sat 9:00–17:00, Sun 10:00–13:00/14:00–17:00) and at 106 Leidsestraat (July–August: daily 10:30–21:00, Easter through June and September: daily 10:30–17:30, October through Easter: Mon–Fri 10:30–17:30, Sat 10:30–21:00). Phone 26 64 44 or write to VVV, P.O. Box 3901, NL-1001 AS Amsterdam.

City transit

The system includes buses, trams, and metro. Find information, map, and tickets at GVB office outside Centraalstation or phone 27 27 27.

Tourist passes *(dagkaart)* for unlimited travel cost little more than three single fares for 24 hours, and about the same as a single for each additional day. Buy 24-hour passes from automats at metro stations or bus and tram drivers, for longer periods at GVB offices; validate in punch clock at first use. (See page 153 for city transport and railway combination passes.) **Multiride tickets** *(strippenkaarten)* for two or ten units are sold by drivers who stamp the required number of units, depending on the number of zones crossed and persons using the ticket. **One-hour tickets** are sold by automats at metro stations and bus and tram drivers; they are valid for one hour with transfer.

Taxis

Tel. 77 77 77

Post, telegraph

Mon–Fri 8:30–18:00 (Thu till 20:30), Sat 9:00–12:00 at Nieuwezijds Voorburgwal 182.

Telephone

Permanent service at Radhuisstraat 46–50.

Help in emergencies

Police: Tel. 22 22 22
Ambulance: Tel. 55 55 555
Physician and dentist:
Tel. 664 21 11
Pharmacies on 24-hour duty:
Tel. 664 21 11

Lost & found:
Inquire at 559 80 05 (police) and 551 49 11 (transit)

Airport
Schiphol Airport. See details on page 280.

Rail connections
All trains use Centraalstation. Additional trains to Schiphol Airport and The Hague also leave from Zuid and RAI stations.
Under 1 hour: The Hague, Utrecht
1 to 2 hours: Hook of Holland, Rotterdam
2 to 3 hours: Antwerp, Brussels, Cologne
5 to 6 hours: Frankfurt, Hamburg
Overnight: Basel, Copenhagen, London, Munich, Paris

Rotterdam

Tourist information
Find information and accommodation at VVV kiosk in Centraalstation (Mon–Sat 9:00–22:00, Sun 10:00–22:00) and Stadhuisplein (Mon–Sat 9:00–18:00 (Fri till 21:00), Sun 10:00–18:00). Phone 413 60 00 or write to VVV, Coolsingel 67, NL-3012 AC Rotterdam.

City transit
Transport modes are bus, tram, and metro. You can obtain information and tickets at RET offices outside Centraalstation and in metro stations.

The **tourist pass** (daagkaart) for one day of unlimited travel costs about the same as three single fares; buy it from automats at metro stations and bus and tram drivers; validate in punch clock at first use. (See page 153 for city transit and railway combination passes.) **Multiride tickets** (strippenkaarten) for two to fifteen units are sold by drivers, 45 units in RET offices. The units used depend on number of zones crossed and persons using the ticket. Have it stamped when boarding vehicule.

Taxis
Tel. 436 12 22

Post, telephone, telegraph
Longest service is Mon–Fri 8:30–19:00, Sat 8:30–12:30 at Delftseplein 31, near Centraalstation.

Help in emergencies
Police: Tel. 414 14 14
Ambulance: Tel. 414 14 14
Physician: Tel. 463 92 22
Pharmacy: Tel. 433 99 33
Lost & found: Inquire at police, tel. 424 94 11

Airport
Rotterdam Airport. City bus No.33 runs from Centraalstation; travel time is 20 minutes. Regular trains run to Schiphol Airport; travel time is 45 minutes.

Rail connections
All trains use the Centraalstation.
Under 1 hour: The Hague, Hook of Holland, Utrecht, Amsterdam

1 to 2 hours: Antwerp, Brussels
3 to 4 hours: Cologne
4 to 5 hours: Paris
5 to 6 hours: Frankfurt
Overnight: Copenhagen, London, Munich, Salzburg

Utrecht

Tourist information

Find information and accommodation at VVV kiosk in Hoog Catharijne, adjacent to Centraalstation (Mon–Fri 9:30–17:30) and at Vredenburg 90 (Mon—Sat 9:00–18:00). Phone 31 41 32 or write to VVV, Vredenburg 90, NL-3511 BD Utrecht.

City transit

Find information on the bus system at VVV tourist offices and in transit office at *Stadsbussen,* below passage from Centraalstation. Use *strippenkaarten* for single trips. Validate two strips inside urban area. **The tourist day pass** *(daagkaart),* valid in all Dutch cities, costs the same as five singles.

Taxis

Tel. 51 51 51

Post, telephone, telegraph

Mon–Fri 8:30–19:00 (Thu till 20:30), Sat 9:00–12:00 in Neude.

Help in emergencies

Police: Tel. 33 33 33
Ambulance, physician, pharmacy: Tel. 33 22 22
Lost & found: Police. Kronstraat 25. Tel. 32 59 11.

Airport

Schiphol Airport (Amsterdam). Regular trains run via Amsterdam CS (transfer); travel time is about one hour.

Rail connections

All trains use Centraalstation.
Under 1 hour: Amsterdam, Rotterdam
2 to 3 hours: Cologne
4 to 5 hours: Frankfurt
Overnight: Basel, Copenhagen, London, Milan, Munich, Zurich

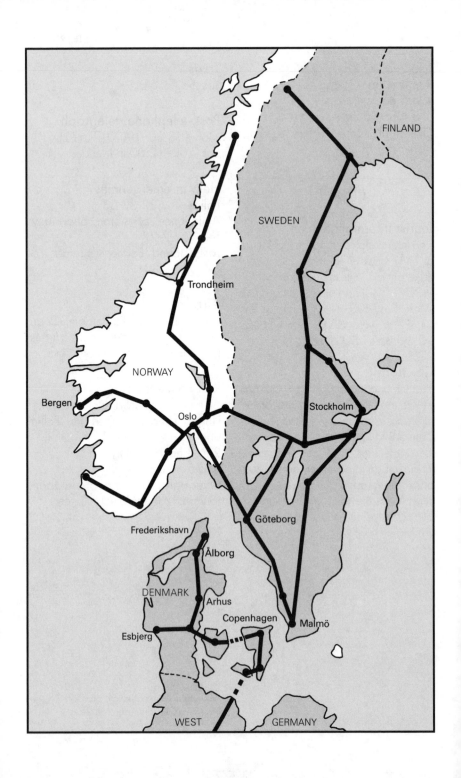

Norwegian State Railways

Norges Statsbaner (NSB)

The railway lines in this country must be popular with artists and engineers. They run past some of the most spectacular scenery in Europe. The tracks go over 3000 bridges and through 775 tunnels; some stretches seem miracles of construction. The Nordlandsbana reaches to Bodø, far above the Arctic Circle, 1300 km from Oslo. The Bergen line is more modest in length, only 470 km, but passes through 200 tunnels and 300 bridges along the way. The barely 20-km-long Flamsbana hugs rock walls and burrows through 20 tunnels to a fjord 2845 feet below the upper terminal.

The statistics don't say anything about the task of upkeep. Tracks run on mountain plateaus above the tree line, or on ledges cut in the steep walls of fjords and the winter snows are never far away. The railway must constantly fight the tough land. Perhaps this is why the NSB is quite expensive to ride, like the Swiss trains which also spend much of their time going through tunnels and over bridges.

The traveler looks at cars, not maintenance problems. And the new generation certainly deserves notice. Nothing has been overlooked for passenger comfort, even for the future: the cars could later be equipped with tilting mechanisms to allow in-creased speeds, currently 130 km/h. They are furnished with new chairs, tables, lights and automatic doors. A service car on each train contains a buffet, telephone, a compartment for the handicapped, a children's compartment, and a first-class conference room. Many special features have always been offered on older trains, too, like compartments with non-allergenic upholstery, amenities provided out of good common sense that should set an example.

Fast trains run every two or three hours between major cities. These are the *ekspresstog* (marked Et. in timetables) with the usual comforts and conveniences of intercity trains and carrying dining cars. The *hurtigtog* (Ht.) are the regular fast trains. Local traffic is served by the slower *persontog* (Pt.) and *lokaltog* (Lt.), most of which have only second-class cars but are of historical interest: some are 1951 vintage.

Information

The NSB publishes tourist literature in several languages and a somewhat vague English explanation in the timetable. You may try to read the more complete Norwegian text with the help of the travel vocabulary included in the timetable. Your good train companion is a set of folders available from the NSB, containing maps of the main routes and descriptions of the sights. In the summer, loudspeaker announcements comment on the scenery outside the train. Both station and train staff speak English.

Schedule changes

Train services may change on the following public holidays (for movable dates, see CALENDAR, page 54):

New Year	January 1
Maundy Thursday	Movable date
Good Friday	Movable date
Easter Monday	Movable date
May Day	May 1
Constitution Day	May 17
Ascension	Movable date
Whit Monday	Movable date
Christmas	December 25–26

Fares

First class costs 50% more than second. Second-class fares in Norwegian crowns (Nkr) and US dollars:

Distance in km	100	200	400
Local prices, Nkr	97	185	343
Eurailtariff, $	16	30	55

Supplements

A supplement is payable on second class of InterCity trains, 40 Nkr.

Reduced fares

Children under four travel free, between four and fifteen pay half fare.

Seniors over 67 pay half fare with proof of age.

Students with ID-card pay half fare on trips over 150 km.

Small groups *(Minigruppe)* of two to nine pay 25% less on trips over 100 km.

A midweek ticket *(Midtuke-billett)* is a flat fare ticket for any distance on second class. It is valid for a total of seven days with stopovers; not on Fridays, Sundays, and holidays, or during Christmas and Easter holidays. It costs 340 Nkr; children pay half.

Go-as-you-please passes

Eurailpasses, Inter-Rail, and **Nordturist Cards** allow unlimited travel on trains. Eurailpass holders get a 20% reduction on DFDS ships between Oslo and Copenhagen. Nordturist entitles you to half fare on ferries: Kristiansand-Hirtshals, Larvik-Frederikshavn, Bergen-Stavanger.

Tickets

Tickets are valid for two months with stopovers on trips above 60 km.

Reservations

Reservation is obligatory on special expresses (Et.) and some fast trains (Ht.), optional on others, and costs 13 Nkr. Reserve from three months to half an hour before departure.

Baggage

Forwarding costs 25 Nkr a piece up to 20 kg (44 lbs), and 50 Nkr up to 50 kg (110 lbs).

Storage costs 5 Nkr a day. Lockers use five- and ten-krone coins, and cost from 10 to 30 Nkr, depending on size.

Meals

Dining cars are carried only on some of the special expresses between Oslo and Bergen. On some other trains, and on the Trondheim-Bodø line, cafeterias serve hot dishes and sandwiches at self-service tables or on trays which you can take to your seat. On expresses between Oslo and Stavanger or Trondheim *togkiosks* serve snacks and drinks. Other trains are served by trolleys.

Meals at stations are good, though not cheap. For picnic meals go outside the station to shop. All alcohol is expensive, even beer which is very good. Unfortunately, food stores tend to close as early as 17:00, even earlier in the summer. Plan ahead!

Night travel

Long distances and low prices make overnight travel a good choice in Norway.

Couchettes run only on international trains. They cost 72 Nkr to Stockholm or Copenhagen, 79 Nkr to Hamburg. Reserve from three months to 30 minutes before departure.

Sleeping cars inside Norway are inexpensive: a place in a three-berth compartment costs the same as a couchette on an international train. On trains going to Sweden or Denmark prices are slightly higher than on inland trains.

Local prices, Nkr	Single	Double	Triple
Inland	320–360	160–180	80
Scandinavia	470	154	103

Eurailtariff, US$	Single	Double	Triple
Inland	55	28	14
Scandinavia	81	26	18

Other services

Train telephones are on special expresses and InterCity trains.

Children's compartments are on long-distance trains, day or night.

Assistance

Special facilities aboard trains are reservable at stations or through travel agents.

Handicapped: Most cars have wide doors, special compartments and toilets accessible by wheelchairs. Special cars also have hydraulic lifts for wheelchairs.

Passengers with allergies may reserve sleeping compartments with special non-allergenic bedding.

Emergencies: On trains contact the conductor, at stations the duty officer, recognizable by the red cap, in the *Vaktcontoret*.

Oslo

Tourist information

Find information and accommodation at Sentralstasjon (daily 7:00–23:00; winter: 8:00–15:00/16:30–23:00) and in Rådhusplassen (Mon–Fri 8:30–19:00, Sat 9:00–17:00; winter Mon–Fri 8:30–16:00, Sat 8:30–14:30). Phone 33 43 86 or write to Oslo Reiselivsråd, Rådhusgata 19, N-0158 Oslo.

City transit

Find information at *Trafikanten* transit office outside Sentralstasjon.

The **tourist pass** *(Turistkort)* for 24 hours of unlimited travel on all buses, trams, metro, local city trains, and the ferry to Bygdøy costs the same as three single fares; buy it at news kiosks, post offices, and transit offices, and validate in punch clock at first use. The **Oslo Card** *(Oslo-Kortet)* is good for free travel, admissions to museums, and many discounts on sightseeing trips, etc. It is sold at transit and tourist offices, hotels, and some banks; the cost is 75 Nkr for one day, 110 Nkr for two, and 140 Nkr for three (less than half for children). **Mini/ Maxi Cards** contain five or twelve coupons, each good for one hour of travel with transfer, and save about 10% on singles; they are sold at transit offices. **Single tickets** are sold aboard buses and trams for one trip, without transfer. At weekends up to four children under 16 may travel free with each adult carrying a Mini, Maxi or Tourist Card.

Taxis

Tel. 38 80 90

Post office

Mon–Fri 8:00–20:00, Sat 9:00–15:00 at Dronningensgate 15 (Prinsensgate corner).

Telephone, telegraph

Mon-Fri 8:00–21:00, Sat 10:00– 21:00 at Kongensgate 12.

Help in emergencies

Police: Tel. 002 or 669 050
Ambulance: Tel. 003 or 112 200
Physician: Tel. 201 090
Dentist: Tel. 674 846
Pharmacy on 24-hour duty: Jernbanetorgets Apotek (near station).
Lost & found: Police: Grønlands-leiret 44. Tel. 66 98 65.
Transit: Tel. 46 24 14.

Airport

Oslo Fornabu Airport. Airport buses run every 15 minutes, city bus every half hour from Sentralstasjon; travel time is 20–25 minutes.

Rail connections

All trains use Sentralstasjon, except those to Drammen-Skien-Nordagutu which leave from Vestbanestasjon. Connection is by taxi only.
4 to 5 hours: Göteborg
Overnight: Bergen, Copenhagen, Stavanger, Stockholm

Station plan
Oslo Sentralstasjon: pp 250–1

Portuguese Railways

Caminhos de Ferro Portugueses (CP)

The transport-minded visitor finds an amazing assortment of conveyances in the Lisbon public transit system. Single- and double-decker and articulated buses, trams of various ages, cable cars, funiculars and even elevators run in three dimensions through this hilly city. The Portuguese Railways, too, operate a wide variety of rolling stock, including luxurious sleeping cars of 1929 vintage and, until recently, some old steam trains on narrow-gauge lines. The reason is not nostalgia but economics; Portugal simply cannot afford to throw out the relics as long as they run. Consequently, the service is mixed, ranging from the finest to the merely functional.

On the credit side is the competent and hospitable personnel who do the best possible with what they have. Now they have more: in recent years spectacular improvements have been made, tracks upgraded to permit higher speeds, and new rolling stock introduced to provide fast service between major centers.

The pride of CP is the *Alfa Service* between Lisbon and Porto at 2–3 hour intervals with few stops, reducing travel time to little over three hours. These are 'business class' trains with special comforts. InterCity *rápidos (intercidades)* also ply the Linha do Norte between Lisbon and Porto, and the southern route to the Algarve.

The frequent electric trains around Lisbon provide excellent access to the nearby resort areas. Down the scale, on other lines, are the *directos* and *semi-directos*, and the regionals, some of which are railcars with one-class accommodation. The system is comprehensive: you can go almost anywhere by train, provided you have the time. The basic fare is very low. The better trains cost a lot more but are still affordable and the speed and quality of service are worth the difference.

Information

It is regrettable that one cannot find out anything about Portuguese rail services before getting there—and

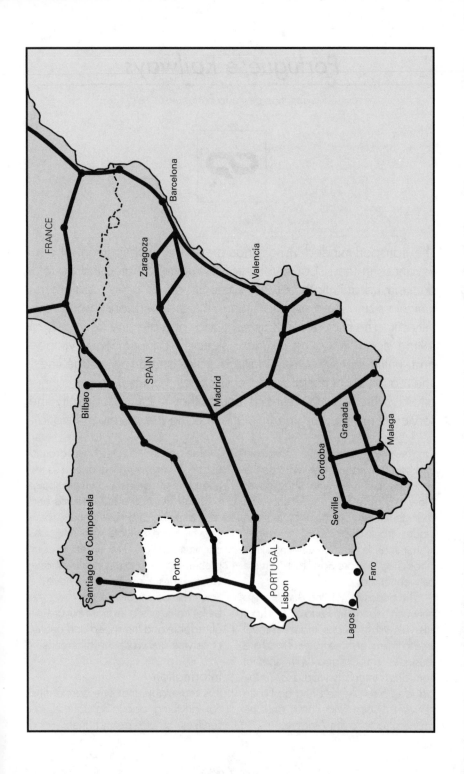

even then with difficulty. The government tourist offices overseas have no information on trains, travel agents have never heard of the very advantageous tourist pass.

In Portugal printed information in English is lacking. Fortunately, the information offices have competent and multilingual staff and keep long hours by telephone. At stations look for the information officer wearing a yellow armband.

Schedule changes

Train services may change on the following public holidays (for movable dates, see CALENDAR, page 54):

New Year	January 1
Shrove Tuesday	Movable date
Good Friday	Movable date
Liberation Day	April 25
May Day	May 1
Camões Day	June 10
Corpus Christi	Movable date
Assumption	August 15
Republic Day	October 5
All Saints	November 1
Independence Day	December 1
Conception	December 8
Christmas	December 25

Portugal is on Western European Time (same as Britain and Ireland, one hour before neighboring Spain). It switches between daylight saving and standard times with the rest of the Continent.

Fares

First class costs 52–64% more than second. The supplement for *rápidos* is automatically added to the basic fare;

Eurailtariff prices include the supplement. Second-class fares in Portuguese escudos (Esc.) and US dollars:

Distance in km	100	200	400
Basic fare, Esc.	445	720	1270
Rápido, Esc.	720	1155	2030
Eurailtariff, $	6	10	17

Supplements

Rápido and InterCity surcharges are included in the total fares above. The supplement for the Alfa Service is 110 Esc. on first class, 30 Esc. on second, for every 50 km. The extra charge between Lisbon and Porto (339 km) is 770 Esc. on first class, 210 Esc. on second.

Reduced fares

Reductions apply only during off-peak times. See the calendar of *dias azuls* (blue days) at stations. Only the basic fare is reduced, the difference for *rápidos* has to be paid in full.

Children under four travel free, four to twelve pay half fare.

Youths between 12 and 26 pay half fare June through September, also at Christmas and Easter on blue days, with the *Cartão Jovem* ID-card; it costs 900 Esc. for a year.

Seniors pay half fare with proof of age. The limit is 65 years for inland traffic, 60 years for international.

In **families** of at least three (including children up to 17) the first person pays full fare, the others half, children under 12 a quarter of the fare. Reductions are granted only on journeys over 150 km. The necessary ID-card with photos costs 290 Esc. for 5 years.

Kilometer tickets *(Cheque Train)* offer a reduction of 15% on the distance purchased in advance without time limit.

Go-as-you-please passes

Eurailpasses and Inter-Rail Cards allow unlimited travel on trains.

The tourist ticket *(Bilhete Turistico)* allows unlimited travel on trains, first or second class. Buy it at stations, travel agencies and TAP Portuguese Airlines offices. Children under 12 and seniors above 65 pay half price.

	7 days	14 days	21 days
Escudos	11,465	18,300	26,140

Tickets

Specify travel date when buying tickets. Regular tickets are valid on the day of issue, return tickets for ten days. *Rápido* tickets must be validated before boarding the train. Stop-overs up to 24 hours are allowed only in Lisbon and Porto. For destinations south of Lisbon, the ticket covers the fare of the ferry to Barreiro station.

Reservations

Reservation is obligatory on international trains for 250 Esc., free on *rápidos*. On InterCity trains the fee is 60 Esc., for Alfa Service 220 Esc. on first class, 120 Esc. on second. Reserve from ten days to 30 minutes before departure.

Baggage

Forwarding costs 165 Esc. a piece up to three pieces and 40 kg (88 lbs). Storage costs 300 Esc. a day. Lockers use 50- and 100-escudo pieces.

Meals

Dining cars are carried on InterCity *rápidos* and international expresses *(Estrella, Lusitania, Sud)*. Tray meals are served at seats aboard the *Luis de Camões* (the Lisbon-Madrid Talgo) and Alfa Service trains. On other long-distance trains trolleys (mini-bars) serve sandwiches and drinks.

Stations with restaurants and *cantinas* are listed in the timetable; their hours are variable and not always convenient. Picnic provisions, snacks, chilled wine and beer are sold at the many bars outside the stations.

Night travel

Couchettes run only in international service on the *Sud Express* to Paris and the *Lusitania* to Madrid. They cost 2891 and 2526 Esc. respectively.

Sleeping cars are all first class but inexpensive. Reserve from ten days before departure.

Local prices, Esc	Single	Double
Porto–Faro	3350	1680
Lisbon–Irun	5335	2300
Lisbon–Madrid	7600	4450

Assistance

Handicapped: Wheelchairs and ramps are available at larger stations; request personal help from the station master *(chefe de estação)* at least 30 minutes before departure. The train information office will make arrangements on personal or telephoned request. At least one car on each long-distance train has a special toilet and space for wheelchairs.

Emergencies: Contact the train information office or the station master at stations, the conductor *(revisor)* on trains.

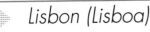
Lisbon (Lisboa)

Tourist information
Find information at Sta. Apolónia station (daily 9:00–14:00/16:00 till last international arrival) and in the central office. Phone 70 63 41 for information in English or write to Direcção-Geral do Turismo, Avenida António Augusto de Aguiar 86, P–1000 Lisboa.

City transit
Find information at kiosks outside Sta. Apolónia and Cais Sodré stations, at Santa Justa Elevator in Rua do Carmo, and metro stations. The system includes buses, trams, metro, cable cars, and elevators. The **tourist pass** *(passe para turistas)* for seven days' unlimited travel on all lines costs the same as 18 single fares. Sold at information kiosks. **Advance purchase** tickets in booklets *(cadernetas)* for 20 short or 10 long trips save about 40%. **Single tickets** *(módulos)* are sold by bus drivers. Metro tickets may be bought singly from automats or in books of ten for about 40% saving. Transfer is not allowed.

Taxis
Tel. 82 50 61

Post, telephone
Permanent services at Praça dos Restauradores and the airport.

Telegraph
All hours at Marconi, Rua de S. Julião.

Help in emergencies
Police: Tel. 36 61 41 or 115
Ambulance: Tel. 115
Physician: Hospital Inglés (private) Tel. 60 20 20
Clinic: Any Centro de Saúde and Postos de Enfermagem.
Pharmacies on 24-hr duty: Check in newspapers.
Lost & found: Police, Rua dos Anjos, 56A. Tel. 36 61 41. Mon–Fri 9:00–12:00/14:00–18:00

Airport
Lisboa Portela Airport. Green buses from railway station; travel time 30-45 minutes.

Rail connections
International and northbound trains leave from Sta. Apolónia. Trains to Coimbra, Figueira de Foz, and Sintra use Rossio, trains to Cascais and Estoril use Cais do Sodré stations. Trains to the south leave from Barreiro station across the river.
3-4 hours: Porto, Tunes*, Faro*
5-6 hours: Lagos*
Overnight: Madrid

Station plan
Lisbon Santa Apolónia: pp 228–9

---

* From Barreiro; add 45 minutes for connection from Terreiro do Paço ferry terminal on the Lisbon side.

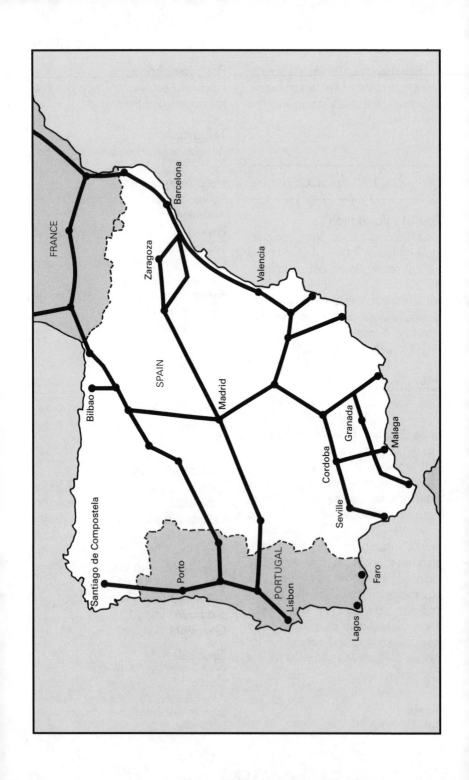

Spanish National Railway System

Red Nacional de los Ferrocariles Españoles (RENFE)

RENFE's spectacular splash for the 1992 World Fair will be a spanking new high-speed train, a French-built TGV, running between Madrid and Sevilla. From this seed should grow lines that eventually link up with the European high-speed network. But the necessary next step, already planned, will be to change the gauge to the European standard, on at least the main lines, which will save the time and bother of transfer at the French border.

The one train that is at home in both countries is the Talgo with wheels that adjust to either gauge and just roll across the border. Designed in the '30s, the Talgo is still one of the most comfortable trains anywhere, with extra space afforded by the wide Spanish gauge. The special suspension and tilting system assure a smooth ride and make the train an excellent candidate for high-speed travel, just 200 km/h for a start. Spain continues to build Talgo sets of various compositions that pamper passengers. The latest is the *Gran Clase* sleepers with showers in single and double compartments. These are slated to run in international service to France and Switzerland.

But the other side of the picture—the countryside—is bleak. The ordi-nary trains are still slow and there are no plans to change that. You are told that the mountains in Spain make better speeds impossible. How have the Swiss managed, you wonder. The extra-fare InterCity trains between Madrid and Valencia cover 490 km in 4 1/2 hours; other trains on a shorter (404-km) route take 5 1/2 to 6 3/4 hours. It's not topography but neglect that slows them down.

A disgruntled travel writer once said that RENFE was a joke. We disagree: RENFE doesn't make one laugh, rather it can be depressing enough to drive one to driving. Buying a high-speed system won't compensate for the traditional lassitude or a management busy with balancing a tariff with five levels of supplement.

Save yourself pain and take the

Talgo. Other trains are the *expresos* (Exp.) and *rápidos* (Rap.) of moderate speed, *Electrotrén* (Elec.) and *TER* railcars. *Tranvía, omnibus, automotor, semidirecto* and *ferrobús* should be mentioned but not boarded unless necessary.

Information

Overseas Spanish tourist offices have no information whatsoever. RENFE prints beautiful brochures in Spanish only. Few information clerks speak English or French.

Pictograms have been posted at new stations.

Schedule changes

Train services may change on the following public holidays (for movable dates, see CALENDAR, page 54):

New Year	January 1
Epiphany	January 6
St. Joseph	March 19
Good Friday	Movable date
Holy Saturday	Movable date
Easter Monday	Movable date
May Day	May 1
Ascension	Movable date
Whit Monday	Movable date
Corpus Christi	Movable date
St. John	June 24
Sts. Peter & Paul	June 29
National Holiday	July 18
St. James	July 25
Assumption	August 15
El Pilar	October 12
All Saints	November 1
Immaculate Conception	December 8
Christmas	December 25–26

Spain is on Central European Time. When traveling to Portugal remember that it is on Western European Time, one hour earlier.

Fares and supplements

First class costs 57% more than second.

The majority of trains are 'qualified' and require a supplement charged by distance. The category of the supplement depends on the quality of the train and the time of operation; for example, a Talgo may require Type A supplement during the day but only Type D as a night train. The timetable is your only guide. On some peak-traffic days, for example December 23, marked in the railway calendar as 'red days' (*días rojos*), the fare is 10% above the normal tariff.

The following table shows total second-class fares (basic fare plus supplements A-E) in Spanish pesetas (ptas) and US dollars. Eurailtariff prices include the highest supplement, Type A:

Distance in km	100	200	400
Basic fare, ptas	420	855	1705
+ Type E, ptas	515	1045	2085
+ Type D, ptas	560	1130	2250
+ Type C, ptas	645	1305	2605
+ Type B, ptas	670	1350	2695
+ Type A, ptas	740	1495	2980
Eurailtariff, $	8	14	27

Reduced fares

Some reductions apply only in off-peak periods or 'blue days' (*días azules*). Supplements must be paid in full.

Children under four travel free, four to twelve pay half fare.

Seniors over 60 pay half fare any day on single journeys above 100 km (or 200 km return) with *Tarjeta Dorada.*

Youths (12 to 26) pay half fare on single journeys over 100 km (or 200 km return) on blue days with a *Tarjeta Joven.*

In **families** the first adult pays full fare, others 50%, children 25%. With *Tarjeta Familiar,* only on blue days.

Return tickets on trips over 100 km in each direction are 20% cheaper on blue days.

Chequetrén vouchers for 21,250 ptas buy 25,000 ptas worth of services for 15% savings. May be used any day for fares, sleepers, etc, and combined with other discounts.

Go-as-you-please passes

Eurailpasses and **Inter-Rail Cards** allow unlimited train travel. Reservations or boarding pass is required for each trip.

The Spain Rail Pass allows unlimited travel on trains. Supplements and reservation fees are not included. Sold only to non-residents by FrenchRail agencies and RENFE offices.

	1st class	2nd class
8 days, ptas	14,000	10,000
15 days, ptas	23,000	16,000
22 days, ptas	27,000	21,000

Tickets

Tickets are sold from two months to two hours before departure for distances over 250 km and to any distance from two hours before till departure. The minimum fare charged on Talgo and InterCity is that corresponding to 250 km, on *Electrotrén* and *TER* 200 km, on *Estrella, Rápido,* and *Expreso* 100 km.

On main routes tickets must be validated before use; passengers with international through tickets or passes need either reservations or a boarding pass.

Reservations

Seats are reservable from two months ahead until departure for 200 ptas.

Baggage

Forwarding is free up to 20 kg (44 lbs). Offices at major stations accept baggage from one hour to 15 minutes before departure time, at smaller stations 30 to 5 minutes. Passengers on Talgo, InterCity, *Electrotrén* and *TER* trains should forward luggage 24 hours in advance; international passengers may have their luggage taken on the same train. Customs clearance should be obtained on international routes.

Storage costs 125–250 ptas. Lockers are in guarded areas and baggage is x-rayed before deposit. Use tokens *(ficha)* in lockers, one in regular, two in large; buy them from the attendant for 125 ptas each.

Meals

Some very good dining cars run on Talgo, *Electrotrén,* and *TER* trains. Most fast trains have bars or buffets. Ordinary trains no services.

Station restaurants and some cafeterias limit their hours to mealtimes. Bars and cafés are open most of the time.

Night travel

Couchettes are not recommended. The cost is 1115 ptas for regular, 1395 ptas for air-conditioned, 1565 ptas for international traffic.

Sleeping car accommodations are numerous in type: *Gran Clase* (large compartment with shower), *Ducha* (with shower), Talgo, regular size, special (small single), and tourist (four berths). When two prices are given in the table below, the first line shows prices for journeys under 550 km, the second for those above 550 km.

Single

Gr. Cl.	Ducha	Talgo	Regular	Special
-	-	6270	4815	3210
11000	9000	7170	5510	3675

Double

Gr. Cl.	Ducha	Talgo	Regular
-	-	2510	1925
6000	4600	2870	2205

Tourist	Talgo	Regular
	2090	1605
	2390	1840

Eurailtariff prices in US dollars:

	Regular	Air-conditioned
Single	40/46	61
Special	27/30	–
Double	16/18	24
Tourist	13/15	20

Other services

First-class lounges *(Sala Rail Club)* at major stations provide a quiet and comfortable waiting area with newspapers, magazines, complimentary coffee and soft drinks, pay phone.

Train departures are announced. Enter with EuroCity or first-class Talgo, InterCity, Electrotrén, or sleeping car ticket.

Train plus packages offered by RENFE: car rental *(Tren+coche)*, hotel *(Tren+hotel)*, boat crossing to and hotel on the Baleares and Canaries *(Tren+barco+hotel)*.

Assistance

Handicapped: Wheelchairs are supplied at most stations. Request assistance at the information office or from the *Subjefe de estación*.

Emergencies: Contact the information office or the *Subjefe de estación*.

Barcelona

Tourist information

Find information at Sants railway station (daily 7:30–22:30), in Plaça de Sant Jaume, and in Gran Via de les Corts Catalanes 658. Phone 010 or write to Patronat Municipal de Turisme, Passeig de Gràcia 35, E-08007 Barcelona. For accommodation, see the hotel agency in Sants (daily 8:00–22:00).

City transit

Find information at tourist offices and metro stations. The system combines buses, metro, Tramvia Blau tram, funiculars, and FGC and RENFE trains.

Multiride tickets *(targeta multiviatge)* are valid for ten trips: the T-1 on buses, metro, FGC trains to

Tibidabo, and Tramvia Blau; the *T-2* is not valid on buses but includes the Funicular de Montjuïc. The savings over single tickets *(bitllet senzill)* is about 45%. Tickets are sold at metro stations and on buses. Validate in punch clocks aboard buses and at metro entrances.

Taxis
Tel. 218 42 12

Post, telegraph
Mon–Sat 9:00–21:00 in Plaça d'Antoní López.

Telephone
Mon–Fri 9:00–21:00 in Carrer Fontanella 2 at Plaça de Catalunya. (Longer hours at Sants station but the rates are higher.)

Help in emergencies
Police: Tel. 092
Ambulance: Tel. 302 33 33
Physician: Tel. 230 70 00
Lost & found: Casa de la Ciutat. Tel. 301 39 23

Airport
Barcelona-Prat Airport. Direct trains run from Sants station every 20 minutes; travel time is 14 minutes.

Rail connections
Estació Terme-França (or Término) will be closed until 1990 for renovations. Until then, all trains use Sants.
3 to 4 hours: Valencia, Zaragoza
Overnight: Basel, Geneva, Lausanne, Madrid, Paris

Madrid

Tourist information
Find information and accommodation at Chamartín station (Mon–Fri 8:00–20:00, Sat 9:00–13:00) and in Plaza Mayor 3. Phone 266 48 74 or write to Oficina Municipal de Información, Plaza Mayor 3, Madrid.

City transit
Find information at *EMT*, Puerta del Sol, (Mon–Fri 7:30–20:30, Sat 10:00–13:00) and Atocha, Retiro and Sol metro stations.

Tourist passes for metro *(Metrotur)* cost the same as 11 single fares for three days, 16 singles for five days. **Multiride tickets** *(bono 10 viajes)* save about 40% on singles. Buy passes and tickets at metro stations and validate in punch clock when first used. **Multiride tickets** *(bono 10 viajes)* for buses save about 40% over singles. Buy them at booths *(casetas)* in Puerta del Sol, Plaza de la Cibeles, Plaza de Castilla, and elsewhere. **Monthly passes** *(Abono-Transportes Mensual)* include bus, metro, and regular trains in the city, and cost the same as 50 singles for one month. Buy them at the EMT information center in Plaza de la Cibeles.

Taxis
Tel. 247 82 00, 405 13 13, 445 90 08

Post, telegraph
Permanent service in Plaza de la Cibeles.

Telephone
Permanent service in Gran Vía 28.

Help in emergencies
Police: Tel. 092
Ambulance: Tel. 734 26 00, 734 55 00
Physician: Hospital La Paz. Tel. 734 26 00
Pharmacy on 24-hour duty: Listed in newspapers.
Lost & found: Plaza de Legazpi 7. Tel. 441 02 14

Airport
Madrid Barajas Airport. Airport bus runs from Plaza de Colón; travel time is 30 minutes.

Rail connections
All international trains use Chamartín station. Some trains to Vigo, La Coruña, Gijon, and Santander in the north leave from Norte (Príncipe Pío) station. At Atocha, only the suburban section operates during complete renovations; it will be the terminal of the Madrid-Sevilla high-speed line in 1992.

3 to 4 hours: Zaragoza

4 to 5 hours: Cordoba

5 to 6 hours: Valencia

Overnight: Barcelona, Granada, Lisbon, Malaga, Paris

Station plans
Barcelona Sants: pp 196–7
Madrid Chamartín: pp 242–3

Swedish State Railways

Statens Järnvägar (SJ)

High-tech and demands of economy have pushed Swedish trains several decades ahead in the space of a few years. While up to date in engineering, they used to have a comfortable, almost old-fashioned air: wood paneling, roomy compartments with movable armchairs and tables, and at the end of each car an elegant glass carafe for drinking water—touches from an older, slower world. But a modern railway cannot afford to appear old and slow when it has to compete with airlines.

When SJ introduced the CityExpress, it invited comparisons with planes. The first-class train catered to business people with an elegant dining car, telephones, conference rooms, secretarial help, and quiet compartments for work. Planes could provide none of that. The race continues with new entrants in 1990 when the still unnamed *snabbtåg* (fast train) cuts the Stockholm-Göteborg trip to three hours. The tilting system of the new cars, and upgraded tracks, will allow a commercial speed of 200 km/h.

Instead of pushing for records, SJ adds conveniences. Reclusive executives appreciate meals and telephones brought to their seats, children the playroom with toys and books. The entire system is being revamped, speed increased, rolling stock modernized. After the success of showers in rebuilt sleepers, the new ones will all feature private bathrooms.

Currently InterCity expresses run hourly on the principal lines from Stockholm to Göteborg and Malmö. Other routes are covered by regional trains running at 160–170 km/h with frequent stops, fast trains (*snälltåg*) and locals (*persontåg*). The transport network extends away from the rails. SJ also operates local buses with train connections. Train tickets and most passes are valid on these lines. Many ferries are run by the railway. These include the boat trains carrying through-cars between Denmark and Sweden.

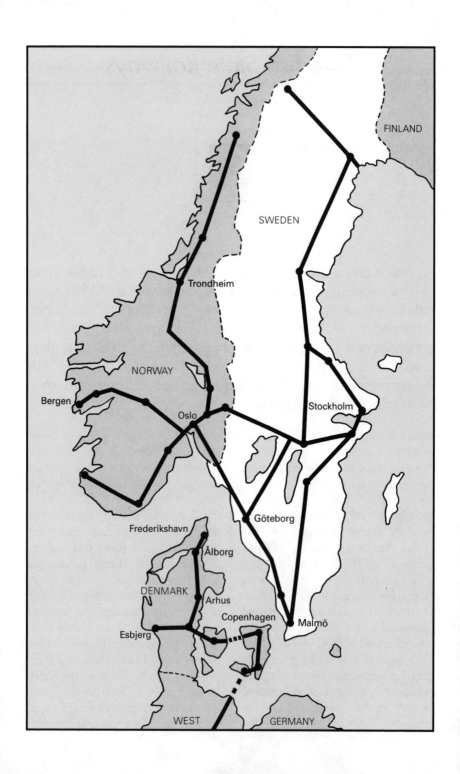

That lamented old-fashioned atmosphere survives in the well-kept stations. The stone and brick in the buildings from the last century are preserved while heating, lighting, movement are modernized. The automatic sliding glass doors contrast well with the old brick walls.

Swedish fares are somewhat higher than the European average but the many discounts offset the price. The railway's policy has been to lower the cost of travel to boost volume and increase revenue.

Information
Brochures in English are available. If you cannot read the timetable, you'll find help on trains and at stations. Most staff speak English. Stations are well marked with pictograms.

Schedule changes
Train services may change on public holidays (for movable dates, see CALENDAR, page 54):

New Year	January 1
Epiphany	January 6
Good Friday	Movable date
Easter Monday	Movable date
May Day	May 1
Ascension	Movable date
Whit Monday	Movable date
Midsummer	Thursday–Saturday nearest June 24
All Saints	November 1
Christmas	December 25–26

Sweden is on Central European Time. When traveling to Finland remember that it is on Eastern European Time, one hour later.

Fares
First class costs 40% more than second. Second-class fares in Swedish crowns (Skr) and US dollars:

Distances in km	100	200	400
Local prices, Skr	80	149	279
Eurailtariff, $	–	22	40

Supplements
On the CityExpress pay 110 Skr on first, 30 Skr on second class.

Reduced fares
Children up to age twelve travel free when accompanied by an adult, from 12 to 16 pay half fare.

Seniors (over 65) get 30% reduction with ID-card.

Students with national ID *(CSN-kort)* pay half fare.

The **low-fare card** *(Sverigekort)* allows 30% discount. The card costs 850 Skr for one year; requires photo.

Inquire about **cheap departures** *(Röda avgångar)* when all tickets are half price.

Go-as-you-please passes
Eurailpasses, Inter-Rail Cards and **Nordturist Tickets** allow unlimited travel on trains and buses. Ferries are free with Eurailpass, half fare with Inter-Rail Card.

Tickets
Single tickets are valid for ten days, returns for one month. Half-fare singles *(röda avgångar)* are valid for 36 hours. SJ buses accept train tickets.

Reservation

Reservation is obligatory on CityExpress and InterCity trains for 15 Skr, optional on others. Reserve from one year ahead to departure time.

	Local price Skr	Overseas $
Special	650	ca.115
Single	450	80
Double	150	26
Triple	100	17

Baggage

Forwarding costs 35 Skr a piece, up to 25 kg (55 lbs). Storage costs 10 Skr a day. Lockers use five-krona coins.

Other services

There are **telephones** are on all CityExpress and InterCity trains.

Car rental (biluthyrning) is available at most larger stations.

Meals

The CityExpress and InterCity trains carry dining cars, most long-distance trains self-service buffets. Both serve everything from drinks to full-course meals. Some long-distance trains have only trolley service.

The station restaurants are excellent but tend to be expensive. Shopping for provisions is easy in the delicatessen and bakery in Stockholm Central, but in other stations there may only be kiosks.

Assistance

Handicapped: Wheelchairs are available at most stations but should be ordered in advance to be ready at both the departure and destination stations. Contact the duty officer (Stationschef). **Children's compartments** (barnkupéer) in second-class cars run on most long-distance trains. Trained nurses look after infants under two.

Emergencies: Contact the duty officer at the Jourexpedition or Stationschef office.

Night travel

Inexpensive night trains are a bonus in Sweden. Berths should be claimed 15 minutes before departure.

Couchettes with second-class tickets cost 70 Skr. Reserve from one year to a few hours before departure.

Sleeping cars have special single-berth compartments, not the Continental small-sized, but new ones with private shower and toilet. Reserve sleepers from one year to a few hours before departure.

Göteborg

Tourist information

Find information near Centralstation, in the Nordstan shopping center (Mon–Fri 9:30–18:00, Sat 9:30–15:00) and in the main office, Basargatan 10 (summer daily 9:00–20:00; shoulder seasons daily 9:00–18:00; winter Mon–Fri 9:00–17:00, Sat 10:00–14:00).

Phone 10 07 40 or write to Turistbyrån i Göteborg, Basargatan 10, S-411 10 Göteborg.

City transit
Find information in tourist offices.

The **Göteborg Card** *(Göteborgskortet)* is good for unlimited travel on buses and trams, free admission to museums and amusements, sightseeing trips, many discounts. It costs 70 Skr for one day, 120 Skr for two, 165 Skr for three, 200 Skr for four. Buy it at tourist offices, hotels, and news kiosks. The **tourist pass** for 24 hours of unlimited travel *(24-timmarskortet)* costs little over two single fares. On weekends, it's valid for one adult and two children under 17. **Tickets** *(kuponger)* in booklets of 11 and 21 save about 40% on singles. Two coupons are needed for a single trip with transfers allowed; return trip is free daily 9:00–15:00. Buy tickets and passes at news kiosks, singles aboard buses and trams. Validate in punch clocks on buses and trams.

Taxis
Tel. 65 00 00

Post, telegraph
Mon–Fri 8:00–19:00, Sat 9:00–15:00 in Nordstan.

Telephone
Mon–Fri 9:00–18:00, Sat 10:00–14:00 at Hvitfeldsplatsen 9.

Help in emergencies
Police, ambulance, physician, dentist: Tel. 90 000

Pharmacy on 24-hour duty: In Nordstan.
Lost & found: Tel. 61 80 00

Airport
Landvetter Airport. Airport buses run from Centralstation; travel time is 30–40 minutes.

Rail connections
All trains use Centralstation.
3 to 4 hours: Frederikshavn (by ferry), Malmö, Stockholm
4 to 5 hours: Copenhagen, Oslo
Overnight: Hamburg

Stockholm

Tourist information
Find information and accommodation at Hotellcentralen in Centralstation (summer: daily 8:00–21:00, winter: 8:00–11:30/13:00–17:00) and in Sverigehuset, Kungsträdgården (summer: Mon–Fri 8:30–18:00, Sat–Sun 8:00–17:00; winter: Mon–Fri 9:00–17:00, Sat–Sun 9:00–14:00). Phone 789 20 00 or write to Stockholm Information Service, P.O.B. 7542, S-103 93 Stockholm.

City transit
Find information, maps, and tickets at SL windows in Centralstation, in Sergels Torg, and Slussen T-bana station.

The **Stockholm Card** *(Stockholmskortet)* is valid for 24 hours of unlimited travel on buses, *tunnelbana* (subway), and local trains, free admission to 64 museums and amusements, and free or half-fare sightseeing tours. It costs 70 Skr (35 Skr under 18) at tourist and transport offices, railway station, and news kiosks. A **tourist pass** *(turistkort)* for 24 hours of unlimited travel in the center costs less than three single fares, for the entire urban area the same as five singles. The 72-hour pass costs less than ten singles and includes the ferry to Djurgården and admission to the Skansen and the Kaknäs Tower. Available from transport offices and news kiosks.

Taxis
Tel. 15 00 00

Post office
Mon—Fri 8:00–20:00, Sat 9:00–15:00 at Vasagatan 28–34.

Telephone, telegraph
Mon—Sun 8:00–24:00 at Skeppsbron 2.

Help in emergencies
Police, ambulance: Tel. 90 000
Physician: Tel. 44 92 00

Dentist: Tel. 54 11 17 till 21:00, then 44 92 00
Pharmacy on 24-hour duty: C.W.Scheele, Klarabergsgatan 64.
Lost & found: Police: Tjärhovsgatan 21. Tel. 41 04 32.
Transit: Rådmansgatan T-station. Tel. 736 07 80.

Airport
Stockholm Arlanda Airport. Airport buses run every 20 minutes from City Terminalen, adjacent to Centralstation; travel time is 40 minutes.

Rail connections
All trains use Centralstation.
3 to 4 hours: Göteborg
Overnight: Hamburg, Copenhagen, Malmö, Oslo

Boat connections
Ferries for Helsinki and Turku leave from Värtahamnen (Silja Line) and Tegelvikshamnen (Viking Line). Overnight sailings to Helsinki, day or night sailings to Turku.

Station plans
Göteborg Centralstation: pp 220–1
Stockholm Centralstation: pp 266–7

Swiss Federal Railways

Schweizerische Bundesbahnen (SBB)/Chemins de fer fédéraux (CFF)/
Ferrovie federali Svizzere (FFS)

The railways of Switzerland lead in many rankings. One of the densest networks in which no place is more than 16 km away from a rail line. One of the busiest—the timetable runs over 2000 pages. The hardest to build, with nearly 6000 bridges and three of the world's longest tunnels. The cleanest running since its complete electrification in the late '30s. The most reliable and punctual. The most expensive. It is also the most diverse. The network, aptly named in promotions the *Swiss Travel System*, consists of the federal company and nearly a hundred private ones running trains, buses, ships, rack railways, funiculars, and cablecars. But since they are all completely integrated, the system is easy to use. You can change from ship to bus to train with little waiting, and use the same ticket or the all-inclusive *Swiss Pass* (see below).

More than ten years ago the SBB planners did what others dream of: they rationalized the entire rail schedule, rewriting it from scratch. The program *Rail 2000* continues to increase the frequency and speed of trains, tightening connections or eliminating them with direct trains. The base of the timetable is an intercity network with half-hourly trains between major centers, hourly between others. International expresses are neatly slotted in. Local feeders make tight connections to intercity trains.

For the relatively short trips the SBB provides a surprising amount of space and high level of comfort. InterCity passenger cars have adjustable seats, movable armrests, tables, and automatic doors. Second class differs only in seating, 2+2 instead of 2+1. The lesser trains are not far behind in comfort.

The private companies serve mostly resort areas. The Rhätische, Furka-Oberalp, and Brig-Visp-Zermatt together run the Glacier Express from St. Moritz to Zermatt across the top of the

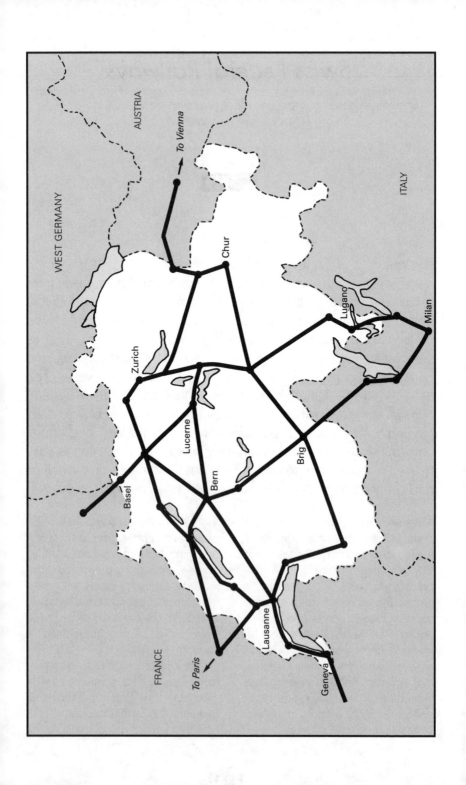

Alps. Other tourist trains and train/bus/ship combinations will take you from alpine snowfields to the palm trees of Ticino.

Information

Most of the printed material appears in several languages. The quinquelingual timetable includes a detailed English explanation of fares, rules, and services. The information offices stock leaflets with schedules, tourist and city transit details. Most staff speak English, German, and French.

Stations are well sign-posted and have many indicator boards. Quick help is available from information officers (yellow cap- and armband) near the trains.

You may find unfamiliar cities listed on indicator boards. Here are their names in the three principal languages:

German	French	Italian
Basel	Bâle	Basilea
Brig	Brigue	Briga
Genf	Genève	Ginevra
Luzern	Lucerne	Lucerna
Zürich	Zurich	Zurigo
Lausanne	Lausanne	Losanna

Schedule changes

Train service may change on the following public holidays (for movable dates, see CALENDAR, page 54):

New Year	January 1–2
Good Friday	Movable date
Easter Monday	Movable date
Ascension	Movable date
Whit Monday	Movable date
Independence Day	August 1
Christmas	December 25–26

Fares

First class costs 55–60% more than second. Second-class fares in Swiss francs (Sfr) and US dollars:

Distance in Km	100	200	400
Local prices, Sfr	24	43	64
Eurailtariff, $	18	31	45

Fares become steeper as the tracks do: the alpine routes served by private companies are more expensive. The SBB charges 15–30 centimes a kilometer on second class. The Furka-Oberalp Bahn climbs to only 35 centimes but each of the nine kilometers up to the 11,332-foot-high Jungfraujoch costs a dizzying Sfr4.88.

Supplements

On the TGV to Paris from Bern, Geneva, or Lausanne the EuroCity supplement is Sfr 24 on first, Sfr 16 on second class. On the Gottardo between Zurich Airport and Milan the EuroCity supplement is Sfr 11 on first, Sfr 8 on second class.

The Alpine sightseeing trains, like the Bernina, Glacier, and Wilhelm Tell Expresses, require special supplements.

Reduced fares

The **Swiss Card**, sold only to non-residents, combines entry and exit with half fare. It covers the fare both ways between a border station or airport and your destination in Switzerland, and allows you to buy all train, bus, and boat tickets at half price (smaller reductions on mountain railways). Buy it through travel agents,

Swiss tourist and Swissair offices overseas or at railway stations in Switzerland.

Adults	1st class	2nd class
Local prices, Sfr	125	100
Overseas, $	80	65

Children (6–16)		
Local prices, Sfr	75	50
Overseas, $	50	35

The **Swiss Transfer Ticket** is a flat fare from a border station or airport to any destination in Switzerland and back. It costs Sfr 125 on first, Sfr 70 on second class.

The **Swiss Half-fare Card** for non-residents buys all tickets at half price for one month, costs Sfr 65. (See yearly half-fare card below.)

Children under six travel free, six to sixteen at half fare.

Return (round-trip) and circular tickets save, depending on distance, 18% to 39%.

Multiride tickets (Mehrfahrten-karte/carte multicours) give twelve single trips for the price of five returns.

Route passes (Streckenabonnement/abonnement de parcours) are valid for unlimited travel on a chosen route for a week, month, or year.

Half-fare cards 1/2-Preis-Abonnement/abonnement 1/2prix) for half-price tickets cost Sfr 110 for a year. With photo.

With **day cards** (Tageskarte/carte journalière), Sfr 170 for six, you get unlimited travel for a day.

Families: with at least one paying adult, children under 16 travel free, under 25 (if unmarried) pay half fare. With Familienkarte/carte de famille.

Network passes for one year (Generalabonnement/abonnement général) are available at various prices, depending on age. Inquire at stations.

Go-as-you-please passes

Eurailpasses and **Inter-Rail Cards** are valid for free travel on trains and most lake ships, and for 20–50% reductions on other ships and private mountain railways.

The **Swiss Pass** gives you the run of the entire Swiss travel system. It allows unlimited travel on trains, buses, ships, and the public transit systems of 24 cities. The Swiss Pass is the only ticket you need for access to all of Switzerland (except some special trains to mountaintops, where you get 25%–50% reductions). The pass is sold only to non-residents at Swiss railway stations (including Geneva and Zurich airport stations). In the U.S. and Canada the pass is sold by French-Rail Inc. When traveling with a parent, children under 16 travel free; under 25 (if unmarried) they can buy the pass at half price.

Local prices	1st class	2nd class
4 days, Sfr	235	160
8 days, Sfr	280	195
15 days, Sfr	335	235
1 month, Sfr	465	325

Overseas prices	1st class	2nd class
4 days, $	-	-
8 days, $	180	125
15 days, $	220	155
1 month, $	300	210

Alternatively the *Flexipass* permits travel on three days within a period of 15.

	1st class	2nd class
Local price in Sfr	235	160
Overseas price in $	149	99

Regional vacation passes *(Regionale Ferienabonnement/abonnement de vacances régional)* allow five days of unlimited travel chosen within a 15-day period and half fare on other days within one of eight regions. They are issued only in the summer; prices vary with region from Sfr 50 for Locarno/Ascona to Sfr 121 for Lake Lucerne. Inquire at travel agencies and railway offices.

Tickets

Single tickets under 80 km are valid on the day of issue, above 80 km for two days. Returns under 36 km are valid on the day of issue, 37–80 km for two days, above 80 km for one month. Circular tour tickets under 72 km are valid on the day of issue, 73–160 km for two days, above 160 km for one month.

Stopovers are allowed without formalities. However, on alpine and rural bus routes let the driver know when you intend to resume the trip.

You may notice the symbol of an all-seeing eye on the side of a local train or in the timetable. It marks a self-service train without a conductor to sell tickets: you must buy your ticket before boarding or an all-seeing inspector will fine you.

Reservation

Reservation is obligatory only on certain EuroCity trains to and from Italy *(Cisalpin, Gottardo, Lemano, Manzoni)*, included where a supplement is charged; optional on other EuroCity, InterCity, and regular trains for Sfr 4. Reserve from two months to a few hours before departure (the time limit varies with station and train).

Baggage

Forwarding costs Sfr 7 a piece or each 30 kg (66 lbs). It's preferable to send a day in advance during peak periods.

The **Fly Rail Baggage** system combines air and rail baggage services for direct transfer. The cost is Sfr 10 a piece. Going to Switzerland, use a green address label (get it from Swissair or a Swiss tourist office) to have your baggage delivered to your destination. Leaving Switzerland, you can forward your baggage from most stations to your flight destination (US carriers excepted).

Storage costs Sfr 2 a day. Lockers use one-franc coins.

Meals

Dining cars are carried on most EuroCity, InterCity and express trains. Seats may be reserved up to 48 hours before departure time; phone (062) 31 85 76. Self-service cafeterias look much better than they sound. There are mini-bars on most inland trains. Not a great selection, but the (real) coffee and fresh sandwich rolls are good.

Station restaurants serve excellent Swiss and international cuisine. Note that "Buffet 1. Klasse" is seldom a buffet but a high-priced luxury restaurant. Bistros, brasseries, and *Stüblis* are affordable.

Picnic ingredients should be bought at a nearby supermarket or *traiteur* (delicatessen); station kiosks sell mainly sandwiches and sausages.

Night travel

There are no inland services. The SBB runs sleepers and couchettes on international routes.

Couchettes cost Sfr 21 in six-berth compartments, Sfr 28 in four-berth compartments reserved for family or group. Reserve from two months to a few hours before departure.

Sleeping car berths have regular international prices, except on the *EC-Pablo-Casals* from Bern to Barcelona: singles and doubles cost Sfr 232 and Sfr 109, respectively, and include breakfast. Reserve sleeping car berths from three months to a few hours before departure.

Single, Sfr	197
Special, Sfr	141
Double, Sfr	85
Triple (T3), Sfr	57

Other services

Airline check-in: Swissair passengers can check in and reserve seats on their flight from the baggage offices in the main stations of Basel, Bern, Geneva, Lausanne, Lugano, Lucerne, Neuchâtel, St. Gallen, and Zurich. They can forward baggage to their destination airport at the same office.

Train telephones are on most Inter-City trains.

Car rental may be arranged at all large stations.

Bicycles can be rented at most SBB stations and some private ones. Reserve in advance from any station.

Assistance

Handicapped: Facilities and services are excellent. Wheelchairs are available at all stations. Most stations have ramps, instead of stairs. The new cars have wide doors and fold-up seats that allow space for wheelchairs. For personal assistance, contact the train information office by mail or phone.

Family and medical help for mothers with babies, elderly or ill passengers, are given at the shelters of the *Bahnhofhilfswerk*.

Emergencies: Contact the duty officer: *sous-chef* in French, *Stationsinspektor* in German.

Basel

Tourist information

Find information and accommodation at the railway station, SBB Bahnhof (Mon–Fri 8:30–19:00, Sat 8:30–12:30/13:30–18:00) and in the main office at Blumenrain 2 (Mon–Fri 8:30–18:00, Sat 8:30–13:00). Phone 25 50 50 or write to Offizielles Verkehrsbüro Basel, Blumenrain 2, CH-4001 Basel.

City transit

Find information at tourist offices and BVB transport offices.

All transit is free with **Swiss Pass** (see page 184).

A **tourist pass** for 24 hours of free travel in the urban area *(Tageskarte)* costs less than three single fares, for the region *(Regio Billett)* the same as five singles. Validate in punch clock at first use. **Multiride tickets** *(Mehrfahrtenkarten*—one for each of the three zones) for 11 rides save 10% on singles. Punch to validate before boarding. **Single tickets** are issued already validated. All tickets and passes are sold by automats at every stop. Fares and period of validity vary by distance. Transfers are allowed.

Taxis
Tel. 22 22 22

Post office
Mon–Fri 6:00–23:00, Sat 6:00–20:00, Sun 9:00–23:00 in Nauenstrasse, next to SBB Bahnhof.

Telephone, telegraph
Mon–Fri 6:30–22:00, Sat–Sun 7:30–22:00 in SBB Bahnhof.

Help in emergencies
Police: Tel. 117
Ambulance: Tel. 144
Physician, dentist: Tel. 25 15 15
Pharmacy on 24-hour duty:
Tel. 25 15 15
Lost & found: Tel. 21 70 34 (city) and 21 89 90 (transit)

Airport
Basel-Mulhouse Airport. City bus No.50 runs every 20 minutes from SBB Bahnhof; travel time is 12 minutes. For airline check-in and to transfer baggage directly to or from airplane, see pp 185 and 186.

Rail connections
It may confuse you to find that timetables list three stations for Basel. But two of these are in one building. Swiss and German trains stop in what is called Basel *SBB*, French trains in the French section, Basel *SNCF*. German trains halt but don't terminate at the small Basel *Badischer Bahnhof,* across the River Rhine.

1 to 2 hours: Bern, Karlsruhe, Strasbourg, Zurich
2 to 3 hours: Frankfurt, Geneva, Lausanne, Mannheim
3 to 4 hours: Luxembourg
4 to 5 hours: Cologne, Paris
5 to 6 hours: Lyon, Milan
Overnight: Amsterdam, Barcelona, Hamburg, Rome, Utrecht, Vienna

Lausanne

Tourist information
Find information and accommodation at the railway station (May through June: daily 14:00–20:00; July to mid-October: 10:00–21:00; October through April: 15:00–19:00) and main office, 2 avenue de Rhodanie, (Easter to mid-October: Mon–Fri 8:00–19:00, Sat–Sun 8:00–12:00/ 13:00–19:00; mid-October to Easter: Mon–Fri 8:00–18:00, Sat–Sun 8:30–12:00/13:00–17:00). Phone 617 14 27 or write to Office du tourisme et des congrès, 2 av. de Rhodanie, CH-1000 Lausanne.

City transit

Find information at tourist offices and metro stops.

All transit is free with **Swiss Pass** (see page 184). **Tourist passes** *(abonnement)* for free travel on all buses, trolleybuses, and metro cost the same for one day as three single fares, for three days the same as eight singles. **Ticket booklets** for ten trips save 25% on singles. Tickets may be valid on all public transport (good for 60 minutes' travel) or on metro only. Buy tickets from automats and metro stops, and validate in punch clock before use.

Taxis

Tel. 141, 23 11 11

Post, telephone, telegraph

Mon – Fri 6:30 – 22:00, Sat 6:30–20:00, Sun 9:00–12:00/ 18:00–22:00 at 43b avenue de la Gare, near railway station.

Telephone, telegraph

Mon–Sat 6:45–21:45, Sun 7:00–21:45 in railway station.

Help in emergencies

Police: Tel. 118
Ambulance: Tel. 122
Physician, dentist: Tel. 32 99 32
Pharmacy on 24-hour duty: Addresses posted on pharmacy doors.
Lost & found: Mon–Fri 7:30–11:45/ 13:00–17:00, Sat 7:30–11:30. 6 rue St-Laurent. Tel. 21 60 58.

Airport

Geneva Cointrin Airport. Trains run about every 20 minutes; travel time is 42 minutes. For airline check-in and to transfer baggage directly to or from airplane, see pages 185 and 186.

Rail connections

All trains use Gare CFF.
Under 1 hour: Geneva
1 to 2 hours: Bern
2 to 3 hours: Basel, Zurich
3 to 4 hours: Milan, Paris
5 to 6 hours: Strasbourg, Luxembourg
Overnight: Brussels, Rome, Venice

Zurich

Tourist information

The central office for information and accommodation is at the railway station, Hauptbahnhof (March through October: Mon–Fri 8:00–22:00, Sat–Sun 8:00–20:30. November through February: Mon–Thu 8:00–20:00, Fri 8:00–22:00, Sat–Sun 9:00–18:00). Phone 211 40 00 or write to Offizielles Verkehrsbüro Zürich, Bahnhofplatz 15, CH-8023 Zürich.

City transit

Information and map are available at the VBZ transit office in ShopVille at Hauptbahnhof.

All transit is free with **Swiss Pass** (see page 184). **Monthly passes** *(Abonnement)* cost the same as 20–30 single fares, depending on the size of area where valid. **Tourist pass** *(Tageskarte)* for 24 hours of free travel costs less than three singles. **Multiride cards** *(Mehrfahrtenkarte)* for 13 rides save about 25% on singles. Day passes and tickets are sold by automats at every stop, singles already stamped; validate others in punch clock at stops before first use. Fares vary by distance, maps on automats show the zones. Transfer is allowed.

Taxis
Tel. 44 44 41

Post, telephone, telegraph
Mon – Sat 6:30 – 23:00, Sun 9:00–23:00 in Kasernenstrasse 95–99.

Help in emergencies
Police: Tel. 117
Ambulance: Tel. 361 61 61
Physician, dentist: Tel. 47 47 00
Pharmacy on 24-hour duty: Bellevue, Bellevue Platz.

Lost & found: Werdmühlestr. 10. Mon – Fri 7:30 – 17:30. Tel. 216 71 11

Airport
Zurich Kloten Airport. Regular trains run from Hauptbahnhof three to five times an hour; travel time is 11 minutes. For airline check-in and to transfer baggage directly to or from airplane, see pages 185 and 186.

Rail connections
All trains use Hauptbahnhof.
1 to 2 hours: Basel, Bern
2 to 3 hours: Geneva, Cologne, Lausanne
3 to 4 hours: Milan
4 to 5 hours: Frankfurt, Munich, Strasbourg
Overnight: Brussels, Hamburg, Paris, Rome, Utrecht, Vienna

Station plans
Basel SBB Bahnhof: pp 198–9
Lausanne Gare CFF: pp 226–7
Zurich Hauptbahnhof: pp 278–9

STATION PLANS

Amsterdam Centraalstation

Travel center	Mon–Fri 9:00–18:00, Sat–Sun 9:00–17:00. *Trans Reisbüro*	D
Train information	In Travel center. Tel. 20 22 66.	
Tickets, inland	All hours	A
Tickets, international	Daily 6:00–22:30	A
Reservations	Mon–Fri 8:00–20:00, Sat–Sun 9:00–17:00	A
Baggage	All hours	E
Lockers	Accessible all hours	E
Lost & found	Daily 7:00–22:00	E
Emergencies	All hours. *Perronopziehter* on platforms	
First aid	See Emergencies.	
Police	All hours. *Spoorwegpolitie*. Track (*Spoor*) 2a	access at C
Help for handicapped	All hours. Contact Baggage office Phone in advance 30/33 12 53.	E
Toilets	All hours. Tracks (*Spoor*) 2a, 2b	access at C
Waiting room	All hours. Tracks (*Spoor*) 7a, 10a, 13a	access at C
Restaurant	Mon–Wed 9:30–23:00, Thu–Sat 9:30–24:00, Sun 10:30–23:00. Track (*Spoor*) 2	access at C
Self-service	Mon–Sat 7:00–20:00, Sun 8:00–20:00. Track (*Spoor*) 2	access at C
Bar, buffet	Daily 7:00–20:00. In main tunnel	B
Tourist info, accommodation	See city page	outside
City transit information	GVB office	outside
Foreign exchange	Mon–Sat 7:00–22:45, Sun 8:00–22:45	E
To airport	Direct trains.	

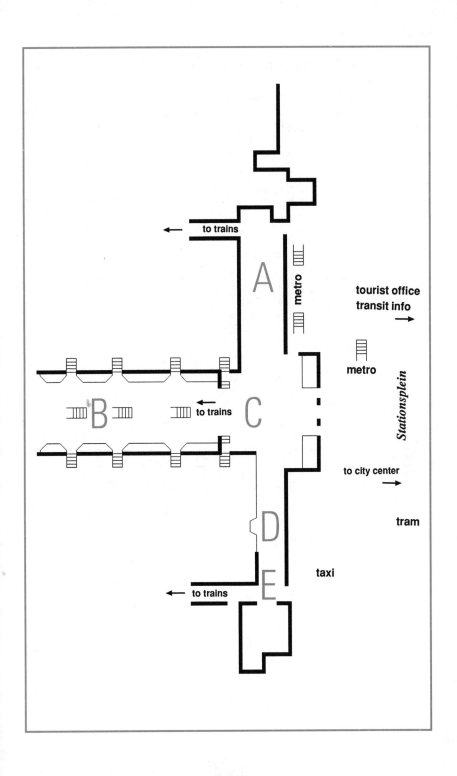

Athens - Athíne Stathmós Larísis

This is the international station for all northern trains to Thessaloniki and beyond. Trains to the south and the Peloponnese (including Patras for the ferry to Italy) leave from the adjacent Stathmós Peloponnísou.

Train information	Daily 7:00–23:00	B
	Tel. 522–2491.	
Tickets, inland	Daily 4:40–23:20	D
Tickets, international	6:00–24:00	D
Tickets, advance	6:30–21:30	D
Reservations	See Tickets, advance	
Eurail aid	In railway head office: OSE, Corolou 1–3	
Baggage	Daily 6:30–22:00	C
Lost & found	See Baggage office. Other times Tourist Police	
Emergencies/First aid	See Train information	D
	Other times Tourist Police	A
Police	Daily 7:00–24:00	A
Help for handicapped	See Tourist Police	A
Toilets	All hours	A
Waiting room	Daily 6:00–24:00	D
Restaurant, bar	Daily 5:00–24:00	C
Tourist information	Daily 7:00–23:00	
	Tourist Police	A
City transit information	See Tourist information or booth outside, daily 8:00–16:00	
Foreign exchange	Daily 8:00–14:15/14:45–21:15	B
Telephone, telegraph	Mon–Fri 7:30–21:30	outside
To other station	Stathmós Peloponnísou is connected by an overpass.	
To airport	Express buses to East and West Terminals	outside

The station is open at all hours.

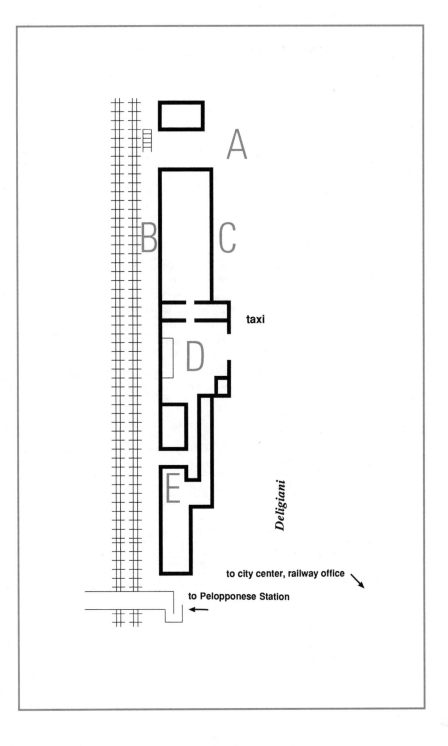

A

B   C

taxi

D

E

Deligiani

to city center, railway office

to Pelopponese Station

Barcelona Estació de Sants

Barely ten years old, the station still has growing pains. The interior is still in flux: the shading on the floor plan (K) covers the commercial area where shops shift with the whim of designers. Sants has a fine waiting area—on a sunny day—just outside in the adjoining park with a lake.

Train information	Daily 6:00–22:30. Tel. 322 41 42	L
Tickets and reservations, inland	All hours. Windows 11–21	H
Tickets and reservations, int'l	Daily 5:30–20:00. Windows 6–9	H
Tickets, suburban	All hours.Note: Take number under the sign *su turno* (national or international); the overhead display will flashyour number and the window to go to.	G
Eurail aid	Daily 5:30–20:00. Window 9	H
Baggage send/pick-up	No service. Go to the baggage car on the train to send or pick up forwarded luggage	
Lockers	Daily 6:30–23:00. Manned storage area; baggage is X–rayed before deposit. Location is temporary.	A
Lost & found	Daily 6:00–22:00. *Cap d'estació*	F
Emergencies, first aid	All hours. Contact guard at ticket barrier	F
Police	All hours	C
Help for handicapped	Daily 10:00–13:00/16:00–20:00. *Missió Trinitaria.* Other times see Train information	C
Toilets	All hours	J
Waiting area	All hours	D
Special waiting room	Sala Rail Club	D
	Daily 8:00–23:00. Attendants let you in with Eurailpass or first-class tickets for EuroCity, Talgo, InterCity, Electrotrén and sleeping cars. Complimentary coffee, soft drinks, magazines; pay phone. Comfortable and quiet.	
Restaurants, self-service, bar, buffet, provisions	Variable hours	B,M
Pharmacy	Mon–Fri 9:00–13:30/16:30–20:00, Sat 9:00–13:30	K
Shopping center, supermarket	Hyper–Sants	outside
Foreign exchange	Mon–Sat 8:00–22:00, Sun 8:00–14:00/16:00–22	K
Telephone, telegraph	Daily 6:45–23:00	N
To other stations	Metro to Terme	E–J
	Regular trains to Passeig de Gràcia	
To airport	Train from Track *(Via)* 4. Tickets at Cercanias.	G

No services when station is closed, after last train or 23:30 to 5:00.

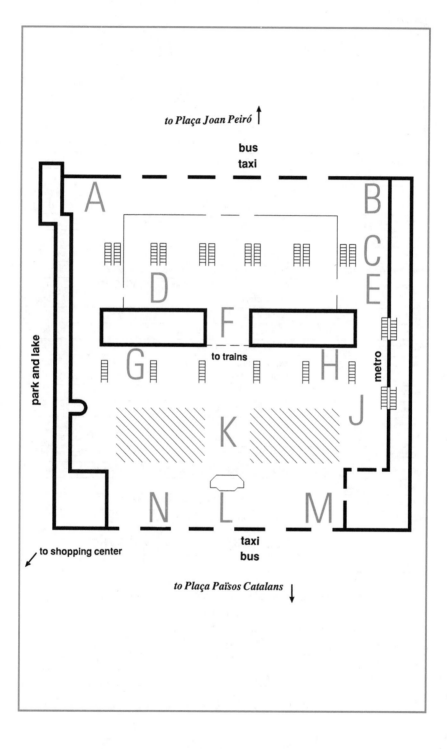

Basel SBB Bahnhof/Basel Gare SNCF

Travel center, Eurail aid	Daily 6:00–22:00 (Nov–Mar 6:00–20:00) *Reisebüro SBB*	E
Train info., reservations	Daily 7:00–20:00 in Travel center. Tel. 23 67 67	E
Tickets	Daily 5:00–00:10	E
Baggage send	Daily 6:00–21:30	G
	To transfer baggage directly to/from airplane, see pp 185–186	
Baggage pick-up	Daily 5:30–23:50	G
Baggage store	Daily 5:30–00:15	H
Lockers	Accessible 4:00–0:30	
	(other times with ticket only)	B,D,F,H
Lost & found	Daily 7:30–19:00. Track *(Gleis)* 4	F
Emergencies, first aid	All hours. *Kundendienst* or *Zugdienstbüro*	F,J
Police	Daily 5:00–1:30. Other times phone 117	Direction K
Help for handicapped	See Baggage. Phone in advance 22 37 23	
Nursery, help	Mon–Fri 8:30–12:30/13:30–17:30, Sat 8:30–12:30.	
	Bahnhofhilfe	C, upstairs
Toilets	All hours	B,J
Shower	Mon–Sat 7:30–18:30, Sat 7:30–17:00	C, upstairs
Waiting room	All hours on platforms	
Restaurant	Daily 11:15–14:15/18:15–23:45	outside
	Daily 6:00–23:40	C
Snack bars, kiosks	5:15–23:00	B,D
Provisions	Outside, across Bahnhofplatz	
Pharmacy	Mon–Fri 7:30–18:30, Sat 7:30–12:30	
	In underground passage	access at E–G
Shopping	In underground passage	access at E–G
Tourist info, accommodation	Mon–Fri 8:30–19:00, Sat 8:30–12:30/13:30–18:00	D
City transit information	See Tourist info	
Foreign exchange	Daily 6:00–21:45 (April–December till 22:15)	E
Post office	Mon–Fri 6:00–23:00, Sat 6:00–20:00,	
	Sun 9:00–23:00	outside
Telephone	Mon–Fri 6:30–22:00, Sat–Sun 7:30–22:00	K
To airport	City bus.	outside

Trains to and from France stop at Basel Gare SNCF (Area A on the floor plan). Passengers go through French passport and customs check here. Tickets, reservations and baggage charges are payable in Swiss currency.

Train information, reservations	Mon–Sat 7:45–19:00, Sun 7:45–18:00	A
Tickets	Daily 6:00–20:30	A
Baggage send, pick-up	All hours	A

No services when station is closed, 0:30–4:00. Enter with ticket at main door.

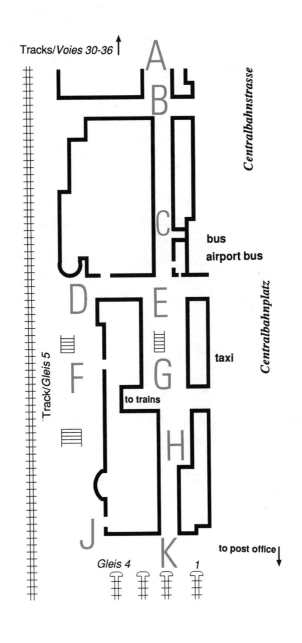

Bologna Stazione Centrale

About ten years ago a rightist group presented its argument here by killing a number of passengers with a bomb. Their 'cause' would be forgotten, but for the memorial to the victims. Bologna is a wise city and has gone on. Its railway station is simple, efficient, and now safe.

Train information	Daily 7:00–23:00. Tel. 24 64 90	E
Tickets, inland	All hours. Windows 1–9	E
Tickets, international	Daily 6:30–21:30. *Biglietteria sussidiaria* Other times see Tickets, inland	B,C
Reservations	Daily 7:00–22:00. Windows 11–15	E
Baggage send/pick-up	All hours	L
Baggage store	All hours	K
Lost & found	Daily 7:00–21:00	B
Emergencies	All hours. *Dirigenti movimento*	N
First aid	Daily 8:00–20:00	C
Police	All hours	B
Help for handicapped	All hours. *Dirigenti movimento*	N
Toilets	All hours	A,M
Bath, shower	Mon–Sat 7:00–21:00, Sun 7:00–20:00. *Albergo diurno*	J
Waiting room	All hours	F
Restaurant	Daily 11:30–22:00	G,J, upstairs
Bar, buffet	Daily 6:00–1:00	G,J
Provisions	See Bar, buffet	
Pharmacy	Mon–Sat 7:30–23:00, Sun 8:00–22:00	C
Tourist info, accommodation	Mon–Sat 9:00–19:00, Sun 9:00–13:00 (summer only)	H
City transit information	Daily 6:00–0:30	outside
Foreign exchange	Daily 7:00–13:00/14:45–20:00	E
Post, telegraph	Mon–Fri 8:15–13:20, Sat 8:15–12:20	D
To airport	City bus.	outside

The station is open at all hours.

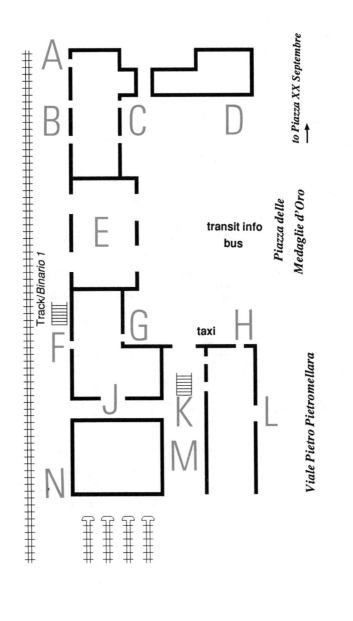

Brussel Centraalstation/Bruxelles Gare Centrale

Central only by location, the station serves mostly commuters. Not all long distance trains stop here. It is nearest to the tourist offices, about five minutes' walk toward Grand'Place. Direct trains connect to the airport, and the east–west metro stops here.

Train information	Daily 6:00–21:00. Tel. 219 28 80	F
Tickets, inland	All hours	C
Tickets, international	Daily 6:00–23:00. Windows 1–2	C
Reservations	Daily 4:00–23:00	C
Baggage	All hours	E
Lockers	Accessible daily 4:00–1:00	E
Lost & found	See Baggage	
Emergencies	All hours. *Sous-chef de gare*	A
First aid	See Emergencies	
Police	Mon–Fri 7:00–21:00 Other times see Emergencies	J
Help for handicapped	See Emergencies. Phone in advance 219 28 80	
Toilets	All hours	G
Waiting room	All hours	K
Restaurants	Mon–Fri 10:30–21:30, Sat 8:30–21:30, Sun 7:00–21:30 and Mon–Sat 7:00–18:30	B, upstairs concourse level, B
Bar, buffet	Daily 11:00–23:30	J
Pharmacy	Mon–Fri 7:00–18:30	H
Shopping	Outside, across Carrefour de l'Europe.	
Tourist info, accommodation	See city page.	outside
City transit info, maps	See Train information	
Foreign exchange	Daily 6:00–21:00	B
Post office	Mon–Fri 9:00–17:00	D
Telephone	Daily 8:00–22:00. 17 Kaiserinlaan	outside
To other stations	Regular trains every 15–20 minutes to Noord and Zuid/Midi stations; travel time 3 minutes	
To airport	Direct trains from Track *(Spoor)* 1a.	L

No services when the station is closed, 1:00–4:00

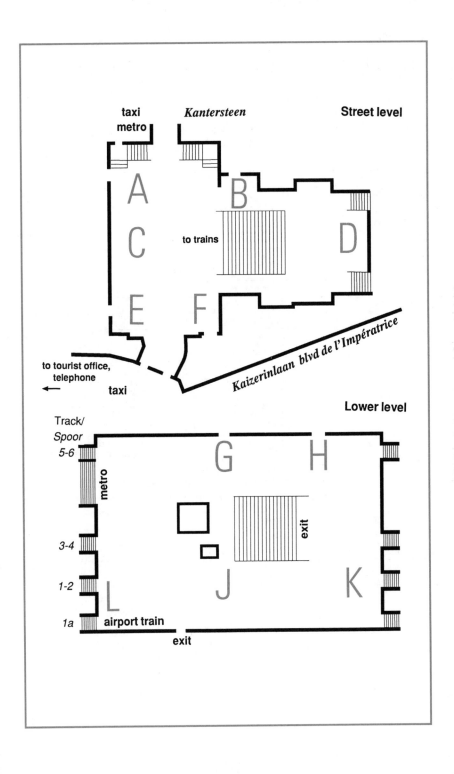

Brussel Noordstation / Bruxelles Gare du Nord

The north station is the first Brussels stop for trains arriving from the north. It's conveniently situated near to hotels and shopping streets. Trains go on to Centraalstation, nearer to the tourist office in the city center. The premetro (underground tram) stop is just below the station concourse.

Train information	Daily 6:30–21:00. Tel. 219 28 80	B
Tickets, inland	Daily 6:00–23:00. Windows 9–13	B
	Other times Windows 6–7	F
Tickets, international	All hours. Windows 6–7	F
Reservations	All hours. Windows 6–7	F
Baggage	All hours	F
Lockers	Accessible daily 4:00–2:00	F
Lost & found	See Baggage	
Emergencies	All hours. Police	B
First aid	See Emergencies	
Police	All hours	B
Help for handicapped	See Train information or Police	
	Phone in advance 219 28 80	
Toilets	All hours in tunnel, between Tracks (Spoor) 5–6	D
Waiting room	All hours in tunnel, between Tracks (Spoor) 9–10	D
Restaurants	Mon–Sat 7:30–22:00, Sun 9:00–23:00	C
	and Mon–Fri 6:30–22:00, Sat–Sun 10:00–22:00	G
Bar, buffet	Daily 7:00–23:00, in tunnel at Tracks 3–4 and 7–8	D
Provisions	Mon–Fri 7:00–18:00, Sat 7:00–20:00,	
	Sun 8:00–17:00	G
Shopping	Outside, in Place Rogier	A
Tourist information	See city page.	
City transit information	Premetro station	E
Foreign exchange	Daily 7:00–23:00	D
Post office	Mon–Fri 9:00–17:00	C
Telephone	Mon–Fri 9:00–17:15. 23a Brabantstraat	outside
To other stations	Regular trains every 15–20 minutes to Centraal and Zuid/Midi stations; travel times 3 and 6 minutes. Premetro to Zuid/Midi.	
To airport	Direct trains; check indicator board for track number.	

No services when the station is closed, 2:00–4:00.

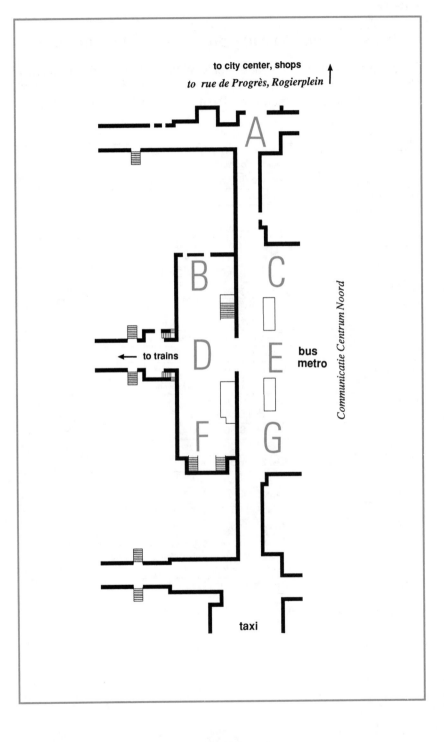

Brussel Zuidstation/Bruxelles Gare du Midi

The busiest of the three, the south station used to handle only trains to the south (that is, France or le Midi) but since tracks were laid to the north (via Centraal), most long distance trains stop here. There are connections to both metro and premetro lines.

Travel center, Eurail aid	Mon–Fri 8:00–20:00, Sat–Sun 9:00–19:00	
	Salon d'accueil	E
Train information	Daily 6:30–22:15. Tel. 219 28 80	D
Tickets, inland	All hours	C
Tickets, international	All hours	D
Reservations	In Travel center	E
Baggage	Mon–Sat 6:00–21:30, Sun 7:00–15:30	G
	Other times Window 9	
Lockers	Accessible daily 4:00–2:00	G
Lost & found	See Baggage	
Emergencies	All hours. Police	F
First aid	See Emergencies	
Help for handicapped	See Emergencies. Phone in advance 219 28 80	
Toilets	All hours	A
Waiting room	All hours on platforms	
Restaurant	Mon–Fri 11:30–15:00	B
Self-service	Daily 8:30–20:00	B
	and daily 6:45–22:00	F
Bar, buffet	Mon–Fri 8:30–19:00	in main concourse, A–H
Pharmacy	Mon–Fri 7:00–18:30	H
Tourist information	See city page.	
City transit information	Mon–Sat 8:30–12:00, 12:30–17:00	D
Foreign exchange	Daily 7:00–23:00	D
Post office	Mon–Sat 8:00–20:00; two offices alternate	outside
Telephone	Mon–Fri 9:00–17:00, Sat 8:00–16:00. In Post office	
To other stations	Regular trains every 15–20 minutes to Centraal and Noord stations; travel times 3 and 6 minutes. Premetro to Noord.	
To airport	See Centraal and Noord stations.	

No services when the station is closed, 2:00–4:00.

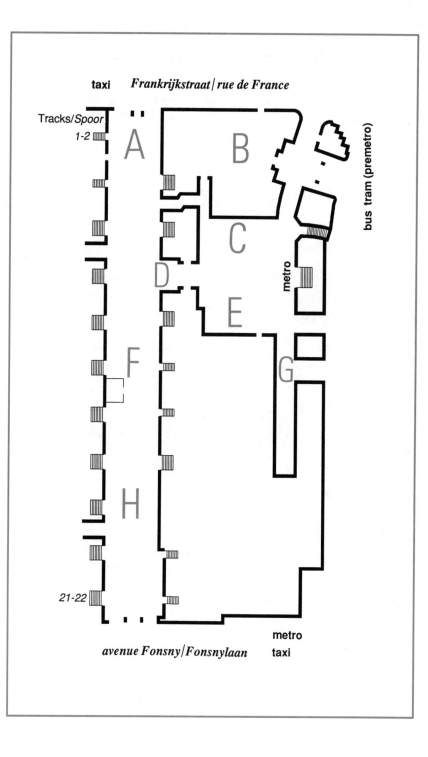

Budapest Déli pályaudvar

The south station is the terminal for trains to the resorts along Lake Balaton, and for the EuroCity Lehár to Vienna. On the lower level (not shown on the plan) find the international section, tourist office and post office. The metro station is another level down.

Train information	All hours. Tel. 1228–049	C
Tickets and reservations, inland	All hours	B
Tickets and reservations, int'l	Mon–Sat 7:15–18:45 (lower level)	
Eurail aid	MÁV Passenger Service. See page 132	
Baggage	All hours (Krisztina side, lower level)	
Lost & found	All hours. At Track (Vágány) 12	A
Emergencies	All hours. Ügyeletes tiszt at Track (Vágány) 1	E
First aid	See Emergencies	E
Police	See Emergencies	E
Help for handicapped	See Emergencies	E
Toilets	All hours	A
Waiting room	All hours	C
Restaurant, self-service	Daily 6:00–20:00	D
Provisions	Supermarkets Mon–Wed 7:00–17:00, Thu–Fri 7:00–19:00, Sat 7:00–14:00	outside
Pharmacy	All hours, ring bell if closed	outside
Tourist information	Mon–Fri 8:00–13:00/14:00–20:00, Sat till 18:00 (lower level).	
Accommodation	Mon–Fri 8:00–13:00/14:00–19:00, Sat till 17:00 (tourist office, lower level).	
City transit information	Daily 6:00–21:00. In metro station.	
Foreign exchange	Mon–Fri 8:00–13:00/14:00–18:00, Sat till 16:00 (tourist office, lower level).	
Post office, telephone	Mon–Fri 8:00–20:00, Sat 8:00–14:00 (lower level).	
To other stations	To Keleti: metro. To Nyugati: metro; change at Deák tér to No. 3	
To airport	Metro to Deák tér station, near Engels tér bus terminal and airport bus stop.	

The station is open at all hours.

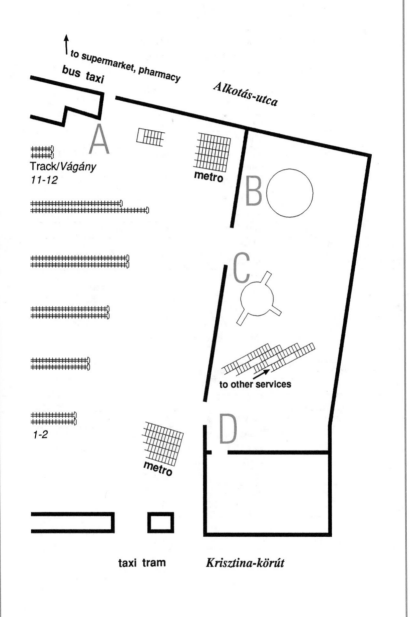

Budapest Keleti pályaudvar

Interestingly, the east station handles western connections, and all Vienna trains except one. This is the principal international terminal, housed in a historic and well-renovated building. Find inland information and tickets under the stairway to the metro, as well as shops on the lower level.

Train information, inland	All hours (below stairs to metro)	
Train information, international	Daily 6:00–20:00. Tel. 1228–049	
Tickets, inland	All hours (advance tickets daily 7:00–18:00) (below stairs to metro)	
Tickets, international	Daily 7:00–18:00	
	Other times for immediate departures only	B
Reservations	Daily 8:00–12:00/13:00–18:00	B
Eurail aid	MÁV Passenger Service. See page 132	
Baggage send/pick-up	All hours	F
Baggage store	All hours	A
Lockers	Accessible at all hours	A
Lost & found	See Baggage office	
Emergencies	All hours. *Ügyeletes tiszt*	C
First aid	Mon–Fri 6:00–18:00	H
	Other times see Emergencies	
Police	All hours	C
Help for handicapped	See Emergencies	
Toilets	All hours	A,G
Waiting room	All hours	A
Restaurant, self-service	Daily 6:00–23:00	G
Provisions	Kiosks on platforms, shops on lower level.	
	Supermarkets Mon–Fri 6:00–20:00 (Wed 7:00–18:30), Sat 6:00–17:00	outside
Tourist information	Daily 8:00–13:00/14:00–19:00 (Sat–Sun till 17:00)	E
Accommodation	Daily 8:00–21:00	E
City transit information	In metro station	
Foreign exchange	Daily 8:00–21:00	E
Post, telegraph, telephone	All hours	outside
To other stations	To Déli: metro.	
	To Nyugati: metro; change at Deák tér to No. 3.	
To airport	Metro to Deák tér station, near Engels tér bus terminal and airport bus stop.	

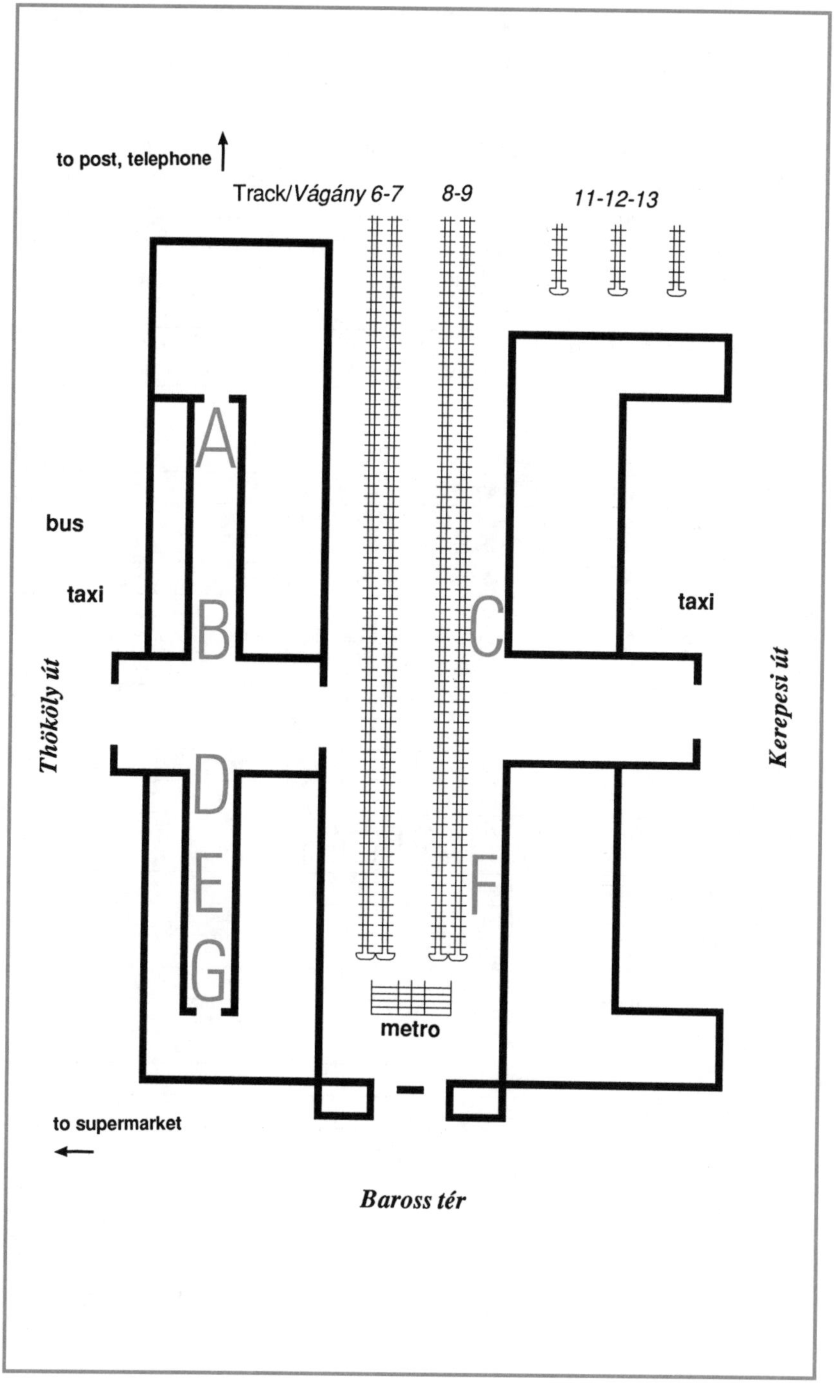

to post, telephone ↑

Track/*Vágány 6-7* *8-9* *11-12-13*

A

bus

taxi

B C taxi

Thököly út *Kerepesi út*

D

E

F

G

metro

to supermarket
←

Baross tér

Cologne - Köln Hauptbahnhof

In the Second World War several bombs, intended to disrupt rail traffic, landed on the cathedral, the legendary Dom, which was damaged but miraculously escaped destruction. The station next door didn't. From the rebuilt Hauptbahnhof it's a few minutes' walk to shopping streets, the old quarter, and the KD landings for ferry and cruise ships on the Rhine.

Travel center; Eurail aid	Daily 6:00–23:00	G
	Services are color coded; check directions outside.	
Train information	In Travel center. Tel. 19 419	G
	Also all hours	B
	and daily 6:00–22:00	F
Tickets, inland	All hours	G
Tickets, international	Mon–Fri 6:00–23:00, Sat–Sun till 22:30	
	In Travel center	G
Reservations	Daily 6:00–21:00. In Travel center	G
Baggage	All hours	H
	To send baggage directly to airplane, see page 111	
Lockers	Accessible 4:00–1:00	J
Lost & found	All hours. *Kundendienst.* Track *(Gleis)* 1	access at F
Emergencies	All hours. *Kundendienst.* Track *(Gleis)* 1	access at F
First aid	Daily 6:00–22:00. *Rotes Kreuz.* Track *(Gleis)* 1	access at F
Police	All hours	A
Help for handicapped, nursery	All hours. *Bahnhofsmission.*	
	Phone in advance 13 15 10. Track *(Gleis)* 1	access at F
Toilets	All hours	D,E
Waiting room	All hours	B–C
Restaurant	Daily 6:30–22:00	K, upstairs
Bar, buffet	Daily 6:00–21:00; all hours in *"Treffpunkt "*	C
Provisions, bakery	Daily 6:00–21:00	B
Pharmacy (cosmetics)	Daily 7:00–22:00	H
Shopping	Daily 7:00–21:00	C–E
Tourist info, accommodation	See city page.	outside
City transit information	In U–Bahn station	K
Foreign exchange	Daily 7:00–21:00	H
Post, telephone	Mon–Sat 7:00–22:00, Sun 10:00–22:00	H
To airport	Airport bus	outside

No services when the station is closed, 1:00–4:00.

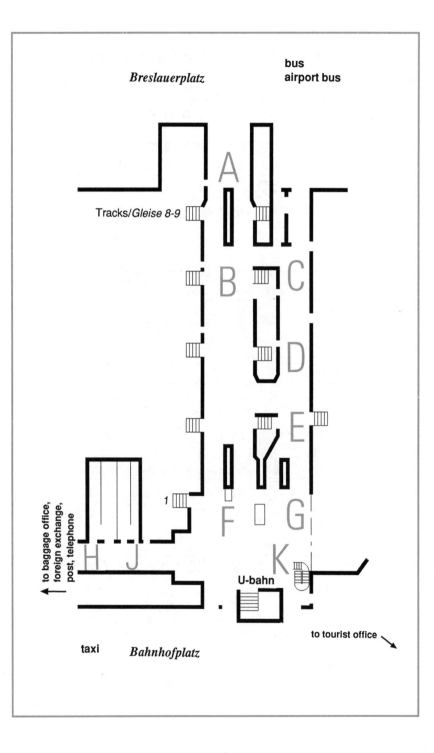

Copenhagen - København H

The hall, its wooden arches evoking the lines of an upside-down Viking ship, houses all services, including a supermarket, a communication center with telephone, telex, fax, and computers, the Inter-Rail Center and IC-Salon.

Travel center, Eurail aid	Daily 6:00–24:00. *DSB Rejsebüro*	H
Train information	Daily 7:00–23:00 (winter: 7:00 –22:00). Tel. 141 701	F
Tickets, inland	Daily 5:30–1:00	E
Tickets, int'l; reservations	In Travel center. Reservations: daily 8:00–21:00	H
Baggage send/pick-up	Daily 6:00–24:00	A
Baggage store	Daily 6:30–0:15	L
Lockers	Accessible daily 4:30–1:30	C–D
Lost & found	Daily 10:00–18:00	J
Emergencies	Mon–Fri 8:00–20:00, Sun 15:00–23:00. *Kundeservice*	J
	Other times *Stationskontor*	J
Police, first aid	All hours	A
Help for handicapped	See Baggage. Phone in advance 140 400 extension 12678	
Toilets, showers	All hours (Showers only in A)	A,D
Waiting room	All hours	L, upstairs
Special waiting rooms		
First-class passengers:	IC Salon with lounge, shower, lockers, phone.	F
	All hours. To enter ask DSB *Kundeservice*.	J
Eurail Youthpass, Inter-Rail:	Inter Rail Center. Daily 6:30–24:00	G
	Dining room, shower, laundry, buffet	
Restaurant, self-service	Daily 7:00–24:00	K
Cafeteria	Daily 6:30–23:45	K, upstairs
	Bar, buffet. Daily 6:30–23:30	C,D,G,K
Supermarket	Daily 8:00–24:00	B
Tourist information	See city page. outside, follow signs to Tivoli Gardens	
Accommodation	Daily 9:00–24:00	H
City transit information	Daily 7:00–21:00. *Kortsalg.*	F
	Other times Tickets, inland	
Foreign exchange	Daily 6:45–22:00 (November–April 7:00–21:00)	G
Banking	Mon–Fri 9:30–16:00 (Thu 18:00)	D
Post office, telephone	Mon–Fri 8:00–22:00, Sat 9:00–16:00,	
	Sun 10:00–17:00, telephone upstairs	B
To ferry	City bus No.28 or No.41 to Havnegade	outside
To airport	Airport bus.	outside

No services when the station is closed, 1:30–4:30.

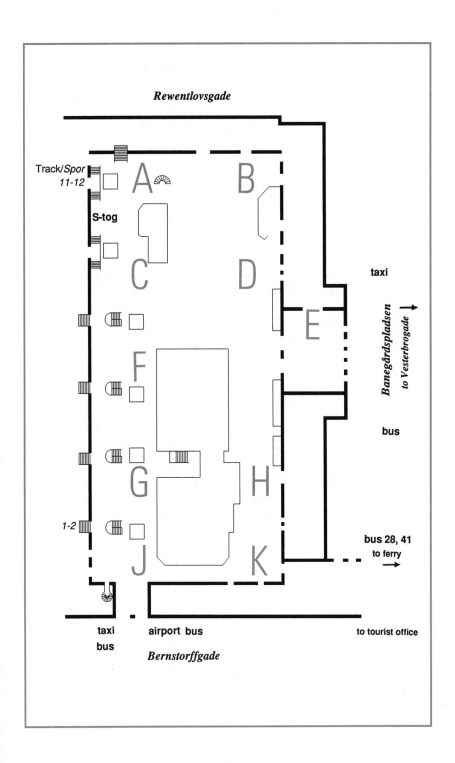

Dublin Connolly Station

In theory, Connolly is an international station, sending trains to Belfast and to Rosslare (ferry port for France). In fact, it's very small and has few services. But you can walk to the city center, or find good connections to the area by bus and rapid transport (DART).

Train information	Mon–Sat 7:30–15:00/16:30–21:30. Tel. 771–871 Other times see ticket windows.	D
Tickets, reservations, inland	Mon–Tue and Thu–Sat 7:30–15:00/16:30–20:15, Wed and Sun 7:30–14:15/20:00–23:30	E
Tickets, reservations, int'l	Iarnród Éireann office, 35 Lower Abbey Street	
Eurail aid	Iarnród Éireann office, 35 Lower Abbey Street	
Baggage	Mon–Sat 7:30–21:30, Sun 9:00–22:00	D
Lost & found	See Baggage office	
Emergencies	All hours. Station master	E
First aid	See Emergencies	
Police	See Emergencies	
Help for handicapped	All hours. Station master Phone 771–871 with advance request	E
Toilets	Mon–Sun 7:00–22:00 Till 23:30 in suburban station	B
Restaurant, bar	Mon–Sat 7:30–19:00	C
Provisions, shopping	Outside, in Talbot Street	
Tourist information	In city tourist office. See page 137	
City transit information	See Train information	
Foreign exchange	Outside, bank in Talbot Street	
To other station	Bus No.90 to Heuston Station	
To airport	Bus from Busaras bus terminal (200 yards from station).	
To ferry	Bus to Ferryport, DART train to Dun Laoghaire.	

No services when the station is closed, 23:00–7:00.

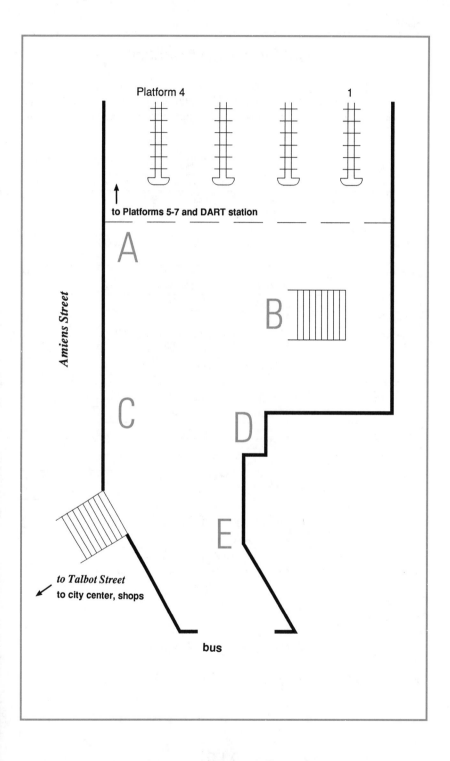

Frankfurt Hauptbahnhof

Europe's biggest and busiest station combines all modes of transport: main line trains inside, buses outside, U–Bahn and S–Bahn below. It also houses a large shopping complex one level below the main concourse. Yet it's surprisingly easy to get around, thanks to excellent signs.

Travel center	Daily 6:00–22:00. *DB-Reisezentrum*	F,H
Train information	See Travel center. Also booths. Tel. 19 419	E,H
Tickets, inland	Daily 6:00–22:30. Windows 1–16	G
	Also vending machines with English text	G
Tickets, int'l; reservations	See Travel center.	
Eurail aid	Mon–Fri 6:00–20:00, Sat–Sun 6:00–16:00	
	Aufsicht der Fahrkartenausgabe	G
Baggage	All hours	D
	To send baggage directly to airplane see page 111	
Lockers	Accessible daily 4:00–1:00	A,D,J,M
Lost & found	All hours. *Fundstelle*	A
Emergencies	All hours. *Kundendienst.* Tracks *(Gleise)* 9–10	E,H
First aid	All hours. *Rotes Kreuz.* Track *(Gleis)* 1	L
Police	All hours. *Bahnpolizei.* Track *(Gleis)* 1	L
Help for handicapped	See First aid, Nursery. Phone in advance 23 44 68	
Nursery, help	All hours. *Bahnhofsmission.* Track *(Gleis)* 1	L
Toilets, bath, shower	All hours (Bath, shower only A,M)	A,E,M
Waiting room	In Self-service with ticket	K
Restaurant	Daily 11:30—23:00	K, upstairs
Self-service	Daily 6:00–23:00	J,K
Bar, buffet	Daily 4:00–22:00	B
	6:00–23:00	K
Provisions	Daily 6:00–22:00. *Markt im Bahnhof*	H
Pharmacy	Mon–Fri 6:30–21:00, Sat–Sun 8:00–21:00	J
Shopping	In lower level passage	access at B,F
Tourist info, accommodation	Mon–Sat 8:00–21:00, Sun 9:30–20:00	A
City transit information	Mon–Fri 6:30–19:00, Sat 8:00–17:00. FVV	
	In lower level passage.	access at B,F
Foreign exchange	Daily 6:30–22:00	M
Post, telephone	All hours	C or E, upstairs
To airport	S-Bahn No.15 on Track *(Gleis)* 21	B
	or No.14 in lower level S-Bahn station.	

No services when the station is closed, 1:00–4:00.

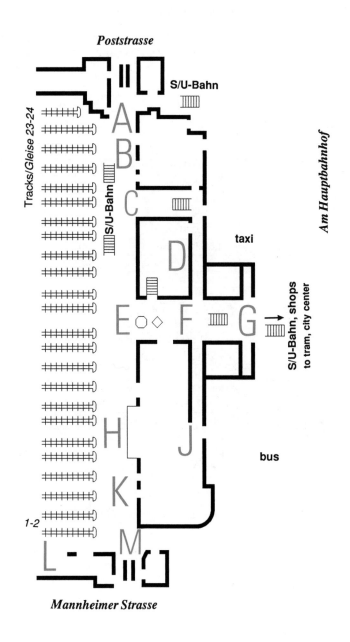

Göteborg Centralstation

What you can't find inside the station, you can reach in minutes: post office in the square (Drottningtorget), telephone, tourist information, shops in the adjacent Nordstan shopping center.

Travel center	Mon–Sat 5:40–22:00, Sun 6:30–23:30	D
Train information	All hours. Tel. 10 30 00	C
Tickets, reservations	In Travel center	D
Baggage	Mon–Fri 6:30–22:00, Sat–Sun 6:30–20:00	(at Track 12)
Lockers	Accessible when station is open (see below)	(at Track 11)
Lost & found	See Baggage office. Other times see Train information	
Emergencies	See Train information or security officer (Ordningsvakt)	
First aid	See Emergencies	
Police	All hours. In Nordstan.	
Help for handicapped	See Train information or phone 10 30 00	
Nursery	Mon–Sat 6:00–22:00, Sun 7:00–22:00	E
Toilets	All hours	E
Bath, shower	All hours	E
Waiting room	In Travel center. All hours	A
	For women and children see Nursery	
Restaurant	Tue–Sat 11:00–2:00, Sun–Mon 11:00–1:00	B
Bar, buffet	Daily 9:00/11:00–20:00/24:00	B,G
Provisions	Daily 7:00–22:00	F
Pharmacy	Permanent service. In Nordstan.	
Shopping	Mon–Fri 9:30–18:00, Sat 9:30–14:00. In Nordstan.	
Tourist information	Mon–Fri 9:30–18:00, Sat 9:30–15:00. In Nordstan.	
City transit information	Daily 7:00–22:00. Pressbyrån kiosk	C
Foreign exchange	Daily 8:00–21:00	D
Post, telephone	Daily 8:00–19:00, Sat 9:00–15:00. In Nordstan.	
To airport	Airport bus.	outside

No services when the station is closed, Mon–Fri 00:00–4:30, Sat 00:00–5:30, Sun 00:00–6:00.

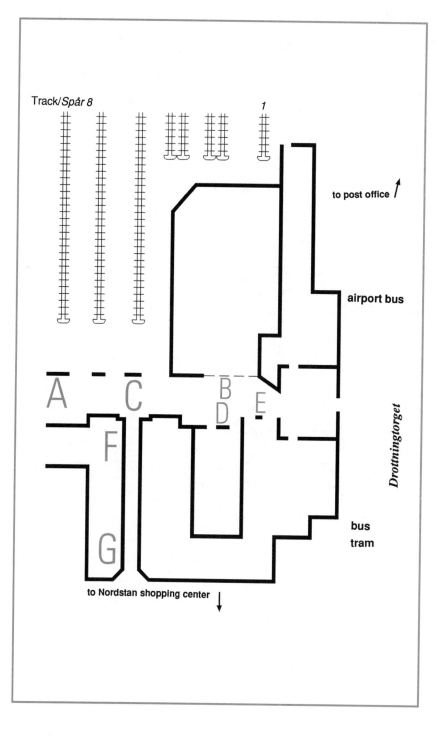

Hamburg Hauptbahnhof

The station has been undergoing renovation and several services are in temporary quarters at the time of writing. A new shopping area is planned for the new bridge over the tracks (shaded area on the plan). When this is completed some of the concessions from the *Südsteg* (H–J–K) may be moved there; some railway services will also be relocated.

Travel center, Eurail aid	Daily 5:30–23:00. *DB–Reisezentrum*	B
Train information	In Travel center. Windows 21–24	
	Also daily 10:00–19:00. Tel. 19 419	H
Tickets, inland	In Travel center. Windows 1–4	
	With reservation Windows 5–6	
Tickets, reservations, int'l	In Travel center. Windows 8–11	
Baggage	Daily 6:00–23:00	B
Lockers	Accessible all hours	B,K
Lost & found	Mon–Fri 8:00–20:00, Sat–Sun 9:00–19:00	B
Emergencies	See Travel center	
First aid	Daily 6:00–22:00	G
Police	All hours	A
Help for handicapped, nursery	Daily 6:00–22:00. *Bahnhofsmission*. Phone 39 79 29	G
Toilets	All hours	C,D,K
Restaurant	Daily 6:30–23:00	D, upstairs
Bar, buffet	Daily 6:30–23:00	D
	Daily 6:00–22:00	J
Provisions	Daily 6:30–23:00	D
Pharmacy	Mon–Fri 8:00–18:00, Sat 9:00–14:00	F
Shopping	Department stores. in Mönckebergstrasse	outside
Tourist info, accommodation	Daily 7:00–21:00	outside, A
City transit information	Daily 7:00–23:00	E
Foreign exchange	Daily 7:30–22:00	D, upstairs
	Also Mon–Sat 7:30–15:00/15:45–20:00,	
	Sun 10:00–13:00/13:45–18:00	H
Post office	Mon–Fri 8:00–18:00, Sat 8:00–13:00, Sun 11:00–12:00	
	Other times ring bell for service at 2.80 DM extra fee	E
Telephone	Daily 7:00–21:45	E
To other stations	Regular trains every 15–20 minutes to Dammtor and Altona; travel times 2 and 10 minutes.	
To airport	Airport bus .	outside

The station is open at all hours.

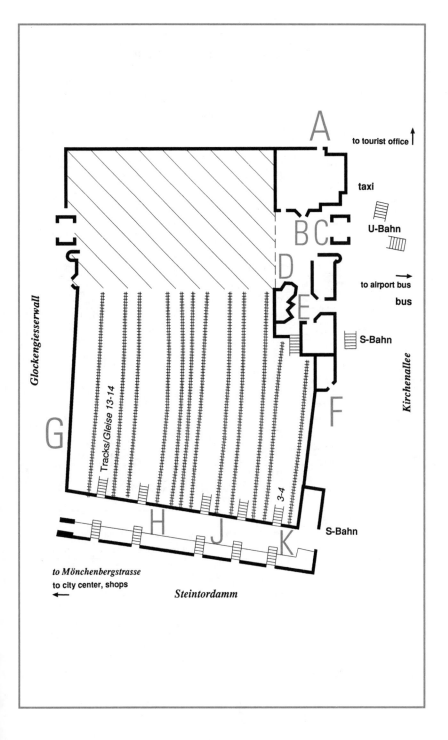

Helsinki Rautatieasema

Eliel Saarinen's elegant building has earned a place in architectural history and the Finnish railways keep it looking as good today as at the 1919 opening. The granite walls are unscarred; interior renovations follow the original design, down to the upholstery of the chairs in the restaurants.

Travel center, Eurail aid	Daily 7:00–21:00	E
Train information, inland	Mon–Fri 7:00–20:00, Sat 7:00–18:00, Sun 9:00–18:00. Tel. 659 244	D
Train information, int'l	Mon–Fri 8:30–16:30 in Travel center. Tel. 659 411	D
Tickets and reservations, inland	Daily 7:00–21:00 in Travel center	E
Tickets and reservations, int'l	Daily 8:30–16:30 in Travel center Note that international reservations may take up to two days and the cost of telex is added to the supplement.	E
Baggage send, pick-up	Daily 6:30–00:15 (Sat till 24:00)	J
Baggage store	Daily 6:15–23:25	H
Lockers	Accessible Mon–Sat 4:40–1:30, Sun 5:20–1:30	H
Lockers in basement (large)	Accessible Mon–Fri 7:00–22:00	H
Lost & found	Mon–Fri 9:20–17:00	H
Emergencies, First aid	See Train information. Other times *Vahtimestari*	A
Police	All hours	F
Help for handicapped	See Emergencies. Phone in advance 707 3422	
Toilets	All hours	B
Restaurants	Daily 9:00–1:00 Mon–Sat 6:30–24:00, Sun 8:00–24:00	A, upstairs C
Self-service	Mon–Sat 6:30–22:00, Sun 8:00–22:00	C
Snackbars	Daily 6:30–23:45	B,G
Supermarket, shopping	Mon–Sat 10:00–22:00, Sun 12:00–22:00 in passage to metro	access at D
Tourist info, accommodation	See city page.	outside
City transit information	Mon 9:00–18:00, Tue–Fri 9:00–16:00 in metro station	D
Foreign exchange	Mon–Fri 9:15–16:15. Banks in metro station	access at D
Post office	Mon–Fri 9:00–17:00. Mannerheimintie 11	outside
Telephone, telegraph	Mon–Fri 7:00–23:00, Sat–Sun 8:00–23:00. Mannerheimintie 11B	outside
To ferries	Bus No. 3B to Olympiaterminalii (Silja). Trams Nos. 4,13 to Katanajokkanterminalii (Viking).	
To airport	Finnair airport bus or bus No.615.	outside

No services when the station is closed, 1:40–4:40. No access to lockers in metro tunnel 23:00–5:15.

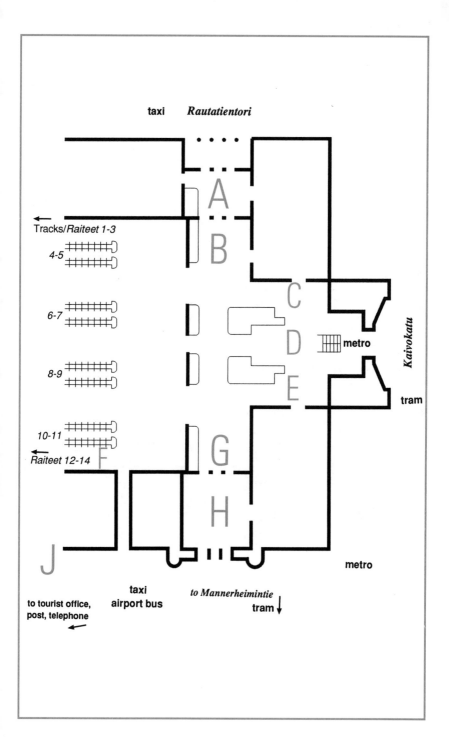

Lausanne Gare CFF

Train information	Daily 7:20–20:30. Tel. 20 80 71	B–C
	Other times see the *sous-chef* (red cap) on platforms.	
Tickets	Daily 5:00–00:15	E
Reservations	Daily 7:20–20:30	B–C
Baggage send	Mon–Fri 6:40–20:50, Sat–Sun 6:40–19:50	G
Baggage pick-up, store	Daily 6:30–23:00	H
	To transfer baggage directly to or from airplane, see pages 185 and 186	
Lockers	Accessible all hours. In tunnels to platforms	
Lost & found	Mon–Fri 8:00–12:00/14:00–19:00, Sat 8:00–13:00	G
	Other times ask at ticket windows	E
Emergencies	*Sous-chef* (red cap) on platform or *Secrétariat*	F
First aid	See Emergencies	
Police	All hours. *Gendarmerie.* Phone 117	D, upstairs
Help for handicapped	See Emergencies. Phone in advance 42 21 41	
Toilets	All hours in tunnel to platform	access at B
Waiting room	All hours. Also on platforms	B
Restaurant	Daily 5:00–24:00	A
Snack bars, kiosks, provisions	Daily 6:30–22:00	A,J
Pharmacy	Mon–Fri 7:45–12:15/13:45–18:30,	
	Sat 9:00–12:30	outside
Shopping	Outside, two blocks from back of station, till 18:45.	
Tourist info, accommodation	May 1–June 30: daily 14:00–20:00; July 1–October 15:	
	10:00–21:00; October 16–April 30: 15:00–19:00	E
City transit information	See Tourist info	
Foreign exchange	Mon–Fri 6:10–20:50, Sat–Sun 6:10–19:50	E
Post office	Mon–Fri 6:30–22:00, Sat 6:30–20:00,	
	Sun 9:00–12:00/18:00–22:00	outside
Telephone, telegraph	Daily 7:00–21:45	C
To airport	Regular trains to Geneva–Cointrin Airport.	

The station is open at all hours.

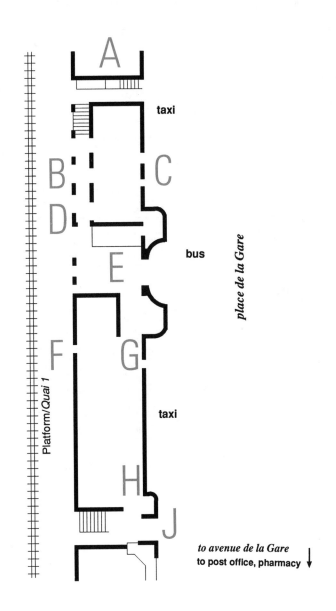

Lisbon - Lisboa Estação de Santa Apolónia

Some long-distance trains stop on tracks outside the station building: *rápidos* to Porto use Tracks *(Linhas)* 1–2, Madrid trains Track 6.

Train information, Eurail aid	Daily 8:00–23:00. Phone 87 60 25	F
Tickets, inland	Daily 6:00–1:00. Windows 1–7	F
Tickets, *Rápido*	Daily 6:00–1:00. Windows 8–10	G
Tickets, International	Daily 6:00–1:00. Window 11	G
Reservations	Daily 8:00–21:00. Window 11	G
Baggage	Daily 7:00–1:00	B
Lockers	Accessible daily 6:00–2:00	E
Lost & found	All hours. *Chefe de estação*	A
Emergencies	All hours. *Chefe de estação*	A
First aid	Daily 7:00–19:00	A
Police	See Emergencies	
Help for handicapped	See Train information or *Chefe de estação*	
Toilets	Men. All hours.	C
	Women. All hours	D
Waiting room	All hours	C
Bar, buffet	Daily 7:00–24:00	D
Provisions	Mon–Sat 7:00–24:00	Direction H
Tourist information	Daily 9:00–14:00/16:00 till last international arrival	F
City transit information	See Train information or kiosk at bus stop in front	
Foreign exchange	Daily 8:30–20:00	G
Post, telephone	Mon–Fri 9:00–19:00	E
To other stations	Buses 9, 39, 46, and 59 to Baixa de Lisboa and Rossio.	
To airport	Bus *(Linha Verde)* in Avda. Infante d'Henrique.	

No services when the station is closed, 2:00–6:00.

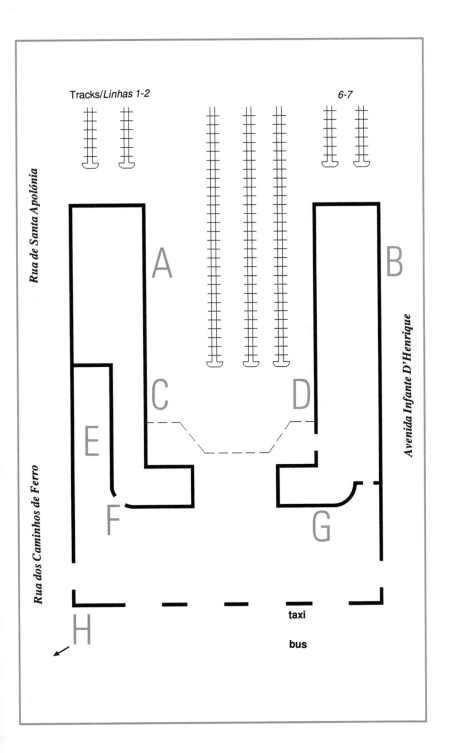

London Euston Station

In our listing, Euston qualifies as an international station with trains to Liverpool and Holyhead, bridgeheads to Ireland, and to Scotland. Through passengers have convenient Tube connections to European trains from Victoria and Liverpool Street stations.

Travel center	All hours. Tel. 387 8541	F
Train information	All hours in Travel center	F
Tickets, inland	All hours in Travel center	F
Tickets, international	Mon–Fri 9:00–18:00, Sat 9:00–16:00 in Travel center	F
Reservations, inland	Daily 8:00–22:00 in Travel center	F
Reservations, international	Mon–Fri 9:00–18:00, Sat 9:00–16:00 in Travel center	F
Eurail aid	At French National Railways, 179 Piccadilly	
Baggage send	No service	
Baggage store	All hours	H
Lost & found	Daily 8:00–20:00	H
Emergencies	Daily 7:00–24:00. Area Manager	G
First aid	Mon–Fri 8:00–16:00 Other times see Emergencies	H
Police	All hours	H
Help for handicapped	See Emergencies. Phone in advance 922 6476	
Toilets	All hours	A,B
Bath, shower	Mon–Fri 7:00–22:00, Sat 11:00–18:00	B, upstairs
Waiting room	All hours. Foodcourt First class	B B, upstairs
Restaurant	Mon–Fri 7:00–22:00, Sat 12:00–19:00	B, upstairs
Self-service, buffet, bar	All hours	B,C
Shopping	Outside concourse	
Tourist information	Mon–Sat 7:15–18:00, Sun 8:15–18:00	D
City transit information	Tube station	access from F
Foreign exchange	Daily 6:30–20:30	B
To other stations	Tube to Charing Cross (Northern Line), King's Cross/St. Pancras (Victoria Line), Liverpool Street (Northern and Central Lines), Paddington (Victoria and Bakerloo Lines) Victoria (Victoria Line), Waterloo (Northern Line).	
To airports	Gatwick Airport: Trains from Victoria Station Heathrow Airport: Tube or Airbus	outside

The station is open at all hours.

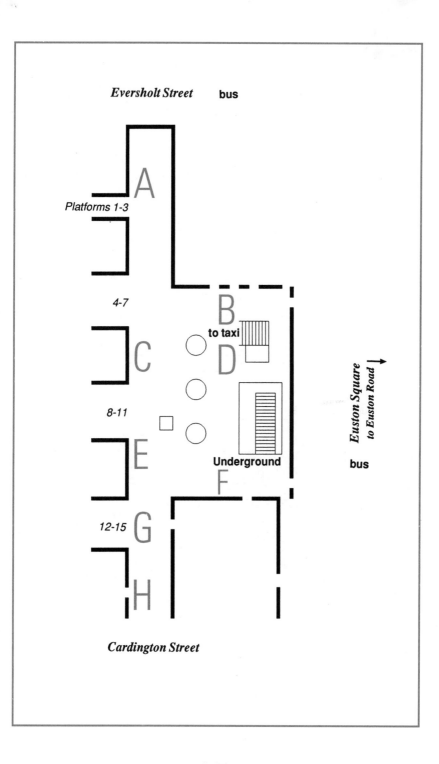

London Liverpool Street Station

This station is the terminal of boat trains to Harwich, connecting with ferries to Hook of Holland, the European bridgehead for the Netherlands, northern Germany, and Scandinavia.

At the time of writing Liverpool Street is being rebuilt as "the station for the 21st century". It'll be a joy to arrive here in 1991. Until then you'll find the din and dust of construction. The listed locations and hours of services may change.

Travel center	Mon–Fri 7:15–22:45, Sat–Sun 7:15–22:30	B
Train information	In Travel center. Tel. 928 5100	
Tickets, inland	All hours	B
Tickets, international	Mon–Sat 8:00–20:00, Sun 8:30–20:00 in Travel center	B
Reservations	Daily 8:00–20:00 in Travel centre	B
Eurail aid	At French National Railways, 179 Piccadilly	
Baggage	All hours except Sat 22:45–Sun 7:00, Sun 22:55–Mon 6:30	E
Lost & found	See Baggage	
Emergencies	All hours. Station Manager	B
First aid	See Police	
Police	All hours	E
Help for handicapped	See Emergencies. Phone in advance 247 7600	
Toilets	All hours	B, downstairs
Self-service, buffet, bar	Mon–Sat 7:00–23:00, Sun 8:00–23:00	F
Tourist information	No service	
Accommodation	Daily 8:00–21:00	D
City transit information	See Tickets, inland	
Foreign exchange	Daily 8:00–21:00	D
To other stations	Tube to Charing Cross, Euston (Central and Northern Lines), King's Cross/St. Pancras, Paddington (Circle or Metropolitan Lines), Victoria (Circle or District Lines), Waterloo (Central and Northern Lines).	
To airports	Gatwick Airport: Trains from Victoria Station. Heathrow Airport: Tube.	

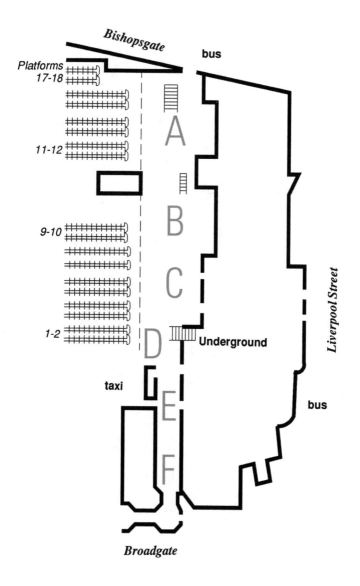

London Victoria Station

Services to the Continent

Travel center, train information	Mon–Sat 8:00–18:00. European Travel Centre	K
Ferry information, tickets	Sealink: Mon–Fri 8:00–18:00, Sat 8:30–14:30	K
	P & O Ferries. Daily 7:10–16:15 Platform 7–8,	H
	Hoverspeed: daily 7:00–16:30 (tickets till 14:30)	H
Tickets, reservations	Daily 7:15–20:55. Travel Today	K
Tickets, reservations, advance	In Travel center	
Eurail aid	At French National Railways, 179 Piccadilly	
Baggage send	Daily 7:00–20:00	K
Baggage pick-up	Mon–Fri 8:15–21:00, Sat–Sun 8:15–20:30. Customs	A

Gatwick Express to airport, Victoria Place

Train information	Daily 9:00–17:00	B, upstairs
Tickets, reservations	Daily 7:00–22:00	B, upstairs
Tickets to airport	Daily 6:00–22:00	D
Foreign exchange	Mon–Sat 7:00–21:30, Sun 7:45–20:30	B, upstairs

Inland services

Train information	All hours. Windows 13–14. Tel. 928 5700	E
Tickets, reservations	All hours. (Reservations, windows 14–15)	E
Baggage send/pick-up	Mon–Fri 7:30–21:45, Sat 8:00–14:00,	
	Sun 8:15–12:45/13:15–15:45. Parcels Point	A
Baggage store	7:45–22:30	Platform 8, G
Lockers	Always accessible	G, upstairs
Lost & found	Mon–Sat 9:00–17:00, Sun 8:00–16:00	G, upstairs
Emergencies	All hours. Area Manager's office	C
Police, First aid	All hours	H
Help for handicapped	Area Manager or Police. Phone in advance 928 5151	C
Toilets	All hours	E
Bath, shower	For women only, daily 7:00–22:00	E
Restaurant, buffets, bars	Daily 5:00–24:00, alternating	B,G,J
Pharmacy	Mon–Fri 8:00–19:00, Sat 9:00–19:00	C
Shopping	Victoria Place	access at B
Tourist info, accommodation	Daily 9:00–20:30	F
City transit information	Daily 8:15–21:30. London Transport	F
Foreign exchange	All hours (Exchange International)	H
	Daily 8:30–24:00 (Berkeley)	F
	Mon–Fri 9:00–17:30, Sat 9:00–12:00 (Thomas Cook)	C
To airports	Gatwick Airport: Direct trains.	D
	Heathrow Airport: Tube or Airbus.	outside

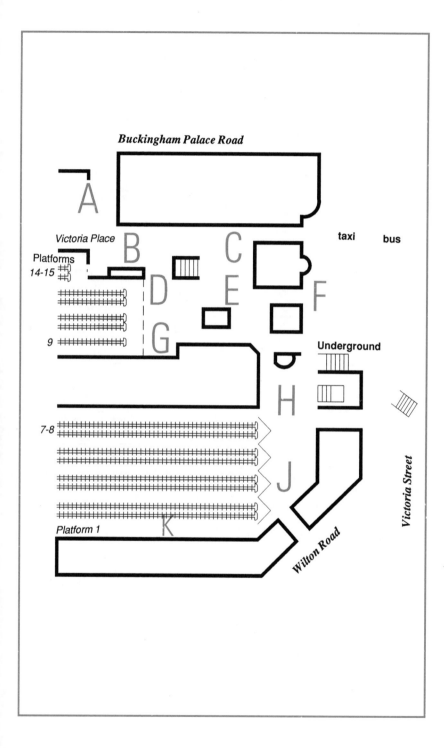

Luxembourg Gare Centrale

Small is not only beautiful, it can also be practical, as in this compact railway station that has most of what you need. Basic necessities are there (shower, money, food and drink) and you have to walk only a corner or two to shop, phone, plan your stay or take a plane. But don't forget to look back and admire the shape of the building.

Travel center	Daily 7:00–20:00. *Railtour Lux*	D
Train information	See Travel center. Other times see Tickets. Phone 49 24 24	
Tickets	All hours	C
Reservations	In Travel center	D
Eurail aid	In Travel center	D
Baggage	All hours	A
Lockers	Accessible daily 4:00–1:30. Other times enter the station with international ticket or pass.	
Lost & found	See Baggage office	
Emergencies	All hours. *Chef de surveillance* on Track *(Voie)* 3	H
First aid	See Emergencies	
Police	All hours	B, outside
Help for handicapped	See Emergencies or information officer	
Nursery	All hours	in tunnel to trains, access at F
Toilets	All hours	in tunnel to trains, access at F
Bath, shower	Daily 7:00–18:30	in tunnel to trains, access at F
Waiting room	All hours	G
Restaurant	Daily 11:00–24:00	G
	Mon–Fri 12:00–14:00	G, upstairs
Self-service	Daily 11:00–22:00	G
Bar, buffet	Daily 5:00–24:00	G
Provisions, shopping	In avenue de la Gare, rue J. Junck, rue de Strasbourg	outside
Tourist information	Daily 9:00–19:30, In winter, daily 9:00–12:00/14:00–18:00, December through March closed Sundays	outside
City transit information	See Tourist information (bus tickets in Baggage office)	
Foreign exchange	Mon–Sat 8:30–21:00, Sun 9:00–21:00 (Train fares may be paid in foreign currency.)	G
Post, telephone	Daily 6:30–22:00	outside
To airport	City bus No.9 or airport bus	outside

No services when the station is closed, 1:30–4:00.

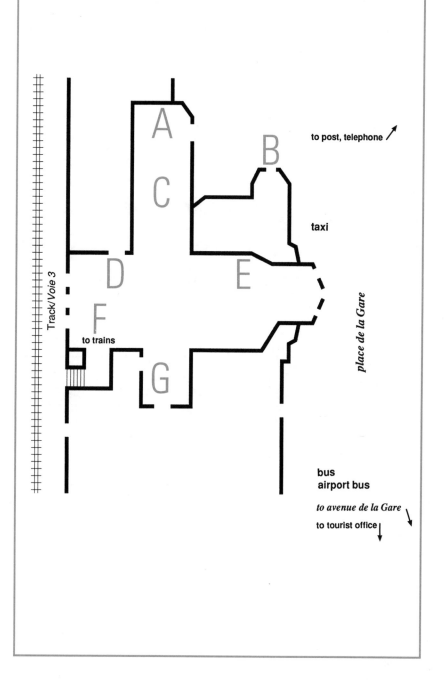

Lyon Gare de Part-Dieu

This new station lies outside the central area but has good access by train, metro, and bus. The *Centre Commercial* across the square offers convenient one-stop shopping.

Travel center	Mon–Sat 8:00–18:30, Sun 9:00–12:00/14:00–18:30	L
Train information	In Travel center. Other times *Accueil*. Tel. 78 92 50 50	F
Tickets, inland	All hours. Windows 6–21	C,E
Tickets, international	All hours. Windows 1–5	G
Reservations	In Travel center. Other times Windows 1–5	G
Baggage	All hours	L
Lockers	Accessible daily 4:45–0:45	B,D
Lost & found	At Perrache station. Inquire at Baggage office	
Emergencies	All hours. *Accueil*	F
First aid	See Emergencies	
Police	All hours	H
Help for handicapped	See Emergencies. Phone in advance 78 37 03 31	
Nursery, help	Mon–Sat 8:00–22:00, Sun 9:00–22:00. *SOS voyageurs*	D
Toilets	All hours	K
Bath, shower	Daily 5:00–1:00	K
Waiting area	All hours	E,J
Restaurant	Daily 6:00–24:00	K
Bar, buffet, provisions	Daily 6:00–20:00 (Fri from 9:30)	A
Supermarket, shopping	Outside, across Porte Vivier-Merle	
Pharmacy	Mon–Fri 10:00–19:00, Sat 11:00–19:00	outside
Tourist information	At Perrache station	
City transit information	Daily 6:30–19:30. Bus terminal	outside
Foreign exchange	Daily 9:30–18:30	D
To other station	Trains to Perrache; travel time is 8–12 minutes.	
To airport	Airport bus.	outside

No services when the station is closed, 00:45–4:45.

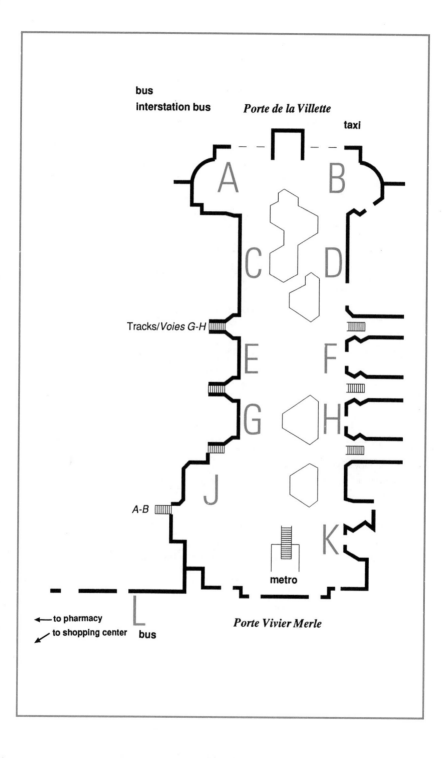

Lyon Gare de Perrache

The 'central station' of Lyon has expanded into a multi-modal terminal. The adjacent *Centre d'Echanges* combines metro station, bus terminal, truck stop, parking, shopping, bank, restaurant, and tourist office. There is also medical/social help at all hours.

Travel center	Mon–Sat 8:00–19:30, Sun 9:00–12:00/14:00–18:30	G
Train information	In Travel center. Other times *Accueil*	C
Tickets	All hours	A
Reservations	In Travel center	
Baggage	Daily 5:00–21:00	F
Lockers	Accessible 5:00–24:00	J
Lost & found	In Travel center	
Emergencies	All hours. *Accueil*	C
First aid	All hours. *Antenne Médicale* in passage to *Centre d'Echanges*	
Police	All hours	F
Help for handicapped	See Emergencies	
Nursery, help	Mon–Fri 8:00–22:00, Sat 8:00–21:00, Sun 16:00–22:00. *SOS voyageurs* Other times see First aid	K
Toilets	All hours	D
Shower	All hours	D
Waiting room	All hours	E,H
Restaurant	Daily 6:00–23:30	L
Bar, buffet, provisions	Daily 6:00–23:00, later take-out only	D
Supermarket, shopping	In *Centre d'Echanges*	
Tourist information	Mon–Sat 9:00–12:30/14:00–18:00 In *Centre d'Echanges*	
City transit information	Metro station in *Centre d'Echanges*	
Foreign exchange	Daily 5:30–21:00	B
To other station	Trains to Part-Dieu; travel time is 8–12 minutes.	
To airport	Airport bus in *Centre d'Echanges*.	

The upper level is always open.
No services on the lower level 00:00–5:00.

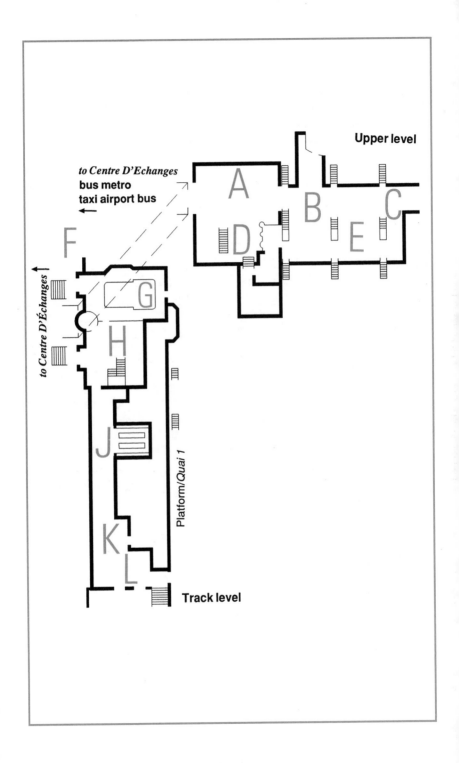

Upper level

to Centre D'Echanges
**bus metro
taxi airport bus**
←

A

B C

D E

F

to Centre D'Échanges ↑

G

H

J

Platform/*Quai 1*

K

L

Track level

Madrid Estación de Chamartín

The station is inconveniently far from the center (access by metro) but it has a shopping center, open daily 7:30–23:30 (F, upper level). Railway services—tickets, reservations with computer link to France, Eurail aid—are available downtown at the RENFE office, Alcalá 44 (near metro).

Train information	Daily 7:00–23:45. Tel. 429 05 18	C
Tickets, reservations	Daily 7:00–23:40	C
	Take number under sign *su turno* (national or international); the overhead display will flash your number and window.	
Eurail aid	RENFE ticket office, Alcalá 44	
Baggage, inland	From first till last train.	F
Baggage, international pick-up	From first till last train. Customs office	outside
Baggage store, lockers	Daily 7:40–23:30. Manned storage area; baggage is X–rayed before deposit	F
Lost & found	All hours. *Jefe de estación viajeros*	C
Emergencies	All hours. *Jefe de estación viajeros*	C
First aid	Daily 7:45–23:45. Medical center at Track (*Via*)1	E
Police, help for handicapped	See Train information or uniformed security officers	
Toilets	All hours	B,C,D, behind stairs
Waiting room	All hours along the concourse	
Special waiting room	Sala Rail Club	E, will move to C
	Daily 8:00–23:00. Attendants let you in with Eurailpass or first-class tickets for EuroCity, Talgo, Intercity, Electrotrén and sleeping cars. Complimentary coffee, soft drinks, magazines; pay phone. Comfortable and quiet.	
Restaurants	Daily 12:30–23:30	D
Restaurants, self-service	Daily 13:00–16:00 and 8:00–22:00	F, upper level
Bar, buffet	Daily 6:30–22:30	A,D
Provisions, shopping	Daily 7:30–23:30	F, upper level
Tourist info, accommodation	Mon–Fri 8:00–20:00, Sat 9:00–13:00	A
City transit information	See Tourist info	
Foreign exchange	Daily 8:00–23:00 (winter till 22:00)	opposite C
Post office	Mon–Fri 9:00–14:00/17:00–21:00	
	(telegraph Sat 9:00–13:00)	C
Telephone	Daily 6:30–23:30	D
To other station	Metro to Norte and Atocha suburban station.	
To airport	Metro to Air Terminal in Plaza de Colón, then bus.	

No services when the station is closed, 0:00–5:00.

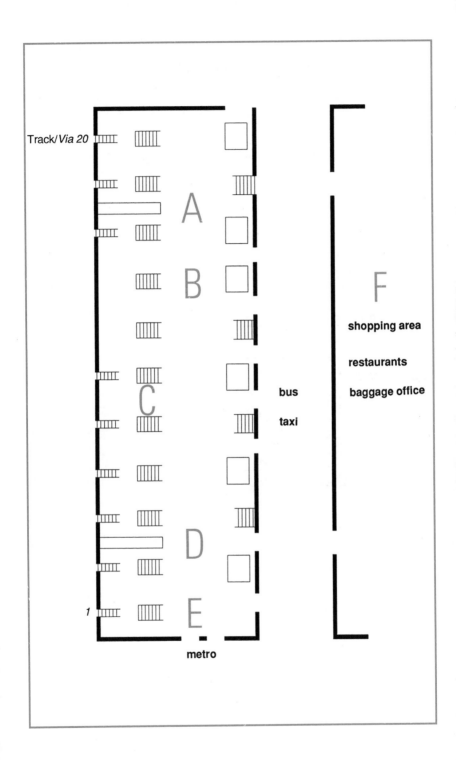

Marseille Gare St-Charles

The second most exciting view on arrival (after Venice) greets you from the top of the 'monumental stairway' as you leave the station. You can walk to shopping areas; reach the Old Port and tourist office by metro.

The plan shows only the track level of the station. In the lower concourse you find ticket windows, the travel center (information, reservations), reservation automats for TGV, and a pub.

Travel center, reservations	Daily 8:00–20:00	lower level
Train information	In Travel center. Also daily 5:00–1:00. *Accueil* Tel. 91 08 50 50	D
Tickets, inland	All hours. Windows 4–14	lower level
Tickets, reservations, int'l	All hours. Windows 15–17	lower level
Tickets, TGV, immed. departure	All hours. Window 7	lower level
Eurail aid	All hours. Windows 15–17	lower level
Baggage send, pick-up	Daily 5:00–0:30	C
Baggage store	All hours	C
Lockers	Accessible daily 5:00–1:00	J
Lost & found	Mon–Fri 8:00–12:00/14:00–17:30	G
Emergencies, first aid	All hours. *Accueil*	D
Police	All hours	H
Help for handicapped	See Emergencies. Phone in advance 91 95 14 94	
Nursery, help	Daily 9:00–12:00/13:00–19:00. *SOS voyageurs*	H
Toilets	All hours	J
Shower	Daily 6:00–20:00	J
Waiting room	All hours	E
Restaurant	Daily 8:00–22:00	lower level
Self-service	Daily 6:00–22:00	C
Provisions	Daily 6:00–22:00	A
Pharmacy	Mon–Sat 7:00–20:00	B
Tourist information	Daily 8:00–20:00 (winter: Mon–Fri 9:00–12:30/14:00–18:30)	F
City transit information	Metro station	two levels down
Foreign exchange	Daily 8:00–18:00	G
Post, telephone	Mon–Fri 8:00–19:00, Sat 8:00–12:00. Rue Honnorat	outside
To airport	Airport bus.	outside

No services when the station is closed, 1:00–5:00.

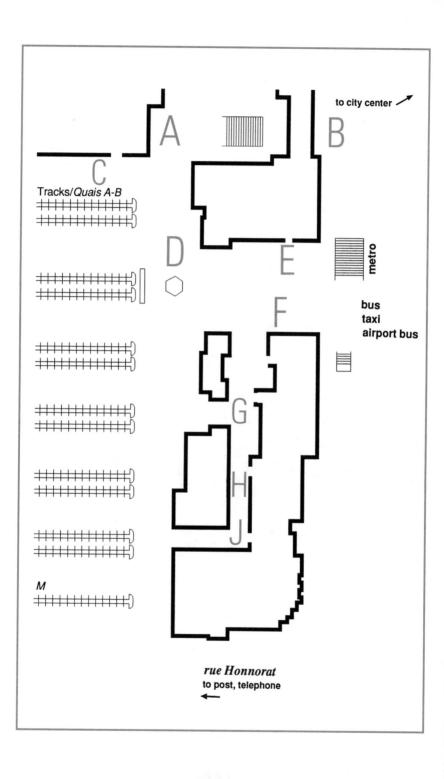

to city center ↗

A

B

C

Tracks/*Quais A-B*

D

E

metro

bus
taxi
airport bus

F

G

H

J

M

rue Honnorat
to post, telephone
←

Milan - Milano Stazione Centrale

The architecture was called Babylonian and other things. The madly anachronistic extravagance of this cathedral of technology embarrasses the railway officials in charge of it. But its countless sculptures, friezes, reliefs, murals, and mosaics offer a whimsical contrast to the sleek high-speed trains. A three-star station, worth a journey.

Travel center (private)	Daily 6:00–20:00. *Italturismo*	O
Train information, Eurail aid	Daily 7:00–23:00	N
Tickets, inland	All hours	H
Tickets, international	All hours. Windows 20–22	L
Reservations	Daily 7:00–20:45	D
Baggage send/pick-up	All hours	P
Baggage store	Daily 4:00–2:00	K
	Also daily 7:00–20:30. *Albergo diurno*	J
Lost & found	Daily 7:00–21:00	B
Emergencies	See Train information. Other times *Polizia Ferroviaria*	B
First aid	All hours. *Ambulatorio*	B
Police	All hours	B
Help for handicapped	See Train information	
Toilets	All hours	B,C,M
Bath, shower, rest rooms	Daily 6:50–20:10. *Albergo diurno*	J
Waiting room	All hours	G
Restaurant	Daily 11:30–15:30/18:30–22:30	C
Bar, buffet, self–service	Daily 7:00–24:00 and 11:30–23:00	C
Provisions	See Bar, buffet. Also outside, across Piazza IV Novembre in Via Fabrio Filzi	
Pharmacy	All hours	K
Tourist info, accommodation	Mon–Sat 9:00–12:30/14:15–18:00	E
City transit information	Mon–Sat 8:00–20:00. ATM. Also metro station	E
Foreign exchange	Daily 8:00–21:30	N
	Other times Tickets, Window 20	H
Post, telegraph	Mon–Fri 8:15–18:00, Sat 8:15–13:00	O
Telephone	Daily 7:00–19:45	E
To other stations	Metro	J
To airports	Airport buses	A

No services when the station is closed, 2:00–4:00.

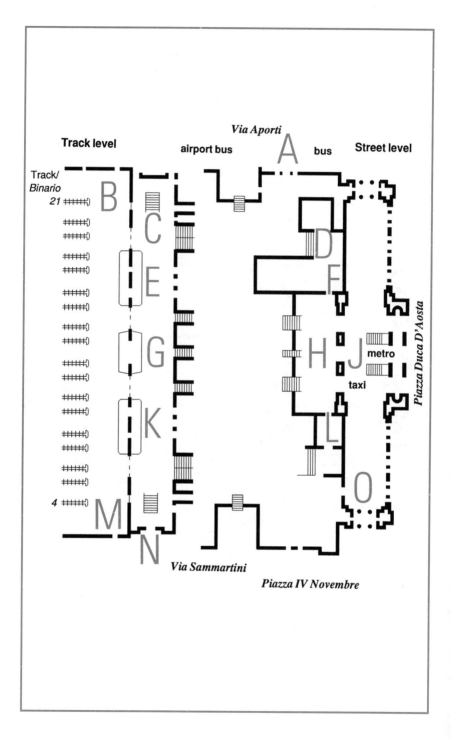

Munich - München Hauptbahnhof

A perfectly central station where the carefree car-free walking street begins right outside and leads to the best sights and shopping in town. The station itself has full services, shopping next door, and rapid transit connections below.

Travel center	Daily 6:00–23:30. DB–*Reisezentrum* Tel. 115 31 35	D,E
Train information	In Travel center. All hours at *Kundendienst*	D
Tickets, reservations	In Travel center. Also Mon–Fri 5:30–23:00, Sat 5:30–22:40, Sun 6:00–22:40 at ticket windows	F
Eurail aid	In Travel center	
Baggage	Mon–Sat 6:00–22:30, Sun 6:15–23:30 To send baggage directly to airplane, see page 111	E
Lockers	Accessible daily 4:30–24:00	C,J
Lost & found	Daily 6:30–23:30	B, upstairs
Emergencies	All hours. *Kundendienst*	D
First aid	Daily 7:00–19:00. *Rotes Kreuz*. Track *(Gleis)* 11	L
Police	All hours. Track *(Gleis)* 11	L
Help for handicapped, nursery	All hours. *Bahnhofsmission*. Track *(Gleis)* 1 Phone in advance 59 50 06.	L
Toilets	All hours	A,L
Waiting room	All hours	B, upstairs
Restaurant	Daily 6:00–23:30	J,K
Bar, buffet	All hours	H,J,K
Provisions	Daily 6:00–22:00	C
Pharmacy	Daily 8:00–18:00	N
Supermarket, shopping	Mon–Fri 9:00–19:30, Sat 9:30–14:00, Sun 9:30–18:00 (access from lower level passage)	outside
Tourist info, accommodation	Daily 8:00–23:00	M
City transit information	See Tourist office or MVV	direction left from A
Foreign exchange	Daily 6:00–23:30	G
Post, telephone	Mon–Fri 8:00–18:00, Sat 8:00–13:00 Other times in main post office	D, upstairs outside
To airport	Airport bus	outside

No services 0:00–4:30, no entry to platforms 1:30–4:30.

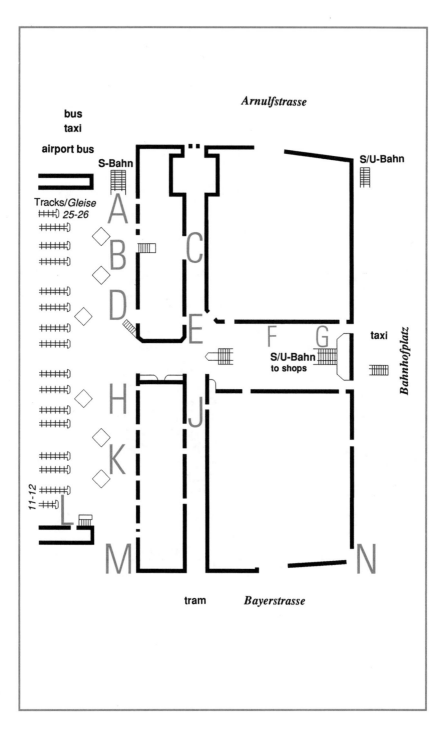

Oslo Sentralstasjon

Train information	Mon–Sat 7:00–23:00, Sun 7:00–23:30	F
Tickets, reservations	Mon–Sat 6:30–23:00, Sun 6:30–23:30	E
Tickets, local trains	Daily 6:30–1:30	E
Eurail aid	See Tickets	
Baggage send/pick-up	Daily 6:30–23:00 (Sun send till 23:30)	D
Baggage store	Lockers only. Accessible daily 7:00–23:00	D
Lost & found	Mon–Fri 9:00–16:00. Outside, in Østbane.	
	Valuables may be held at *Vaktkontoret*, all hours	A
Emergencies	All hours. *Vaktkontoret*	A
First aid	See Train information or Emergencies.	
Police	Mon–Fri 7:00–23:00, Sat–Sun 8:00–12:00. *Politi*	D
Help for handicapped	See Train information or Emergencies. Phone 36 80 00	
Toilets	All hours at Track (*Spoor*) 4–5	A–B
Waiting room	All hours	C
Restaurant	Mon–Fri 7:00–22:00, Sat 7:00–14:00,	
	Sun 15:00–22:00	D, upstairs
	Also daily 12:00–19:00 in Østbane	
Self-service	Mon–Sat 7:00–21:00, Sun 10:00–21:00	G
	Daily 7:00–23:00	D
	Also Mon–Fri 6:00–19:00, Sat–Sun 8:00–19:00 in Østbane	
Bar, buffet	Mon–Sat 7:15/10:30–22:30/23:00,	
	Sun 11:00–23:00	B,D
Provisions, shopping	Mon–Fri 9:00–20:00, Sat 9:00–18:00.	
	Outside, in Oslo City, next to station	
Pharmacy	All hours. Jernbanetorgets Apotek. Opposite station	
Tourist info, accommodation	Daily 7:00–23:00	
	(winter: 8:00–15:00/16:30–23:00)	G
City transit information	Mon–Fri 7:00–20:00, Sat–Sun 8:00–18:00.	
	In front of station	outside
Foreign exchange	Mon–Fri 8:00–19:30, Sat 8:00–19:30,	
	Sun 12:00–18:00	G
Post office	Mon–Fri 7:00–17:30, Sat 9:00–14:00	G
To other station	City buses to Vestbanestasjon.	
To airport	City bus from in front of station; airport bus from	
	Havnegata, left when leaving station.	

No services when station is closed, 1:30–4:30.

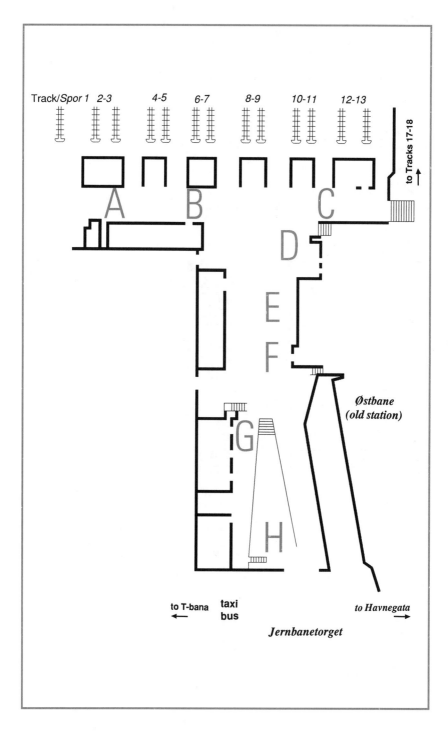

Paris Gare d'Austerlitz

The terminal for south and southwest (Spain, Portugal) also has direct RER trains to Orly Airport.

Travel center	Daily 7:00–24:00. *Bureau de voyages*	G
Train information	Daily 6:00–24:00. *Accueil* Tel. 45 82 50 50	B
Tickets, inland	All hours	G
Tickets, international	In Travel center	G
Reservations, inland, int'l	Daily 7:00–21:00 in Travel center Other times at ticket windows	G
Baggage send	All hours	J
Baggage pick-up	Daily 6:00–24:30	J
Lockers	Accessible daily 6:30–0:30	J
Lost & found	Mon–Fri 8:00–12:00/13:00–17:00	B
Emergencies	All hours. *Accueil*	B,H
First aid	Mon–Fri 8:00–12:00/13:00–17:00. Or *Accueil*	D
Police	All hours	A
Help for handicapped	See Emergencies. Tel. 45 84 14 18, extension 11173	
Toilets	Daily 6:00–24:00	B,F
Bath, shower	Daily 6:00–21:00	C, downstairs
Waiting room	All hours	D
Restaurants	Daily 11:45–14:00/18:30–21:30	H, upstairs
	Daily 6:00–24:00	H
Bar, buffet	Daily 6:00–24:00	K
Provisions	Daily 7:00–23:00	K
Pharmacy	Mon–Fri 8:00–19:00	E
Shopping	Gare Banlieue, lower level	access at C, J
Tourist information	Mon–Sat 8:00–22:00 (winter: Sat till 15:00)	B
City transit information	Metro station	J
Foreign exchange	Daily 7:00–21:00	H
Post, telephone	Mon–Fri 8:00–19:00, Sat 8:00–12:00	(blvd de l'Hôpital)
Telegraph	Daily 5:30–24:15	D
To other stations	SNCF interstation bus. Gare de l'Est and Gare du Nord by metro. Gare de Lyon by bus Nos. 24, 57, 61, 63, 65, 91	
To airports	Charles-de-Gaulle Airport: From Gare du Nord. Orly Airport: RER trains.	

No services when the station is closed, 0:30–5:30.

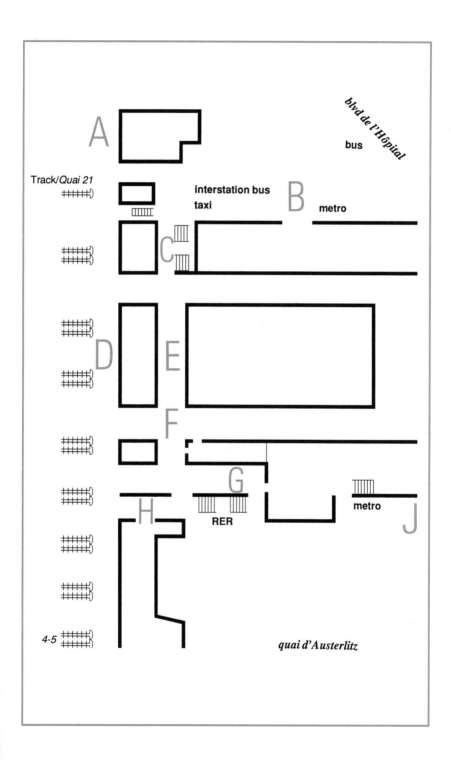

Paris Gare de l'Est

Trains to Germany, Switzerland, and points beyond depart from here. This station shares with the Gare du Nord an excellent food shopping area within a few minutes' walk, in the market hall at rue du 8 mai and rue de Faubourg-St-Denis.

Travel center	Mon–Sat 7:00–21:00, Sun 8:00–20:00	G
Train information	See Travel center. Other times at *Accueil* Tel. 45 82 50 50	A,F
Tickets, inland	Daily 6:00–24:00	G
Tickets, int'l; reservations	See Travel center. Other times at Windows 5–10	G
Baggage send, pick-up	Daily 6:00–23:00 (pick-up until 0:30)	E
Baggage store	Daily 6:00–24:00	E
Lockers	Accessible daily 5:00–1:00	E
Lost & found	Daily 9:00–18:00	passerelle, stairs at C, F
Emergencies, First aid	All hours. *Accueil* or*Secrétariat*	A,F passerelle, stairs at C, F
Police	All hours	A
Help for handicapped	See Emergencies. Tel. 42 03 96 31, extension 12106	
Nursery, help	Mon–Fri 9:00–20:00. *SOS voyageurs* Saturdays see Gare du Nord	A
Toilets, bath, shower	All hours (Bath, shower: daily 6:15–22:00)	C
Waiting room	All hours	D
Restaurants	Daily 6:00–24:00	B,D
Bar, buffet	Daily 6:00–24:00	platform entrances, C–F
Pharmacy	Mon–Fri 7:30–20:00, Sat 8:00–15:00	C
Provisions	Supermarket and market hall: rue du 8 mai and rue de Faubourg-St-Denis	outside
Shopping	In passage to metro	D
Tourist info, accommodation	Mon–Sat 8:00–13:00, 17:00–20:00	A
City transit information	Mon–Fri 8:00–17:00. RATP kiosk in metro	D
Foreign exchange	Daily 7:00–21:00	B
Post, telephone	Mon–Fri 8:00–19:00, Sat 8:00–12:00: rue de Faubourg–St-Martin	outside
To other stations	SNCF interstation bus. Gare d'Austerlitz by metro. Gare de Lyon by bus No. 65 or metro No. 5 to Bastille, then No.1. Gare du Nord by metro No. 5 or walk 1/2 mile.	
To airport	Charles-de-Gaulle Airport: From Gare du Nord. Orly Airport: From Gare d'Austerlitz.	

No services when the station is closed, 1:00–5:00.

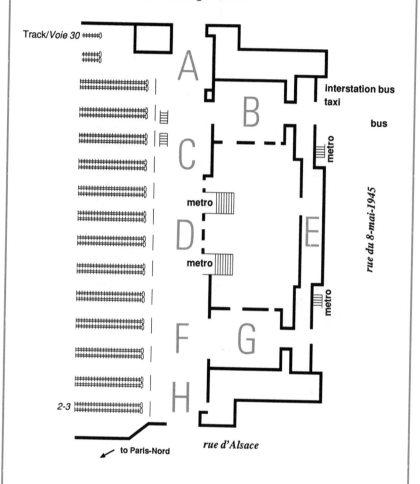

Paris Gare de Lyon

This station houses the restaurant *Le Train Bleu*, officially classified a historical monument for its interior decor. The station is the terminal for the *TGV Sud–Est*. Information, tickets and reservations are duplicated in the below-ground *Gare TGV*, with entrances from rue de Chalon (A) and rue de Bercy (B). One level down is the metro/RER/suburban station complex.

Travel center	Mon–Sat 7:00–21:00, Sun 8:00–20:00	C
Train information	Travel center. Other times *Accueil*. Tel. 45 82 50 50	H
Tickets, inland	Daily 5:30–24:30. Windows 33–44	D
	Daily 5:45–22:00 in *Gare TGV*	A
	Mon–Sat 7:15–20:15 at rue de Bercy entrance	B
Tickets, international	Travel center. Also daily 5:45–0:30 at windows 29–32	D
Reservations	See Travel center. Daily 5:45–22:00 in *Gare TGV*	A
	Daily 7:00–20:15 at rue de Bercy entrance	B
Baggage send	Daily 6:00–23:45	C
Baggage pick-up	Daily 6:00–21:45	C
Baggage store	Daily 6:00–23:45	lower level, at H
Lockers	Accessible daily 3:30–1:30	lower level, at G,H
Lost & found	Mon–Fri 8:00–18:30	rue de Bercy side
Emergencies	All hours. *Accueil*	H
First aid	See Emergencies or Police	
Police	All hours	rue de Bercy side
Help for handicapped	See Emergencies or Police. Phone in advance 40 19 17 19	
Toilets	All hours	lower level, at A, F–H
Bath, shower, nursery	Daily 6:00–20:30	lower level, at F
Waiting room	All hours	A–B, lower level, at E
Restaurants	Daily 6:00–23:30	G
Bar, buffet	Daily 6:00–23:30	C–D
Tourist info, accommodation	Mon–Sat 8:00–13:00/17:00–22:00 (winter: till 20:00)	H
City transit information	In metro station	access at E
Foreign exchange	Daily 6:30–23:00	F
Post, telephone	Mon–Fri 8:00–19:00, Sat 8:00–12:00: rue Diderot	outside
To other stations	All by metro or SNCF interstation bus.	
	Gare d'Austerlitz by bus Nos. 24, 57, 61, 63, 65, 91.	
	Gare de l'Est and Gare du Nord by bus No. 65.	
To airports	Charles-de-Gaulle Airport: RER trains.	
	Orly Airport: From Gare d'Austerlitz.	

No services when the station is closed, 1:30–3:30.

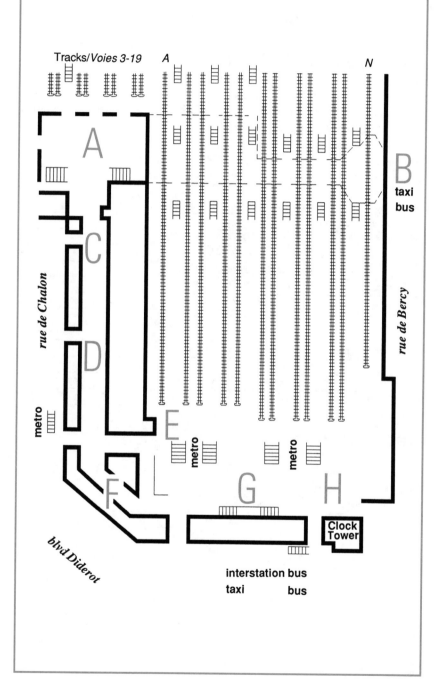

Paris Gare du Nord

The restaurants around this gateway to Flanders and Belgium smell of the north with oysters and beer. Bring a taste of France from the market hall at the rue du 8 mai and rue de Faubourg-St-Denis. Trains for Britain depart from here and Sealink has a desk in the travel center. There is a large and complicated underground suburban station where, if you are lucky, you'll find the RER train to Charles-de-Gaulle Airport.

Travel center, Eurail aid	Daily 8:00–20:00	G
Train information	See Travel center. Other times *Accueil* Tel. 45 82 50 50	G
Tickets, inland	Daily 6:00–23:00. Also in Travel center	F
Tickets, int'l, reservations	See Travel center. Also daily 6:00–23:00	F
Baggage send/pick-up	Daily 5:00–24:45	J
Baggage store	Daily 6:00–23:45	H
Lockers	Accessible daily 6:00–23:45	H
Lost & found	Mon–Fri 10:00–13:00/15:00–18:30	passerelle, E
Emergencies	All hours. *Service clientèle*	passerelle, E
First aid	All hours. *Accueil* or see Police	G
Police	All hours	passerelle, E
Help for handicapped	All hours. *Accueil*. Tel. 42 80 63 63, extension 11811	G
Toilets	All hours	metro level, B, E
Shower	Daily 7:00–20:30	metro level, E
Waiting room	All hours	G
Restaurants	Daily 6:00–23:00	C
	Mon–Fri 11:30–14:30/18:30–21:45	D
Provisions	Supermarket and market hall: rue du 8 mai and rue de Faubourg-St-Denis	outside
Pharmacy	Mon–Fri 7:30–20:00, Sat 9:00–12:30/14:00–18:00	B
Tourist info, accommodation	Daily 6:30–21:45	C
City transit information	In metro station	E
Foreign exchange	Daily 6:30–22:00	E
Post, telephone	Mon–Fri 8:00–19:00, Sat 8:00–12:00: rue de Faubourg-St-Denis	outside
To other stations	SNCF interstation bus. Gare d'Austerlitz by metro. Gare de l'Est by metro or walk 1/2 mile. Gare du Lyon by metro or bus No. 65.	
To airports	Charles-de-Gaulle Airport: RER trains. Orly Airport: From Gare d'Austerlitz.	

No services when the station is closed, 0:15–4:30.

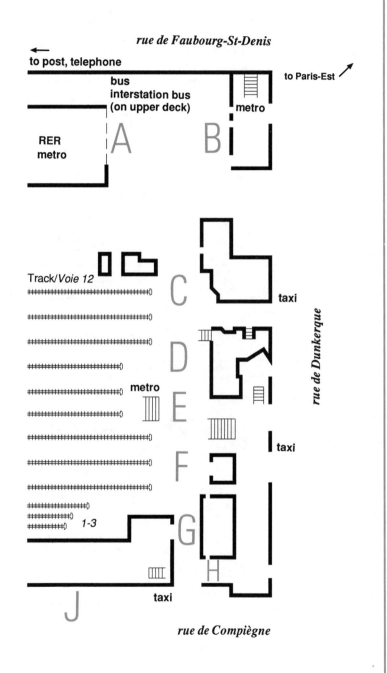

Rome - Roma Stazione di Termini

While hugging a wall built by Emperor Severus, the station is of the 20th century and Roman only in Rome's negative aspects. It's full of visibly non-Roman drifters, passengers anxious about thieves, and magnificently uniformed cops chatting over a smoke. Lots of space, many services, but expect to stand in line for everything.

Travel center	CIT Agency. Mon–Fri 9:00–13:00/14:00–17:30	C
Train information, Eurail aid	Daily 7:00–23:30. Phone 4775	E
Tickets, inland	All hours. Windows 7–30	E
	With credit card at Windows 14–16	E
Tickets, international	All hours. Windows 1–2	E
Reservations	Daily 7:00–22:00. Windows 33–43	E
Baggage send	All hours	A, outside
Baggage pickup	All hours	M, outside
Baggage store, lost & found	All hours	K
Emergencies	See Train information	
First aid	All hours. *Soccorso*	K
Police	All hours. *Polizia ferroviaria*	J
Help for handicapped	See Tickets. Clerk will contact station master.	E
Toilets	All hours	K
Bath, shower	Daily 6:40–20:40. *Albergo diurno*	F,G
Waiting room	All hours	K
Restaurant, self-service	Daily 10:30–22:30	J
Bar, buffet	Daily 7:00–23:30	J
	Also daily 7:20–20:40 in *Albergo diurno*	F,G
Provisions	Outside, off Via Giolitti	A
Pharmacy	Daily 7:00–23:30	D
Shopping	In station concourse	D–F
Tourist info, accommodation	Daily 9:00–13:00/15:00–20:00. (Opposite G, inside ticket barrier)	
City transit information	ATAC booth at bus stop opposite station	outside
Foreign exchange	Mon–Fri 8:30–19:30, Sat 8:30–16:30, Sun 8:00–14:15	F
	Also daily 8:00–12:30/15:00–20:00 in Train information	
Post office	Mon–Sat 8:00–19:30, Sun 8:00–12:30	C
Telephone	All hours	H
To other stations	Metro and regular trains to Ostiense, bus to Tiburtina.	
To airport	Airport bus from air terminal in Via Giolitti.	A

No services when the station is closed, 1:00–5:00.

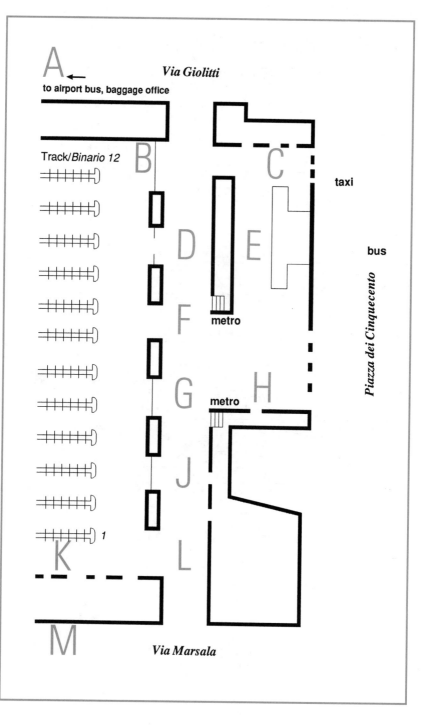

Rotterdam Centraalstation

Travel center	Mon–Fri 8:00–18:30, Sat 9:00–17:00, Sun 10:00–17:00	B
Train information	Mon–Fri 8:00–22:00, Sat 9:00–18:00, Sun 10:00–17:00. NS *inlichtingenbureau.* Tel. 411 7100	B
Tickets, inland	All hours Also daily 7:00–23:00 on *Blijdorpsijd,* back of station	D
Tickets, international	Mon–Sat 5:15–23:30, Sun from 6:15. Windows 11–13	D
Reservations	Mon–Fri 8:00–20:00, Sat 9:00–17:00, Sun 10:00–17:00	B
Baggage send/pick-up	Mon–Fri 7:30–16:00 Other times contact the conductor of your train	C
Baggage store	All hours	C
Lockers	Accessible daily 5:00–1:45	C
Lost & found	All hours. Window 14	D
Emergencies	See Train information	
First aid	See Train information	
Police	All hours	C
Help for handicapped	See Train information. Phone in advance 30/33 12 53	
Toilets	All hours	F
Waiting room	All hours on platforms.	
Self-service	Daily 6:00–22:00. Track (*Spoor*) 1	access at F
Bar, buffet	Mon–Fri 6:30–22:00, Sat–Sun 7:00–22:00 On platforms at Tracks 1, 6–7, 8–9, 11–12; also	F
Tourist info, accommodation	Mon–Sat 9:00–22:00, Sun 10:00–22:00	E
City transit information	RET booth in front of station	
Foreign exchange	Mon–Sat 7:30–22:00, Sun 9:00–22:00	A
Post, telephone, telegraph	Mon–Fri 8:30–19:00, Sat 8:30–12:30 (outside)	
To airport	City bus No.33 to Rotterdam Airport; regular trains to Schiphol Airport	

No services when the station is closed, 1:45–5:00.

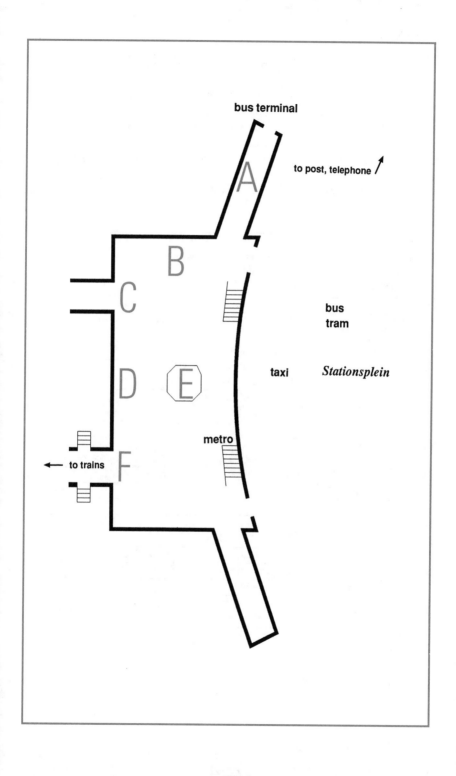

Salzburg Hauptbahnhof

Services are in two areas. Find train information, ticketing, reservations, and foreign exchange in the entrance hall (H on plan). On the *Mittelbahnsteig* (center platform, A–D on plan) are restaurants, tourist information, and emergency services, as well as passport control and customs for passengers to Germany.

Be careful with the numbering of platforms: 2 and 9 are adjacent on one side, 4, 5, and 7 on the other.

The station is a long walk from downtown but most city buses stop right across the street.

Travel center, Eurail aid	Daily 7:00–20:30. *Reisebüro am Bahnhof*	H
Train information	In Travel center. Other times tel. 1717	H
Tickets, inland	All hours. Windows 3–6	H
Tickets to Germany	All hours.	H
Tickets, international	In Travel center. Other times Windows 3–6	H
Reservations	Daily 8:00–19:00 in Travel center	H
Baggage	All hours	G
Lockers	Accessible all hours in tunnel at	H,G
Lost & found	Mon–Fri 8:30–12:00, 13:30–16:30. Platform *(Bahnsteig)* 1	E
Emergencies	All hours. *Fahrdienstleitung*	D
First aid	Daily 8:00–17:00. Other times see Emergencies	C
Police	All hours	outside, F
Help for handicapped	Daily 8:00–17:00. *Bahnhofsmission* Other times see Emergencies. Phone in advance 71 240	C
Nursery, help	Daily 8:00–17:00. *Bahnhofsmission*	C
Toilets	All hours.	In tunnels and B
Waiting room	All hours	A
Restaurants	Daily 6:00–23:00	B
Bar, buffet	Daily 5:30–20:00	H
Provisions	Mon–Sat 5:00–22:30, Sun 7:00–20:00	A,H
Supermarket	Mon–Fri 7:30–18:00, Sat 7:30–12:00	outside
Tourist info, accommodations	Daily 8:00–19:00	B
City transit information	See Tourist information or bus terminal	outside
Foreign exchange	Daily 7:00–22:00	H
Post, telephone	All hours	outside, J
To airport	City bus No. 77.	outside

The station is open at all hours.

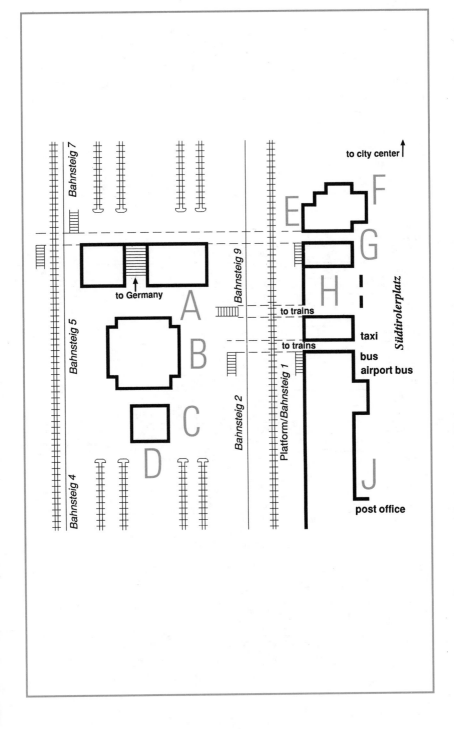

Stockholm Centralstation

A multimodal terminal *(City Terminalen)* has been added to the station for convenient connections to intercity and airport buses. On the station's Klarabergsviadukt side A the upper level concourse houses ticketing and reservation services, mostly for inland and suburban traffic, and snack bars.

Train information	Daily 8:00–21:00 (Sat till 18:30). Tel. 22 50 60	J
Tickets, reservations, inland	Mon–Sat 6:00–23:45, Sun 6:35–23:45	J
	Also shorter hours on upper level	access at A,D
Tickets, reservations, int'l; Eurail aid	Mon–Fri 8:00–20:00, Sat 9:00–18:00, Sun 10:00–18:00	
	Reservations by phone: 7:00–22:00. Tel. 22 79 40	J
Baggage send/pick-up	Mon–Sat 6:00–22:00, Sun 7:45–22:00 with breaks	C
Baggage store	Daily 7:00–23:30	C
Lockers	Accessible daily 4:30–1:00	lower level, access at F
Lost & found	Mon–Fri 9:00–19:00	C
Emergencies, first aid	Mon–Sat 6:00–23:15, Sun 7:00–23:15. *Kundservice*	D
Police	See Emergencies	
Help for handicapped	See Emergencies or phone 762 25 80	
Nursery	All hours in family waiting room	E
Toilets	All hours	lower level, access at F
Shower	See Toilets. Also in family waiting room	E
Restaurants	Mon–Sat 6:30–24:00, Sun 11:30–24:00	K
Self-service	Mon–Sat 6:30–23:30, Sun 7:00–23:30	A,K
Bar, buffet	Mon–Sat 6:30–22:30, Sun 7:00–22:30	A,K
Snack bars	Daily 6:00/8:00–22:30	upper level, access at A; lower level, access at F,G
Provisions	Mon–Fri 7:00–23:00, Sat 8:00–23:00, Sun 9:00–23:00	lower level, access at F,G
Pharmacy	Permanent service. Klarabergsgatan 64	outside
Supermarket, shopping	AHLENS in Klarabergsgatan	outside
Tourist info, accommodation	Daily 8:00–21:00 (winter: daily 8:00–11:30/13:00–17:00)	H
City transit information	Daily 6:30–21:00 with breaks. SL windows (lower level, access at G; upper level, access at A,D)	
Foreign exchange	Daily 8:00–21:00	G
Post office	Mon–Fri 7:00–21:00, Sat 9:00–13:00	F
Telephone, telegraph	Mon–Fri 8:00–20:00, Sat 9:00–13:00	E
To airport	Airport bus from City Terminalen	outside, access at A
To ferry docks	Värtahamnen by T–bana to Ropsten, then bus. Tegelvikshamnen by T–bana to Slussen, then bus.	

No services when the station is closed, 1:00–4:30.

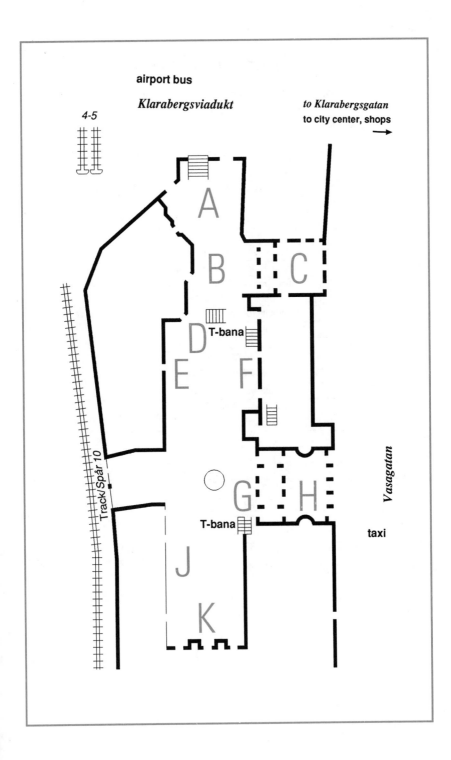

Strasbourg Gare

The station building, completed in 1883, looks nearly as Gothic as the other classic one in Metz, even after modernization which fortunately didn't touch the stained-glass windows. The restaurant is a joy to wait in.

Travel center	Mon–Fri 7:30–20:00, Sat 7:30–19:00, Sun 9:00–19:00	C
Train information	Daily 6:00–22:00. *Accueil*. Tel. 88 22 50 50	B
Tickets	All hours	B
Reservations	See Travel center. Other times at Windows 1–4	B
Baggage	All hours	E
Lockers	Accessible at all hours	G
Lost & found	Mon–Fri 8:00–12:00/14:00–17:45	G
Emergencies	See Train information. Other times *Chef de service voyageurs* (officer in white cap) on Platform (*Quai*) 3	
First aid	See Emergencies	
Police	All hours	H
Help for handicapped	All hours. *SOS voyageurs*. Tel. 88 32 12 59	H, ring bell
Nursery	All hours. Platform (*Quai*) 1	access from D
Toilets	All hours. Platform (*Quai*) 1 Also daily 6:00–22:00	access from D E
Bath, showers	All hours. Platform (*Quai*) 1	access from D
Waiting room	All hours. Platforms	
Restaurants	Daily 6:00–24:00	A
Bar, buffet	Daily 6:00–24:00. Platform (*Quai*) 1	access from D
Provisions	Shops in rue du Maire Kuss	outside, opposite station
Tourist information,	Daily 8:00–19:00	
Accommodation	(winter: Mon–Fri 9:00–12:30/14:45–18:00)	outside
City transit information	Mon–Fri 6:15–19:00	F
Foreign exchange	Daily 9:00–20:00	F
Post, telephone	Mon–Fri 8:00–19:00, Sat 8:00–12:00	A
To airport	Airport bus	outside

The station is accessible with tickets at all hours.

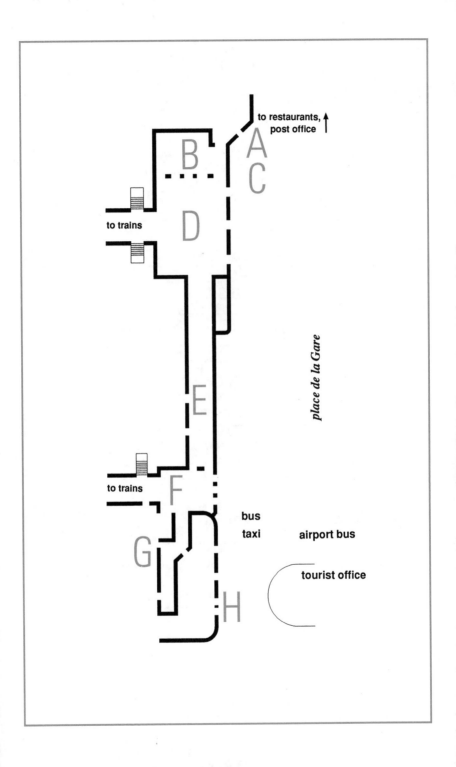

Utrecht Centraalstation

Travel center	Daily 7:00–23:00	E
Train information	In Travel center. Also Mon–Sat 9:00–17:00 Other times *Perronopziehter* on platforms. Tel. 31 58 14	D
Tickets, inland	All hours	C
Tickets, international	Mon–Fri 7:00–21:30, Sat 7:15–21:30, Sun 8:15–21:30. In Travel center Other times see Tickets, inland	E C
Reservations	Mon–Fri 8:00–19:45, Sat–Sun 9:00–19:45 In Travel center	E
Eurail aid	In Travel center or Receptie	E D
Baggage	Mon–Sat 6:00–23:00, Sun 8:00–23:00	K
Lockers	Accessible all hours	
Lost & found	See Baggage office	
Emergencies	All hours. *Perronopziehter* on platforms	
First aid	See Emergencies	
Police	All hours	G
Help for handicapped	See Emergencies. Phone in advance 33 12 53	
Toilets	All hours	J
Waiting room	All hours on platforms.	
Restaurant	Daily 11:00–21:00	H
Self-service	Daily 6:00–23:00	H
Bar, buffet	Daily 6:30–23:00 Mon–Sat 10:00/11:00–19:00/20:00 More in Direction L	B D
Provisions	Mon–Fri 7:00–20:00, Sat 8:00–20:00, Sun 11:00–18:30	F; more in Direction L
Pharmacy	Mon–Fri 7:30–18:00, Sat 7:30–17:00	Direction L
Tourist info, accommodation	Mon–Sat 9:00–17:00 See also city office	D Direction L
City transit information	Booth at Stadsbussen	Direction L
Foreign exchange	Mon–Sat 8:00–21:00, Sun 10:00–18:00	A
Post, telephone	Mon–Fri 7:30–18:00, Sat 7:30–17:00	Direction L
To airport	Regular trains to Schiphol Airport with change in Amsterdam.	

The station is open at all hours.

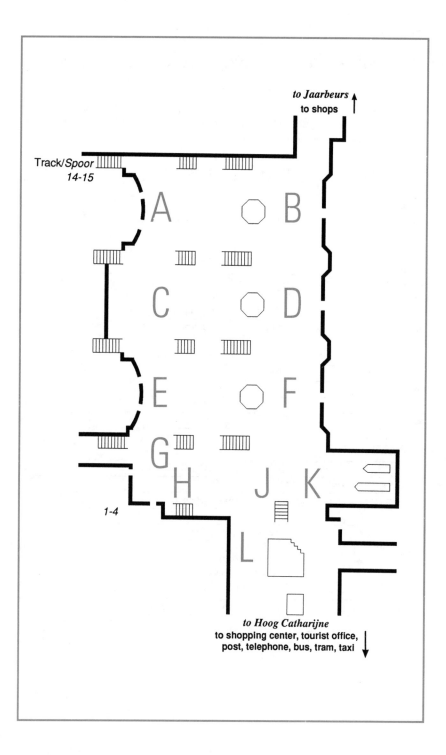

Venice - Venezia Stazione di Santa Lucia

The romantic name doesn't fit this flat, boxy structure. It's clean, well-organized, efficient, and has all amenities from showers to good food. But the best part is the wide glass door opening to the view of the Grand Canal. There with a few steps you walk into another century.

Train information	Daily 7:00–21:30. Tel. 71 55 55	C,D
Tickets, inland	All hours. Windows 2–5	H
Tickets, international	All hours. Window 7	H
Reservations	Daily 7:00–21:15. Windows 9–10 (Minimum 3 hours before departure; sleeping cars one day before)	H
Eurail aid	Mon–Fri 8:00–17:30 in Train information	C,D
Baggage send/pick-up	Daily 6:15–20:30	J
Baggage store	Daily 6:15–20:30	F
Lost & found	Mon–Fri 8:00–12:00/14:00—17:20	M
	Other times see Baggage office	J
Emergencies	See Train info. Other times *Dirigenti movimento*	L
First aid	Mon–Sat 8:00–14:00	A
	Other times see Train information or *Dirigenti movimento*	L
Police	All hours	F
Help for handicapped	All hours. *Dirigenti movimento*	L
Toilets	All hours	A pay, L free
Bath, shower	Daily 6:30–20:30	A
Waiting room	All hours	B
Restaurant	Daily 11:30–15:00, summer only	B,D
Self-service	Daily 11:30–15:00/18:30–21:30	B,D
Bar, buffet, provisions	Daily 6:00–22:00	B,D
Pharmacy, shopping, provisions	Outside, in Lista di Spagna	
Tourist information	Daily 8:00–20:00	E
City transit information	Outside, at vaporetto stops	
Foreign exchange	Daily 7:30–20:30 in Train information	C,D
	Also daily 8:00–19:00	G
	Other times at Window 7	H
Post, telephone	Mon–Fri 8:00–20:00, Sat 8:00–14:00	H,K
To other station	Regular trains to Venezia–Mestre	
To airport	Boats from Piazza San Marco, buses from Piazzale Roma.	

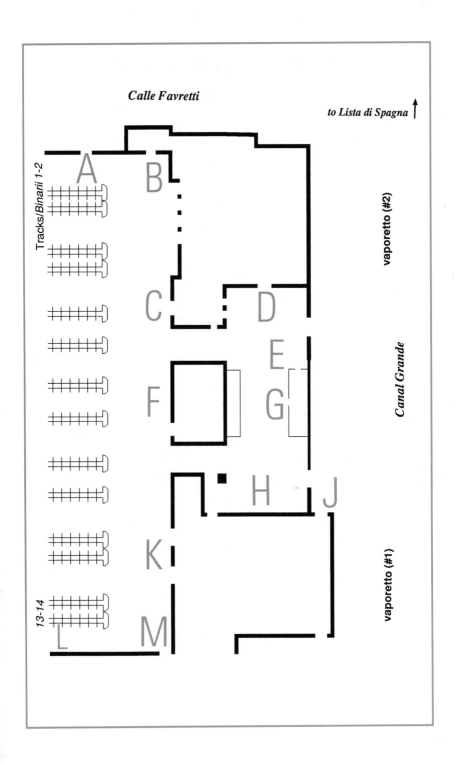

Vienna - Wien Südbahnhof

Once called the Südostbahnhof (south–east station), the station serves two areas. The Ostbahn section, top concourse (Tracks 1–9, D on plan), handles trains from the east (Czechoslovakia, Hungary, Poland). The Südbahn section, middle concourse (Tracks 11–19, B on plan) is the terminal for the south (Italy, Yugoslavia). Most services are in the street level concourse. The *Schnellbahn* offers quick connection to the center.

Travel center, train information	Daily 6:30–21:20. *Reisebüro am Bahnhof*	C
	Other times ticket windows. Tel. 1717	C
Tickets, inland	In Travel center. Other times Windows 8–15	C
Tickets, international	In Travel center. Other times Windows 4–5	C
Reservations	Mon–Fri 7:00–19:00, Sat 7:00–12:00 in Travel center	C
	Other times Windows 7–8	C
Baggage	All hours	C
Lockers	Accessible daily 4:00–24:00	G
Lost & found	Mon–Fri 7:00–15:30	G
	Other times Window 29	C
Emergencies	All hours. *Fahrdienstleitung.* Track *(Gleis)* 1	D
	Abfahrt, Ankunft. Track *(Gleis)* 11 or 19	B
First aid, Nursery	Daily 7:00–20:00. *Bahnhof–Sozialdienst*	G
	Other times see Emergencies	
Police	All hours	outside, H
Help for handicapped	See Emergencies. Phone in advance 5650 3999	
Toilets	All hours	D,E
Bath, shower	Daily 6:00–19:00	E
Waiting room	All hours	B,D
Restaurants	Daily 6:00–23:30 and 11:00–19:00	D,E
Bar, buffet	Daily 6:00–23:30	B,D,F
Provisions	Daily 5:30–23:00	E
Pharmacy	Mon–Fri 8:00–12:00, 14:00–18:00,	
	Sat 8:00–12:00	outside
Tourist info, accommodations	Daily 6:30–22:00. *Verkehrsbüro*	E,G
City transit info, tickets	In Travel center and Windows 9–15	C
Foreign exchange	See Tourist info. Tickets only: all hours at Windows 4–5	C
Post, telephone	Daily 6:00–24:00	outside, A
To other station	Tram No.18 to Westbahnhof.	
To airport	Airport bus.	outside, A

No services when the station is closed, 0:00–4:00.

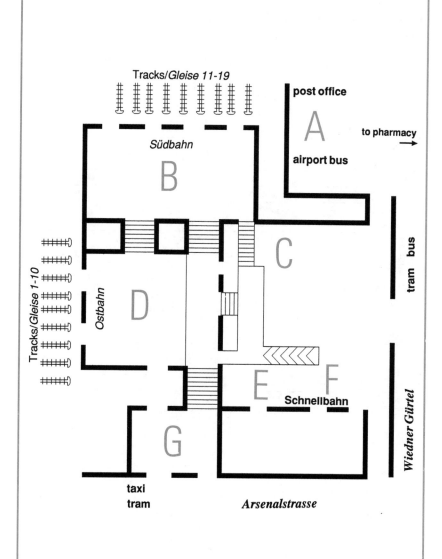

Vienna - Wien Westbahnhof

A well-equipped station at the top end of a major shopping street. Supermarkets are just outside, department stores within two blocks. It's not on a *Schnellbahn* line—allow time to get there by slower tram or *Stadtbahn*.

Travel center, Eurail Aid	Mon–Fri 8:00–19:00, Sat 8:00–13:00.	
	Reisebüro am Bahnhof	D
Train information	In Travel center. Tel. 1717. Other times ticket windows	F
Tickets, inland	All hours. Windows 6–12	F
Tickets, international	In Travel center. Other times Windows 1–3	F
Reservations	In Travel center. Other times Windows 4–5	F
Baggage send, pick-up	All hours	D
Baggage store	All hours	J
Lockers	Accessible daily 4:00–1:00	B,D,H,K
Lost & found	Mon–Fri 8:00–15.30. Langauergasse	K
	Other times see Emergencies.	
Emergencies	All hours. *Fahrdienstleitung.* Track *(Gleis)* 1	G
First aid	See Emergencies.	
Police	All hours	outside, A
Help for handicapped	See Emergencies.	
Nursery, help	All hours. *Bahnhof-Sozialdienst.* Track *(Gleis)* 1	G
Toilets	All hours	B,J
Bath, shower	Mon–Sat 7:00–20.00, Sun 8:00–13:00	D
Waiting room	All hours	H
Restaurants	Daily 6:00–23:30, 12:00–21:30	J,H
Bar, buffet	Daily 6:00–23:30	E,J
Provisions	Daily 6:00–23:00	E,J
Supermarkets	Mon–Fri 8:00–18:30/20:00,	
	Sat 7:30–12:30	outside, Mariahilferstrasse,K
Pharmacy	Mon–Fri 8:00–12:00/14:00–18:00	
	Sat 8:00–12:00	outside, K
Shopping	"Stafa" department store	outside, Mariahilferstrasse
Tourist info, accommodation	Daily 6:15–23:30	C
City transit info, tickets	All hours. Windows 6–12	F
Foreign exchange	Daily 7:00–22:00	C
	Other times Post Office	K
	For tickets only: daily 6:00–24:00 at Windows 13–14	F
Post, telephone	All hours	K
To other station	Tram No. 18 to Südbahnhof	outside: Europaplatz
To airport	Airport bus	outside, A

No services when the station is closed, 1:00–4:00.

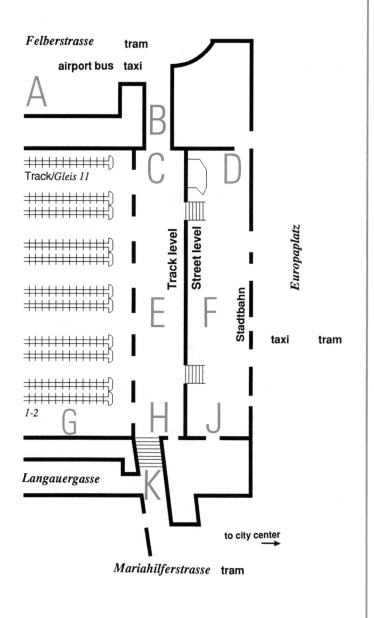

Zürich Hauptbahnhof

The underground S–Bahn station was completed in 1989 but renovations in the main hall will continue for the next few years. Find shops, bath, public transit office under Bahnhofplatz in ShopVille, reached by escalator.

Travel center	Daily 6:30–21:00. *Reisebüro SBB*	H
Train information, Eurail aid	In Travel center. Tel. 211 50 10	
Tickets	All hours. Windows 1–10	H
Reservations	Daily 6:30–21:00	H
Baggage send, pick-up	Daily 6:00–21:50 To transfer baggage directly to or from airplane, see pages 185 and 186.	F
Baggage store	Daily 6:00–23:50	F
Lockers	Accessible daily 4:00–0:10	F
Lost & found	Mon–Fri 6:45–20:45, Sat 7:00–12:00/13:00–17:30, Sun 7:50–12:40/14:10–19:00	F, upstairs
Emergencies, First aid	See Travel center. Other times the *sous–chef* (red cap) on platforms	
Police	All hours	F, upstairs
Help for handicapped	See Emergencies. Phone in advance 211 92 77	
Nursery	Mon–Fri 7:00–20:30, Sat 8:00–20:00, Sat 12:00–20:00 *Bahnhofhilfswerk*	F, upstairs
Toilets	All hours	A
Bath, shower	Daily 6:00–23:00. In ShopVille	access from D
Waiting room	Daily 6:00–23:55	B
Restaurants	Daily 8:00–23:30 and 6:00/11:00–23:30	D, upstairs B,C
Snack bars, self-service	Daily 5:30–23:30	B.F,G
Provisions, shopping	In ShopVille	access from D
Tourist info, accommodation	March through October: Mon–Fri 8:00–22:00, Sat–Sun 8:00–20:30. November through February: Mon–Thu 8:00–20:00, Fri 8:00–22:00, Sat–Sun 9:00–18:00	E
City transit information	Mon–Fri 7:00–19:00, Sat 7:00–18:00, Sun 8:00–19:00 VBZ booth on street, office in ShopVille	
Foreign exchange	Daily 6:15–22:45	G
Post office	Mon–Fri 7:30–18:30, Sat 7:30–11:00	H
Telephone	Mon–Fri 7:00–22:30, Sat–Sun 9:00–18:00	D
To airport	Frequent regular trains.	

No services when the station is closed, 0:10–4:00.

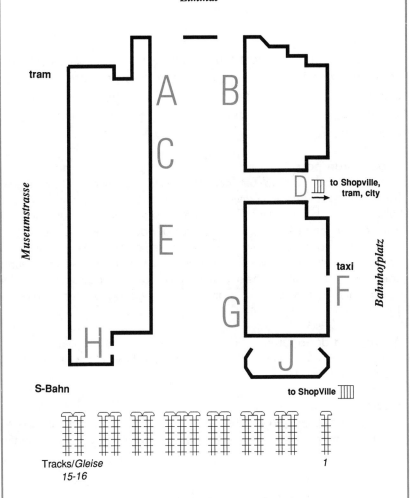

GATEWAY AIRPORTS

Without a transoceanic train tunnel, even the most faithful rail travelers fly to Europe. Airports, like railway stations, are cities within cities, complicated enough to require a guide. In this section we tell you what to expect at the gateway airports — and how to get in and out.

Ground transport
We recommend rail travel between airport and city wherever it's available. Trains usually run faster than anything on the road, and they are impervious to traffic jams and bad weather. They also cost less than airport buses—and only a fraction of the taxi fare. Note that the railway stations at some airports (Amsterdam, Frankfurt, Geneva, and Zurich) are part of the intercity, and even the international, rail networks. If your destination is another city, you can usually take a direct train right from the airport and have your baggage sent ahead. The German and Swiss railways offer direct rail/air baggage services (see pages 111 and 186).

Arrival and departure
We give a walk-through description of the shortest route between the plane and the city center.

Services
We don't give opening hours in this section. Airports never shut down completely and always provide some amenities at least until the departure of the last plane.

Amsterdam Schiphol Airport

An airport built on the bottom of a lake, the site of a 16th-century naval battle? Why not, in a country where boats cross highways *above* the cars. Otherwise this is a rational place: well laid out and marked, easy to use. The duty-free shops have the lowest prices in Europe.

Ground transport

Trains run from 5:30 till 23:30 every 12–18 minutes (about hourly all night) between Amsterdam Centraalstation and the airport; travel time is 17–22 minutes. Schiphol is on the intercity network and has direct connections with The Hague and Rotterdam. Other rail services to the airport are from Amsterdam Zuidstation and RAI. Airport buses (KLM) serve major hotels.

Arrival

Moving walkways take you from the plane to the central building. For connecting flights go to the transfer desk in the piers or in the central transit area. To exit, go through passport control, then down to baggage claim area. TV monitors show carousels for each flight. Baggage from intercontinental flights is usually on belts 8–14. Baggage carts may be taken on escalators but should be braked.

Exit through customs to arrival hall. An escalator in the center descends to the railway station. Buses and taxis stop outside. Train information, tickets, and reservations can be found at the railway station.

Departure

Take the train from Amsterdam Centraalstation, Zuidstation, RAI, or any city along the routes to The Hague–Rotterdam–Vlissingen, Enschede, Groningen and Leeuwarden. Arriving at the airport station, find baggage carts on the platform (carts can be used on escalators). Follow the airplane signs to the departure hall. You can check in at any desk in the North Hall, and at your airline's desk in the South Hall (check indicator board). Go through passport control behind desks 6–7 or 12–13 to transit area. Gates 1–20 are in Pier A, Gates 21–33 in Pier B, Gates 34–39 in Pier C, Gates 48–55 in Pier D.

Note: This is a *quiet airport* where flights are not announced. Watch the indicator for green lights signaling boarding time.

Services

Airline information	Arrival hall, center; departure hall, center; transit area, left.
Airline tickets	Departure hall, center and front wall.
Train information, tickets	Railway station.
First aid	Pier D (enter from arrival hall or transit area).
Lost & found	Baggage claim area; lower level baggage store.
Help for handicapped	Arrival hall (IHD service); transit area, center KLM desk
Nursery	Transit area, Pier D and between Piers A and B.
Toilets	Arrival hall, far end; departure hall, both ends; railway station; transit area, piers, baggage claim area.
Showers	Transit area, lower level, between Piers A and B (hotel).

Rest rooms	Transit area, lower level, between Piers A and B (hotel).
Restaurant, self-service	Top level, departure and transit areas.
Bar, buffet	Arrival hall, center; departure hall, left; railway station; transit area, piers.
Provisions, shopping	Railway station.
Duty-free shops	Transit area, upper level, center and in Pier D.
Tourist information	See national and city offices downtown.
Accommodation	Arrival hall, KLM desk.
Foreign exchange	Arrival hall, near exit from customs; transit area, baggage claim area, center lounge, Pier B.
Post, telephone	Outside, right of exit; transit area, upper level, center.

Brussels National Airport (Zaventem)

Ground transport
The airport railway station is under the terminal building (validate your Eurailpass at the tourist information desk in the baggage claim area while waiting). Trains run every 30 minutes from 5:30 till 23:45 between the airport and Noord and Centraal stations; travel times are 12 and 17 minutes, respectively. Buses and taxis stop outside the arrival hall.

Arrival
From the plane, walk to the transit hall. There are service desks near the exits for those with connecting flights. Go through passport control to the baggage claim area. TV monitors show the carousel for your flight. Baggage carts cost 20 BF; insert three 20-franc pieces (the machine changes 100-franc bills), leave carts at collection spots near exits for 40 BF refund. Exit through customs to arrival hall; the escalator from the center takes you down to the train.

Departure
From Centraal, Track *(Spoor)* 1a or Noord (find track on indicator board), take the train to the airport. On arrival take the elevator or follow the signs to the escalator up to the departure hall. The flight indicator (over rows C and D) shows the check-in desk for each flight. After check-in, enter through passport control to transit hall and passages to gates.

Services
Airline information	Transit hall; satellite (Gates 1–24); arrival hall; departure hall.
Airline tickets	Transit hall; departure hall.

Train information, tickets	Station under the terminal building.
First aid	Any airport employee.
Police	Baggage claim area; departure hall.
Lost & found	Baggage claim area; arrival hall.
Help for handicapped	Contact an employee of your airline.
Nursery	Passage to satellite (near Sabena Club)
Toilets	Near gates; baggage claim area; departure hall; train station.
Restaurants, self-service	Transit hall; end of departure hall.
Bar, buffet	Transit hall; satellite; arrival hall.
Duty-free shops	Transit hall; satellite.
Tourist and city transit information, accommodation	Baggage claim area.
Foreign exchange	Baggage claim area; arrival hall.
Post office	Baggage claim area; arrival hall.
Telephone	Arrival hall (post office).

Frankfurt Airport

The Continent's busiest airport crams all its passenger services into one building, yet it's easy to move through, thanks to the excellent signs. We follow those short-hand signs in our list: "Departures B" refers to departure level, area B.
Note: Frankfurt is a *quiet airport* where flights are not called over loudspeakers; watch the indicator boards for flashing green lights signaling your departure.

Ground transport
Rapid transit (S-Bahn) trains run from 4:10 till 00:40. Between the airport station and Frankfurt Hauptbahnhof (main station) trains run every 10–15 minutes; travel time is 11 minutes. Trains to Mainz and Wiesbaden run every 15–30 minutes; travel times are 26 and 42 minutes, respectively. There are also direct trains, EuroCity and InterCity, to Amsterdam, Dortmund, Hanover, Klagenfurt, Cologne, Munich, Nuremberg, and Vienna.

Arrival
Overseas flights arrive at Piers B and C. For connecting flights or Lufthansa Airport Express go to the Lufthansa desk (Transit, Departures B).

Exit through passport control, and follow the signs down to baggage claim (Arrivals B or C). The indicator board shows the carousel for your flight. Pass through customs. In Arrivals B the sign *Fahrkartenausgabe* marks the counter for train information, tickets, and baggage forwarding. Buy S-Bahn tickets to Frankfurt at the blue automat (tickets are not sold aboard the trains). The station is two levels below the arrival hall. Trains for Frankfurt leave from Track 1.

Departure

Take S-Bahn Line No. 14 from Frankfurt (stops at Konstablerwache, Hauptwache, Taunusanlage, lower level in Hauptbahnhof) or Line No. 15 from Hauptbahnhof. Check a timetable for trains from other cities. Arriving at the airport station take the escalator up to next level (marked *Unterm Flughafen*). Find your airline on the "Check-in" display; you can check in on this level or proceed up to the departure level (follow blue lines on the floor). After check-in, go through passport control in Departures B for Gates 31–59 or Departures C for Gates 60–67.

Services

Airline information	Arrivals B; Transit B.
	Departures A and B; Transit B.
Airline tickets	Departures A, B, C.
Train information, tickets	Arrivals B.
First aid	Arrivals, in passage between B and C.
Police	Call 100 on green phone.
Lost baggage (tracing)	Arrivals B (baggage claim area).
Lost & found	Arrivals A.
Help for handicapped	Any information or check-in desk.
Nursery	Arrivals B; Departures Pier A and area C; Transit B.
Toilets	All levels: near entrances to piers; train station.
Showers	Departures B at entrance to transit.
Restaurants	Arrivals B; Departures A, B, C; *Unterm Flughafen*; above Transit B.
Provisions, shopping	Supermarkets on *Unterm Flughafen* level.
Duty-free shops	Transit B, Piers A and C.
Pharmacy	Departures, shopping area between B and C; *Unterm Flughafen*.
Tourist information	Arrivals B; Departures C.
Foreign exchange	Arrivals B and C; Departures A and B; Transit B.

London Gatwick Airport

Gatwick is smooth, comfortable, and silent—no announcements: watch the indicator board for your departure warning. The North Terminal handles Air France, Air New Zealand, British Airways, Lufthansa, and SAS; the South Terminal all other airlines. The two terminals are connected by rail transit.

Ground transport: the Gatwick Express

Trains run between Gatwick Airport South Terminal and Victoria Station every 15 minutes (half-hourly or hourly at night); travel time is 30 minutes.

Arrival

North Terminal: From the plane walk to the immigration area. There is a transfer desk for connecting flights. A TV monitor shows when baggage from your flight has arrived. Go down escalator to collect baggage and out through customs to the arrival hall. Go back up to the first floor and take the transit mono-rail to the South Terminal and trains.

South Terminal: From the plane walk to the immigration area; arriving at the Satellite (Gates 31–38), take the shuttle. For connecting flights, go to the transfer desk in the departure lounge.

Go through passport control to the buffer lounge. TV monitor shows when baggage from your flight has arrived. Go up escalator to collect baggage and out through customs to the arrival hall. The exits to the railway station and buses are slightly to the right.

Departure

At Victoria Station, passengers of British Airways, or airlines handled by them, can check in on the upper level, accessible by escalator from Platform 14. Use the rear section of the train for the North Terminal, the front section for the South Terminal.

North Terminal: From the station follow direction signs to North Terminal. There take the escalator or elevator up to the check-in area. Go through security and passport control to the departure area, then down the ramps to gates.

South Terminal: From the station go up to the bridge and moving walkway to the departure hall and check-in. For late check-in and special assistance go to last desk at the BA counter (right). Go through security and passport control behind check-in desks. The duty-free shop is on the left, buffet on the right. If departing from the Satellite, take the shuttle there; there are duty-free shop, bar and buffet in the waiting area.

Services

Airline information	Both terminals: Arrival halls.
Airline tickets	Both terminals: Departure halls.
Train information, tickets	North: Entrance to transit station. South: Baggage claim area, train station.
First aid	North: Arrival hall. South: Gatwick Village.
Police	Any airport employee will call.
Lost & found	South: Downstairs from departure hall.
Help for handicapped	Contact your airline.
Nursery	North: Transit area, The Avenue. South: Transit area, Gatwick Village, satellite.
Toilets	North: Arrival hall, The Avenue, departure hall. South: Satellite, arrival hall, Gatwick Village, departure hall.
Showers	North: Toilets. South: Gatwick Village.
Restaurant	South: Gatwick Village.
Self-service, bar	North: Transit area, The Avenue. South: Transit area, arrival hall, Gatwick Village.
Shopping	North: The Avenue. South: Gatwick Village.
Duty-free shops	Both terminals: Transit areas.
Tourist information	South: Arrival hall, near train station.
Accommodation	Both terminals: Arrival halls.
Foreign exchange	North: Arrival hall, The Avenue. South: Arrival and departure halls.
Post office	South: Gatwick Village.

London Heathrow Airport

Heathrow, one of the busiest airports in the world, is confusing, not a user-friendly place. Be prepared for crowds and bad sign-posting. Terminal 1 handles European airlines' Continental flights, Terminal 2 British Airways' domestic and European flights. Terminal 3 handles most intercontinental flights except BA which are at Terminal 4, with BA Amsterdam and Paris flights, as well as KLM, NLM, and Air Malta. This logical arrangement may change after modifications at Terminal 3.

Ground transport

The Piccadilly Line of London Underground has two stations at the airport, Terminal 4 and Terminals 1,2,3 combined. Trains run every 3–7 minutes from 5:00 till 1:00. Travel time between Heathrow and Central London (Piccadilly

Circus) is 47 minutes. London Transport's Airbuses run every 20–30 minutes from 6:00 till 21:30. Line A1 goes to Victoria Bus Station, Line A3 to Euston Station; travel times are 60 and 65–80 minutes, respectively. Inquire at information desks or Underground station about other stops.

Arrival

Terminal 3: In the immigration hall, after passport control, check the indicator for your flight number and the corresponding baggage belt; stairs down to the baggage claim area are numbered the same as the belts. Exit through customs to arrival hall, turn left to ramp and escalators to Underground station and trains to the city. Airbuses stop outside the concourse.

Terminal 4: From the immigration hall go downstairs to the baggage claim area, exit through customs to arrival hall, turn right to escalators to Underground station and trains to the city. Airbuses stop outside the concourse.

Departure

Terminal 3: From the Tube station take walkway and ramp up to check-in area (buses stop outside). Look for your airline's desk to check in. Go up to next level and through passport control to the departure lounge.

Terminal 4: From the Tube station take escalators up to departure level to check in. Go through passport control behind check-in desks and into the transit area.

Services

Airline information	Both terminals: Arrival halls and transit areas.
Airline tickets	Both terminals: Departure halls and transit areas.
Train information	Both terminals: Arrival halls.
First aid	Airport Information desks or phone 745-7047.
Lost & found	Ground floor exit of Car Park 2, opposite Terminal 2.
Help for handicapped	Contact your airline or Airport Information Desk.
Nursery	Terminal 3: Departure hall (upper level). Terminal 4: Departure hall (check-in area); transit area.
Toilets	Both terminals: Both levels.
Restaurants, bars	Both terminals: Departure halls (upper level).
Duty-free shops	Both terminals: Transit areas.
Tourist info., accommodation	Both terminals: Arrival halls.
City transit information	Underground station for Terminals 1,2,3.
Foreign exchange	Terminal 3: Arrival hall; transit area. Terminal 4: Arrival hall; check-in area.
Post office	Terminal 4: Departure hall.

Luxembourg Findel Airport

A simple and small airport and a railway station to match just manage to cope with the periodic inundations of travelers who pack the bargain Icelandair flights and connecting trains to Paris and Swiss cities.

Ground transport

City bus No.9 runs every 20 minutes, airport bus every hour between the airport and the railway station; travel time is about 20 minutes. You may pay the fare in foreign currency. On the city bus buy a ticket for baggage.

Arrival

Walk from the plane or ride the bus to arrival gates. For connecting flights proceed to transfer desk, then up to the transit lounge.

To exit, go through passport control, then up the escalator to the baggage claim area. TV monitors over carousels show flight numbers for arriving baggage. Exit through customs to front hall. The city bus stops on the other side of the front plaza, airport bus just outside the exit.

Departure

Take city or airport bus from outside the railway station; arrive in front of airport terminal. Entering the concourse, ticket counters to the left, check-in desks opposite. Desks 1 and 2 handle last-minute departures. Go through passport control in center of front hall to transit lounge.

Services

Airline information	Concourse, center.
Airline tickets	Concourse, left.
Train information	Limited; see Tourist info.
Lost & found	Baggage claim area; concourse, left.
Help for handicapped	Contact any airport employee.
Nursery	Transit area, upper level.
Toilets	Concourse, center; Transit area, arrival hall and upper level.
Restaurant	Concourse, upper level; Transit area, upper level.
Duty-free shops	Transit area.
Tourist info	Concourse, center.
Foreign exchange	Concourse, upper level; Transit area, upper level.
Post, telephone	Concourse, upper level; Transit area, upper level.

Paris Roissy-Charles-de-Gaulle Airport

Aérogare 1 handles transatlantic flights by airlines other than Air France, Aérogare 2 (Terminal A) handles Air France flights, including the Concorde.

Ground transport

Rapid transit trains *(Roissyrail,* RER Line B) run from 5:05 till 11:45 every 15 minutes between the airport station (Roissy-Charles-de-Gaulle) and six stations in Paris. Travel time between the airport and Gare du Nord is 35 minutes. Other Paris stops are Châtelet-les-Halles, St-Michel, Luxembourg, Port Royal, Denfert-Rochereau, Cité Universitaire. Roissyrail trains are marked ECHO, EDEN, ELAN, ERIC, ETAL or ETEL. A free shuttle bus *(navette)* runs between the airport station and terminal buildings. The fare to Gare du Nord is covered by Eurail and Paris tourist passes.

City buses (RATP) run every 20 minutes between the airport and Gare de l'Est (No.350) and Place de la Nation (No.351). Travel time is 50 minutes.

Airport buses (Air France) run from 6:00 to 23:00 every 12 minutes between the airport and Arc de Triomphe/Avenue Carnot, stopping at Porte Maillot. Travel time is 40 minutes.

Aérogare 1
Arrival

From the plane take the moving walkway to the transit level of the central building. To transfer go to a connecting flights desk.

Go through passport control, then up to arrival level and baggage claim area where TV monitors over carousels show flight numbers. Exit through customs to outer hall. Find rail information and validate Eurailpass at SNCF desk near Gate 28. Take the shuttle bus from Gate 28/30 to the airport railway station and transfer to train for the city.

Departure

Arriving from the city at the airport railway station take shuttle bus to the terminal; arrive on departure level. TV monitor shows the check-in desk for each flight. After check-in take moving walkway up to the transit level, go through passport control to transit area and walkways to satellites.

Services

Airline information	ADP desk on arrival level at Gates 34–36.
Airline tickets	Departure level check-in area.
Train information, tickets	SNCF desk on arrival level at Gate 28.
First aid	Boutiquaire level (elevator at Gate 34).

Lost & found	Boutiquaire level baggage store, or ADP duty office.
Help for handicapped	Bel-Air desk on departure level at Gates 8/10. Elevators at Gates 14/16 and 34/36.
Nursery	Boutiquaire level; transit area
Toilets	Arrival level, at Gates 4, 18, 24; boutiquaire level.
Showers	Transit area.
Restaurant, self-service	Boutiquaire level; transit area.
Bar, buffet	Arrival level at Gates 34/36; transit area; boutiquaire level.
Shopping	Boutiquaire level.
Duty-free shops	Transit area. Note: purchases at duty-free prices in shops on the boutiquaire level are delivered to the transit area.
Tourist information	ADP desk on arrival level at Gates 34/36.
Foreign exchange	Arrival level at Gate 18. Departure level at Gates 24/28.
Post, telephone	Boutiquaire level; transit area.

Aérogare 2, Terminal A
Arrival
Enter transit area from the piers. For connecting flights go down to lower level. Go through passport control to baggage claim area; TV monitors indicate belt numbers. Exit through customs. Take the shuttle bus from Gate A5 to airport railway station and transfer there to train for the city.

Departure
Arriving from the city at the airport railway station take the shuttle bus to the terminal; arrive outside concourse. Find check-in desks at Gates A3 and A8; TV monitors show positions by flight numbers. After check-in go through passport control opposite Gate 4 or 7 to the transit area.

Services

Airline information	ADP desk on main level between Gates A5 and A6. Transfer desks on lower level in transit area.
Airline tickets	Check-in areas on main level at Gates A3 and A8.
Train information, tickets	SNCF desk on lower level at Gate A10 (Boutiquaire).
First aid	Lower level at Gate A1.
Lost & found	Main level at Gate A1. Near customs in transit area.
Help for handicapped	Telephone on main level outside Gates A4 and A5 or ADP desk.
Nursery	Lower level, by elevator between Gates A5 and A6.
Toilets	Main and lower levels near Gates A2 and A8; main and lower levels at both ends of transit area.

Showers	Lower level, by elevator between Gates A5 and A6.
Restaurant, self-service	Main level at Gate A10; mezzanine in transit area.
Shopping	Lower level between Gates A10 and B1 (Boutiquaire).
Duty-free shops	Main and lower levels in transit area.
Pharmacy	Lower level at Gate B1 (Boutiquaire).
Tourist information	ADP desk on main level between Gates A5 and A6.
Foreign exchange	Main level, facing Gate A5.
Post, telephone	Lower level at Gate A10 (Boutiquaire).

Paris Orly Airport, Orly Sud

International flights are handled at Orly Sud, domestic at Orly Ouest.

The Orly Sud terminal building has five levels. We have followed the French system of numbering floors (for example, European first floor or *premier étage* is the equivalent of the second floor in the US), to conform with airport signs.

Ground transport

Rapid transit trains (*Orlyrail*, RER Line C) run from 5:30 to 21:00 every 15–30 minutes between the airport station (Pont de Rungis) and eight stations in Paris. Travel time between Gare d'Austerlitz and the airport is 35 minutes. Other Paris stops are Pont St-Michel, Quai d'Orsay, Invalides, Pont de l'Alma, Champ de Mars, Javel, Blvd. Victor; airport trains are marked ROMI or MONA. A free shuttle bus *(navette)* runs between the airport station and terminal building. The fare to Gare du Nord is covered by Eurail and Paris tourist passes.

City buses (RATP's *Orlybus*) run from 6:00 to 21:00 every 15 minutes between the airport and Denfert-Rochereau métro station. Travel time is 25 minutes.

Airport buses (Air France) run from 5:50 to 23:00 every 12 minutes between the airport and Les Invalides, with stops at Montparnasse, Porte d'Orléans, and Duroc. Travel time is 30 minutes.

Arrival

From the plane, enter the transit area on the first floor. For connecting flights, go to the transfer desk. Exit through passport control and go downstairs to find the baggage claim area to your right, past the meeting point. Flight numbers are displayed above belts. Go out through customs. Take shuttle bus at Gate I to the airport railway station and transfer there to train for the city.

Departure

Arriving at the airport railway station take the shuttle bus to the terminal; arrive outside concourse. Check-in desks are in three areas; enter Gates K–L for Area 1, Gate N for Area 2, Gate R for Area 3. TV monitors show check-in desks for flights. After check-in follow signs *Salon Espace* to stairway in the center, Area 1. Access to the upper level public area is only allowed with boarding pass, although you may take guests. Go through passport control here. Departing flights are listed on an indicator facing passport control and in the center of the next floor.

Services

Airline information	ADP desk on main floor, opposite Gate H. Transit area, 1st floor.
Airline tickets	Main floor.
Train information	SNCF desk on main floor, near Gate H.
First aid	1st floor, stairway 1.
Lost & found	Main floor, opposite Gates F-H.
Help for handicapped	Telephone at Gate N or contact any airport employee.
Nursery	Transit area, 2nd floor, *Salon Espace*.
Toilets	Basement, under Gates H, M; Transit area, 1st and 2nd floors.
Showers	Transit area, 2nd floor, *Salon Espace*.
Restaurant	Transit area, 3rd floor.
Bar, buffet	Landside and transit areas, all floors.
Provisions, shopping	Supermarket in basement.
Duty-free shops	Transit area, 1st floor.
Pharmacy	Basement.
Tourist information	ADP desk on main floor, opposite Gate H.
Foreign exchange	Main floor, near Gate F.
Post, telephone	1st floor; Basement; Orly Ouest Arrivals; Transit area, 1st floor.

Rome Leonardo da Vinci Airport (Fiumicino)

Ground transport

Trains run every 20 minutes between the airport and Roma-Ostiense station; travel time is 20 minutes.

Buses run every 15 minutes from 7:00 till 24:00, then hourly all night between the airport (outside the arrival area of the International Terminal) and Termini railway station (bus terminal in Via Giolitti); travel time is about 50 minutes.

Arrival

Coming from the plane through the pier or by bus, you arrive in the transit area and go through passport control on the ground floor. The baggage claim area is on the left. TV monitors show carousel numbers for each flight. After passing through customs, turn left and take the elevator to the upper level, then the moving walkway to the train station. The bus ticket office is on the right in the arrival area. Taxis stop in the center, outside.

Departure

Trains leave from Roma-Ostiense station. At the airport station, go straight ahead from the platform to the International Terminal. In the departure area there are five rows of check-in desks, A and B reserved for Alitalia. TV monitors show the check-in desk for each flight. Go through passport control behind row A or C. In the transit area TV monitors show the gate numbers for flights.

Services

Airline information	Departure hall, opposite row A; arrival hall, right from exit; transit area, centre.
Airline tickets	Departure hall, opposite check-in rows.
Train information, tickets	Airport train station; CIT office in arrival area, left from exit.
First aid	Call 6012 3133 on the house phone.
Police	Call 60121 on the house phone.
Lost & found	Baggage claim area, far end.
Help for handicapped	Transit area, near Gate 35 or contact your airline.
Nursery	Transit area, near Gate 35.
Toilets	Arrival hall, both ends; departure hall, near row A; transit area, near gates.
Restaurant	Transit area, upper level.
Bar buffet	Arrival hall, left of customs; departure hall, near row E; transit area, center.
Duty-free shops	Transit area, center.
Tourist information, accommodation	Arrival hall, left of customs.
Foreign exchange	Arrival hall, left after passport control; transit area, near Gate 34.
Post Office	Departure hall, opposite row D (also in Domestic Terminal).
Telephone	Assisted only for long distance calls, transit area, opposite Gate 32.

Zurich Kloten Airport

Kloten is a sociable airport. Its shops, supermarket, and restaurants are patronized by townspeople, much like the Hauptbahnhof, especially on Sundays when the city shuts down. Of course, the airport has its own railway station.

Terminals A (Europe and US) and B (other international flights) are joined by Parkhaus B which houses the *Plaza* shopping area and the railway station underneath.

Ground transport

Trains run between the airport and Hauptbahnhof from 5:16 to 23:48 at intervals from 3 to 25 minutes; travel time is 10–12 minutes. The airport station is on the main rail line and has direct intercity trains to Basel, Bern, Geneva, Lausanne, Lucerne, Lugano, St. Gallen, and Winterthur. With the *Fly-Rail Baggage* system you can forward baggage from the arrival halls to any destination in Switzerland.

Arrival

Terminal A: Walk along pier to passport control. For connecting flights find transfer desks before customs. Baggage claim is to the right; TV monitors show belt number for each flight. Go through customs to the arrival hall. Buses and taxis stop outside. The railway desk for baggage forwarding is to your right. Follow signs to the station.

Terminal B: The pier leads to the transit area. For connecting flights find transfer desks to the left.

Go through passport control, then down to baggage claim area on the right. Flight numbers are shown over belts. Exit through customs to the arrival hall. Buses and taxis stop outside. The railway desk for baggage forwarding is in the center. Follow signs to the upper level and across bridge to the station.

Departure

Arriving at the airport station follow signs up to the departure level (baggage carts may be taken on escalators) of either terminal.

Terminal A: In the departure hall US airlines' check-in desks are to the right. Go through passport control in the center. Duty-free shops are on the arrival level, below, and in the pier.

Terminal B: Information desks are on the right, check-in desks in the center and left. Go through passport control behind rows 3–4 and down to the transit level. The pier is ahead, shopping and waiting areas behind the stairs.

Services

Airline information	A: arrival hall, center; transit area, pier. B: arrival hall, right; departure hall, left; transit area, at pier entrance.
Airline tickets	A: departure hall, right. B: departure hall, left.
Train information, tickets	A: arrival hall, right. B: arrival hall, center. Railway station, Parkhaus B, lower level.
First aid	A: arrival hall, left end. B: departure hall, left end (if closed, use telephone).
Police	Parkhaus B, railway station level.
Lost & found	Both terminals: baggage claim areas.
Help for handicapped	Both terminals: contact any airport employee.
Nursery	A: transit area, pier entrance. B: transit area, left from stairs.
Toilets	Both terminals: arrival and departure halls; transit areas, both levels and in pier; Plaza.
Restaurants	A: departure hall; transit area, arrival level. B: departure hall; transit area, right from stairs; Plaza; railway station.
Bar, buffet	Both terminals: both levels, transit areas, Pier A, Plaza.
Provisions, shopping	Plaza and Bahnhofhalle in Parkhaus B. Pharmacy—Plaza.
Duty-free shops	A: transit area, arrival level and in pier. B: transit area, middle level.
Tourist information	A: arrival hall, right (if closed, Terminal B). B: arrival hall, left from customs exit.
Foreign exchange	A: arrival hall; transit area, baggage claim area. B: arrival hall, right; departure hall, right; transit area, right from stairs.
Post, telephone	A: transit area, arrival level; Plaza.

THE GREAT ROUTES

A hundred and fifty years ago the first short stretches of uneven rails were laid near the highways. In those days a pair of good horses could easily overtake the wheezing little steam engines dragging rickety carriages. But the experiment gradually turned into the fastest and most comfortable way to travel. The tracks were extended and connected, then the single pairs of rails doubled for two-way traffic. The new iron roads followed the trade routes. These 'great routes' form the basis of the modern European railway network. Today's trains still follow the old paths of mail wagons and link all major cities.

Holiday travel is more than just getting from one point to another as quickly as possible. You can enjoy it for its own sake. Even if you travel on business, you should relieve the pressure of a hectic schedule by taking the occasional slow train, with a stop-off in a picturesque village. And if the train should stop on the open track in the middle of nowhere, open the window and breathe in the silence of the countryside.

In this section you'll find what to expect in the way of services, and notes on the scenery along the tracks. While the great routes follow the demands of trade rather than esthetics, many take you past spectacular sights, such as the Rhine Valley, the hills of Tuscany or the mountains and lakes of Switzerland.

North to Northwest

Helsinki–Stockholm–Copenhagen–Hamburg–Amsterdam–London
To say that there isn't much worth seeing between Helsinki and London sounds arrogant. But let's admit that the flat and boring stretches don't particularly invite daytime travel. However, there are beautiful cities along the way where you can—and should—stop for a day, continuing the journey at night to the next. Three days of sightseeing break the long journey into four night rides: Helsinki–Stockholm, Stockholm–Copenhagen, Copenhagen–Amsterdam, and Amsterdam–London.

Helsinki–Stockholm

There are three ways to travel this leg: expensively by air, interminably by train (thirty hours around the Gulf of Bothnia) or pleasantly by boat. With a Eurailpass you travel free on Silja Lines between Stockholm, Turku and Helsinki, and at half fare between Helsinki and Lübeck-Travemünde. The refurbished Silja ships offer more than transportation: these floating hotels have restaurants, nightclubs, casinos, saunas, and swimming pools.

Unlike many sea voyages, the Helsinki–Stockholm route keeps you on deck with spectacular scenery. Outside Helsinki and near Stockholm the ship weaves its way between hundreds of islands, smooth bare rocks or covered with forest, dotted with cottages along the shores. The night ferries sail from Helsinki at 18:00, still in bright daylight in the northern summer. There is ample time to enjoy the view before going below to stock up at the duty-free shop, eat your way through the mile-long smorgasbord, dance in the disco or relax in the bar before going to sleep (cabins cost about $50 per person, double occupancy).

The ferries from Turku take an even more scenic route, passing among the countless islands of the Ålands and making a brief stop at Mariehamn. The morning boat leaves at 10:00, the night ferry at 21:30 (trains from Helsinki to Turku take 2 hours 25 minutes). The night ferry from Helsinki arrives in Stockholm at 9:00, from Turku at 7:00, leaving a long day at your disposal to see some of the city.

Stockholm–Copenhagen/Malmö

The forested, lake-dotted Swedish landscape is magnificent and you can gaze upon it for over seven hours from one of the day trains to Malmö or Copenhagen. Trains run right through to Copenhagen, taken on board the ferry between Helsingborg and Helsingør. Buffet cars with self-service are carried on all trains.

If you find a day of unrelenting beauty too much to bear, then enjoy Stockholm, take a night train, and sleep through Sweden. The night trains carry first and second-class sleepers and couchettes. While couchettes may be the budget traveler's instinctive choice, the tourist triples are only slightly more expensive, and outside peak travel times it's rare to find more than two beds occupied. Night trains have no meal services.

The route offers an optional visit to Malmö, a pretty town with a beautifully restored old quarter. Include it in your itinerary if you have an extra day. Also, if you want to spend a night, Malmö is less expensive than Copenhagen. The catamaran service between the two cities takes 45 minutes.

The night trains arrive quite early, giving you plenty of time for a shower and breakfast at the station before setting out.

Copenhagen–Amsterdam

There are many day trains to Hamburg but the EC-*Merkur* is the most comfortable and the fastest, getting there in about five hours. It's an interesting trip. The train crosses several bridges between islands until Rødby, where it rolls aboard the ferry for the hour-long sea voyage to Puttgarden. You can stroll on deck, have a short lunch, or visit the duty-free shop which sells, besides liquor and cigarettes, sides of smoked salmon, smoked eel and cheeses.

Unfortunately, the Hamburg–Amsterdam leg takes up to six hours through flat industrial landscape. Quite boring and with scarce meal services. Unless you want to see Hamburg, take the overnight Nord-West Express from Copenhagen (second-class couchettes only). The train goes via Rotterdam to Hook of Holland and connects to the day sailing to Harwich. For Amsterdam, change at Amersfoort.

Amsterdam–London

Crossing the Channel where it's narrow wastes most of a day or turns a night into misery (see THE CHANNEL page 299). The distance between Hook and Harwich allows a decent night's sleep. A place in a two-berth cabin with shower and toilet costs $26; first-class singles start at $51. Don't touch the food on board!

The Harwich–London train is a rather nondescript one, usually crowded, but fortunately you have to bear with it for only an hour and a quarter before arriving at Liverpool Street Station.

Helsinki–Hamburg

You can travel through Scandinavia on a round trip instead of backtracking if you go directly from Finland to Germany by sea. Silja Lines provides the fastest passage with the Finnjet, the world's only jet-powered passenger ship. The middle of the Baltic offers less to see but there is plenty of entertainment on board. Watch films, try your luck at the blackjack or roulette tables, go shopping, dance in the disco, sample from the endless smorgasbord table. The ship also has a sauna and a piano bar.

The trip between Helsinki and Lübeck-Travemünde takes two nights in low season but between June 13 and August 20 the gas turbines kick in and move the giant at 56 km/h, to cover the distance in 23 hours. With a Eurailpass you pay half fare, about $90 in a four-berth C cabin, about $115 in a two-berth B cabin. Reserve at least a week in advance. For information and reservations contact Bergen Line in the US (tel. 1-800-323-7436), or Silja Line in Canada (tel. 1-800-268-3700).

The Channel

The trip between Britain and the Continent is nothing to write home about. It is mentioned in letters only when the crossing was rough, that is, when the elements added more unpleasantness to an already wearying journey. It takes too long with cumbersome transfers.

Both the past and future of cross-channel services look better than the present. Once one could cross in a civilized way aboard the train called Night Ferry. Passengers took to sleeping berths in the evening, right in the middle of London or Paris or Brussels, to wake up in another city after a full night's sleep. The sleeping cars rolled aboard the ferry and sailed right through. In 1993 direct service returns when the trains go through the Channel Tunnel, without change between London and Paris or Brussels, but in three hours instead of overnight. Planes and passenger ferries will be mothballed. You'll be able to board a morning train in London, settle down with a newspaper, or look at the countryside (except for the brief time under the sea), and arrive in the middle of Paris by ten. After a day of business or shopping you can have dinner, then hop back on the train and home and bed by eleven. Or you could just change trains and get to Marseille, ready to wade into the Mediterranean at about three in the afternoon.

Currently the boat trains run from London Victoria, Paris Nord, and Brussels Zuid/Midi, the day ferries between Dover or Folkestone and Boulogne, Calais, or Ostend. The same warning applies to all crossings: approach restaurant food aboard ferries with caution and only if you are desperate!

London–Paris

City to city travel takes up to seven and a half hours by rail and ship. The fast service by hovercraft takes six hours, about 90 minutes less; the crossing itself is only 35 minutes, but travel time is long because of inconvenient bus transfers between trains and hoverports, handy only to cars. There are four crossings a day by ship and four by hovercraft (these may change).

The night crossing via Newhaven–Dieppe takes over nine hours with transfers before dawn. The Portsmouth–Le Havre night service lets you sleep till about seven.

London–Brussels

Ship and train take under eight hours by day, eight and a half hours at night (docking before dawn). There are two day crossings, one at night. The fast jetfoil service takes less than five hours. Three jet-foil arrivals are met by trains running through to Cologne via Brussels. There are four crossings a day.

London–Rotterdam/Amsterdam via Harwich and Hook of Holland

This long crossing allows a good night's sleep in inexpensive cabins. Some long-distance expresses connect directly to the boat at Hook of Holland, then go through Rotterdam (Schiedam or West station, not Centraal) to points east without touching Amsterdam. Boat trains leave from London Liverpool Street, Rotterdam West, and Amsterdam CS.

Flanders to the Riviera overnight

Amsterdam–Brussels–Paris–Marseille–Nice–Ventimiglia

The journey takes nearly twenty hours, not only because it spans most of Europe, but because of frequent stops, designed to collect passengers from most of northwestern Europe on their way to the sun. Nowadays few travelers dedicate that much time to a single trip, especially if it means passing through Brussels and Paris without stopping for a visit. But the Flandres-Riviera is a classic. It has always been a tempting escape from the damp and cold of the North Sea for a few weeks under a friendlier clime. As the train clattered through the rainy afternoon it would gradually fill with Dutch burgher families, Belgian businessmen and French vacationers on their way to the Mediterranean sun next morning.

The train leaves Amsterdam at 15:54 (on most days; check a current schedule). It carries only day cars and couchettes till Brussels, where it picks up sleepers. It joins the Calais train at Paris-Nord. You have half an hour here to buy something for a midnight snack and breakfast before the night-long haul begins.

The train is in no hurry: a TGV would make it to Lyon by 1:00, but the Flandres-Riviera stops just past 4:00 to pick up some early birds. If you're lucky, they won't claim a berth in your compartment for a couple of hours of sleep.

Move to the window after leaving Marseille around eight. On the right side of the train the Mediterranean sparkles, on the left spread rocky slopes and subtropical green. The view compensates for the skimpy meal service, a mini-bar trolley till Nice, nothing after that.

After 45 minutes you pass Toulon, an hour later St-Raphaël. Then the train stops every 10–20 minutes at the playgrounds of the Riviera: Cannes, Juan-les-Pins, Antibes. The Calais cars are taken off in Nice, the rest go on to Beaulieu-sur-Mer, Monaco-Monte Carlo, Menton and finally Ventimiglia, the Italian border.

The Flandres-Riviera Express is now a workhorse that has seen better days. It is slow and suffers from a lack of proper meal services: nothing during the week, a dining car from Brussels to Ventimiglia on Fridays and Saturdays, back on Saturdays and Sundays only. But if you catch it when it's not crowded (which, however, it always is around holiday times), you can enjoy a taste of leisurely travel.

A London connection leaves Victoria at 14:30. Passengers may move into their through sleepers or couchette in Calais.

Riviera

Marseille–Cannes–Nice–Ventimiglia

Europe's playground lies along the 113-km stretch between St-Raphaël and San Remo. On one side of the tracks the Mediterranean crashes against the rocks and washes the beach; on the other side craggy cliffs and semi-tropical greenery alternate. Trains cross the Riviera in two hours or less, not enough time for passengers to savor the scenery. But you can explore the coast in a leisurely way by stopping at each pretty place for a few hours. Cannes, Antibes, Juan-les-Pins, Nice, Beaulieu, Monaco, Menton, Ventimiglia, San Remo are only 10–15 minutes apart.

Through trains from Paris to Ventimiglia on the Italian border used to run day and night until the TGV knocked them off the track. From Paris eleven high-speed trains a day reach Marseille in less than five hours. Only one a day runs through to Nice, more often you have to change in Marseille. Night expresses still run, though, from Paris, Brussels, and Amsterdam; these usually go as far as Nice.

However, there are plenty of trains from Marseille or Toulon to Nice, overlapping with others from Cannes to Ventimiglia, the Italian border, and beyond to San Remo, some to Genoa or Milan. You can hop off the train to visit a town without having to wait long for the next. Make sure that you sit on the right side of eastbound trains and left on westbound; that's where the sun and the sea are, the reasons for going there.

Service aboard the trains doesn't match the glamour evoked by the names of stations. None of them carry dining cars, some not even a buffet. But you can stop for a seafood platter in Nice, then have dessert in Antibes, and enjoy namedropping for years to come ("As I was sipping a St-Raphaël in St-Raphaël...").

The River Rhine

According to nationality, and preference for Strauss or Wagner, Europeans choose the Danube or the Rhine for queen of the rivers. The Danube walzes from the Black Forest through Central and Eastern Europe to the Black Sea; drops of it may wash over to the Asian shore. The Rhine is all Western European, starting from the Bodensee (Lake Constance), marking the Swiss-German border for a while, then turning north at Basel, serving again as a border between France and Germany, flowing through the German Rhineland, and crossing into the Netherlands on its way to the southernmost part of the North Sea at Rotterdam. It has been a busy road since before Roman times, front line in wars, inspiration of poems, source of many legends, and a favorite destination of travelers attracted by its natural beauty, romantic ruins, and fine wines.

Lest we forget the Rheingold

The legendary treasure of the river, the Rheingold, gave its name to an opera and a train. With an apology to Wagner fans, we'll commemorate the fine train that doesn't exist anymore.

The *Rheingold* started in the 1930s, when the speed and comfort of a grand express easily surpassed that of cars on bad roads and rickety planes. While the great night trains were dubbed hotels on wheels, the *Rheingold* on its daylight run was more like an elegant club. The members sprawled in armchairs, savored haute cuisine in the restaurant, then relaxed while watching the ever-changing view from the dome car. Only station marshallers hated the train: it took a lot of handling. Cars came from Hook of Holland, Amsterdam, Berlin and Hanover to be joined for the spectacular run through the Rhine Valley, then split apart in Basel on their way to Geneva, Chur and Milan. During the post-war rail renaissance the *Rheingold* received special attention and became a Trans-Europ-Express that featured not only a dining car but a club car with bar, full table service, and occasional entertainment. When the TEEs began to disappear, downgraded into two-class trains, the *Rheingold* stayed on as the pride of the German Federal Railroad, *"der Komfortzug der Bahn"*. But this fine showpiece cost too much to run and the accountants finally had their way. The great express stopped. One ray of hope: the German railway has reserved the use of the name of the train, perhaps not out of respect for the deceased, but with the idea of resurrecting it one day.

Successor trains

As many as ten EuroCity trains pass Lorelei Rock and the most romantic section of the river between Cologne and Mainz. Of these, the *Erasmus* and *Frans Hals* follow the *Rheingold*'s route from Amsterdam to Frankfurt before turning off toward Munich via Würzburg. The *Leonardo da Vinci* follows the route of the old summer section to Munich via Stuttgart (ending in Milan). But if you want to relive the golden days, ride the *Rembrandt* from Amsterdam through Basel to Chur. Take a table on the left side of the dining car (going south) for the river view.

Flying the Rhine

Four times a day the Lufthansa Airport Express speeds past the Rhine at ground level. See page 112.

The River Road

The best use of a train ticket here is to exchange it for one on a ship. For a truly unforgettable day (or two) of scenery and leisure, take the river road aboard a Köln-Düsseldorfer ship. All ships have good restaurants, lots of lounging space on several decks, and, of course, a close view of the river-life around you.

The non-stop trip from Mainz to Cologne takes ten hours. Going upstream you have to take the journey in segments, with transfers. The Cologne ship reaches Koblenz at 17:00, leaving you time for a stroll through the town and along the Rhine or Mosel before settling down to taste Germany's best wines. Overnight accommodation is not expensive in the many small hotels near the railway station. The morning boat leaves Koblenz for Mainz at 11:00. Other ships make frequent stops at towns where you can board, or disembark to continue by train.

Train tickets are valid with an exchange fee, payable at any KD landing stage. Travel is free with Eurailpasses and GermanRail Tourist Cards, half fare with Eurail Youthpass and Inter-Rail Card. Cruise ships with cabin accommodations are not included. For three to five-day cruises inquire at KD offices landing stages or in overseas German tourist offices.

Holland–France

Amsterdam–Brussels–Paris

From the lowlands of the Netherlands to the flatlands of Flanders, train passengers turn from the windows to other entertainment. This route has always been known for good food, as you would expect between Brussels and Paris. The tradition of fine Trans-Europ-Express dining cars has been maintained by the EuroCity trains.

InterCity trains run nearly hourly between Amsterdam and Brussels, taking little over three hours. These are also the best services to Rotterdam and Antwerp. Four of the Amsterdam trains continue from Brussels to Paris and another seven from Brussels provide an almost hourly service to Paris in two and a half hours.

The best train from Amsterdam is the EC-*Étoile du Nord*. As on other InterCity trains, the meal service consists solely of snacks between Amsterdam and Brussels. Most trains carry dining cars only between Brussels and Paris. Three ex-TEEs, the *Brabant*, the *Ile de France*, and the *Rubens*, run between Brussels and Paris. Perhaps in consideration of the well-heeled clientele on this section, the usual EuroCity rule of two classes is not enforced: the *Ile de France* and *Rubens* have only first-class cars.

The night train between Amsterdam and Paris ambles along for over eight hours and gives you just about enough time for a decent night's sleep. It stops in Brussels after 1:00 one way and after 4:00 the other for those desperate to get there early—or late. Its main attraction for Eurailpass travelers is that it carries very comfortable first-class couchettes which cost less than half as much as a hotel room in either Paris or Amsterdam.

Trains stop at Brussels Noord and Zuid/Midi (some, not all, at Centraal), and arrive in Gare du Nord in Paris.

France South-East

Paris–Dijon–Lyon–Avignon–Marseille–Nice

The high-speed trains sweep through rolling meadows, fly above wide valleys on long viaducts. But gourmets would rather walk in pious pilgrimage. This is Burgundy, where every other name speaks to the palate: Bresse chicken and blue cheese, Charolais beef, Dijon mustard (and Kir, the drink of the mayor, Canon Kir), dishes *à la bourguignonne* and everything to drink with them. A small, nondescript new train station gains a special appeal by being named Mâcon. As a train passenger you only gaze at the countryside that brings forth these wonders, and make do with microwaved fare till you reach the culinary capital, Lyon.

The route from Paris to Lyon and beyond to Marseille has always had good service. Once it was run by the glamorous Paris-Lyon-Mediterranée company that conveyed vacationers to the Riviera in romantic trains like *Le Train Bleu*. Now you travel in less luxury, but with more speed, on the orange *Train à Grande Vitesse*.

The TGV *Sud-Est*

The first high-speed train in Europe, and until recently with the highest commercial speed in the world at 275 km/h (172 mph), runs on tracks laid and reserved for passenger traffic. The new line goes to Lyon, France's second largest city, but many trains bypass Lyon on their way to major cities to the east and south.

The Paris–Lyon service (travel time: two hours) consists of twenty-four trains a day, half-hourly at peak times, other times hourly. The Paris–Midi run has nineteen trains to Avignon, six to Montpellier, eleven to Marseille; two continue to Nice. On the Paris–Jura route ten trains go to Dijon, four to Lausanne, one to Bern. The Paris–Savoie service has five trains daily to Geneva, three to Annecy, five to Chambéry; occasional trains go to Grenoble.

Each train has 386 seats; at peak times two sets run coupled together for a capacity of over 750. The only difference between classes is in seating: two on each side of the aisle in second class, two and one in first. Unfortunately, the French adopted an American design—inspired by buses—for the interior and installed seats facing one way. But enough passengers voiced their dislike of economizing at the cost of the quality of travel to get better design in the second-generation TGV *Atlantique*.

The smooth ride seems to disappoint travelers who expect something exciting. "Oh, the TGV," they say, "it's just like any other train." Exactly. You don't want to feel like an astronaut or a stock-car driver, or have your wine spilled as you get where you want to be in half the time.

Catering is on the economical and practical side with minimal staff. Buffets are carried on all trains, accessible from both first and second class. They serve sandwiches, pizza and *croque monsieur* (tasty grilled sandwiches), coffee and drinks. Full meals are served at the passengers' seats in first class; these have to be ordered in advance. Cold meals are served at seats in second class.

Departures from Paris are from the Gare du Lyon, which has a new section with direct access to the TGV platforms. The fares are the same as on ordinary trains with a supplement only at peak times, weekday mornings, Friday evenings and some holidays. Reservation is compulsory but included in the fare. Last-minute passengers can reserve at automats within 90 minutes of departure, as long as seats are available. Handicapped passengers in wheel chairs are accommodated in one of the first-class cars at second-class fare.

Other trains

When the TGV service began in 1981, it cut the travel time between Paris and Lyon in half. Before the end of the year passengers averaged 14,000 a day; at the end of 1983 there were 33,800 a day. In three years 28 million people traveled on the TGV. There have been no accidents.

Obviously, the conventional service was affected. The famous TEE-*Mistral* and several through trains have disappeared, as has the Geneva night train. One daytime *rapide* completes the old route from Paris to Ventimiglia, others stop at Valence, Avignon or Marseille. The daytime way to the Riviera is by TGV to Marseille or Toulon, then change (see RIVIERA, page 301).

The night trains still offer the surprise of waking up in your berth to the light of the sunny Med. The *Train Bleu*, not as plush as before but still very comfortable, and *L'Esterel* run every day with first and second-class couchettes and sleeping cars, including second-class doubles (T2). Several others fill in on busy weekends during the summer.

France Atlantic

Paris–Bordeaux and Paris–Brittany

France's second busiest route is from Paris to the southwest. Until the TGV *Sud-Est* started service on the other side of the country, Europe's fastest trains ran here, the Trans-Europ-Expresses *Aquitaine* and *L'Etendard,* that swallowed the 580 km to Bordeaux in less than four hours. Top speed returned in 1989 with the *TGV Atlantique.*

The new line begins at Paris-Montparnasse, then splits into two branches at about 130 km from Paris. The west branch goes to Brittany with trains to Brest, Quimper, Nantes, and St-Nazaire. The southwest branch serves primarily Bordeaux, reaching it in less than three hours, with direct trains continuing to Hendaye, Tarbes, Toulouse.

The rolling stock is second-generation TGV, faster and better. Its top commercial speed is 300 km/h (186 mph). It reaches that on the new stretch of track between Paris and Le Mans, running alongside to the autoroute. The conductor announces the speed over the public address system somewhat gleefully as the train slips by the longest, widest Citroëns fighting it out with the BMWs.

But it's not the extra speed that makes the new TGV look like something out of the 21st century. The interior has been completely redesigned, this time catering to human needs rather than economic considerations. There is a choice of seating patterns from *Le Coach*—airplane-style open saloons—to *Le Quatro* compartments for four with a large table in the center. You can also reserve a *Carre, Kiosque, Club,* or *Duo,* if you've done your homework and memorized the pictures of the various arrangements in the guide booklet; obviously, the promotion boys have been busy inventing new, sexy, but utterly confusing terms. However, what's important is that the designers of the interior successfully combined comfort and good looks. The new train is a pleasure to ride and a thrill to explore, from its card telephone (you can call home at 300 km/h) to the electronic displays over the doors showing the name of the next station and the route. The simple and functional bar serves familiar-looking fast food under strange new names. Meals served at seats on first class also have arcane tags but show more of an effort to good catering.

Currently the Breton route has eight–nine trains a day, with weekends well covered for holidaymakers going to the seashore. With the opening of the Bordeaux line in 1990 the schedule of regular trains may change.

The fare on the *TGV Atlantique* is slightly higher than on other trains, but not painfully so unless you travel at peak times. You don't pay a supplement—the promoting experts got rid of that negative term—but buy reservation called *RESA*

300 that may cost as much again as the fare during certain periods. Check the date, day, and hour of your departure in *Le guide voyageurs TGV Atlantique*, a handy booklet which is distributed free at stations, to avoid unwelcome surprises.

Iberia

Spain and Portugal, now in the European Community, are still far from Europe. Waiting for a connection at the Spanish border may take nearly two hours because the proud Spanish don't fancy coordinating their schedules with Europe. You have to change because of the different gauge, unless you are on a Talgo with adjustable wheels.

The major points of departure to the Iberian Peninsula are Paris and Geneva. The Atlantic approach from Paris—via Bordeaux—takes truly long-range trains: Madrid at 1930 km is over 13—18 hours, Lisbon at 2375 km 24 hours. But you can reach Barcelona on the Mediterranean faster: from Paris or Geneva in less than 12 hours.

Going to Madrid or Barcelona, take a Talgo for a taste of fine trains. In the 1930s when they were first built, Talgos were a breakthrough in comfort and speed, and they have stood the test of time with successive technical improvements. You'll appreciate the clever details in the interior, the sensible use of space, and the smooth ride. Also, since Talgos are the pride of RENFE, the Spanish railways, they keep better time than any other train. The night Talgos (*Talgo Camas*) carry dining cars and bars. Single and double sleepers are all first class, tourist compartments with four berths are second. New *Gran Clase* compartments, single and double, have private showers and toilets. Talgos in international service are all EuroCity trains.

Paris—Madrid

For Paris—Bordeaux services, see FRANCE ATLANTIC, page 306.
South of Bordeaux travel slows down. Most through trains are that only by name. Passengers have to change trains at the border (the adjoining stations are Hendaye in France, Irún on the Spanish side). The exceptions are the through couchette cars which are put on broad-gauge bogies at Irún and the Talgos with adjustable wheels that just roll across. Regular trains take up to 18 hours with transfer at Irún. The choice train is the nightly Paris—Madrid Talgo, comfortable and the fastest at twelve and a half hours. It leaves Paris-Austerlitz at 20:00, Madrid-Chamartín at 19:40.

Paris—Barcelona

Day trains on this route via Toulouse stop at every house. The best way to go is at night with the Barcelona Talgo in less than twelve hours, leaving Paris-Austerlitz at 21:00 or Barcelona-Sants at 20:55.

Basel—Bern—Geneva—Barcelona

The day train, the Catalan Talgo, leaves Genève-Cornavin at 11:27, arrives in Barcelona-Sants at 21:18 (leaves Barcelona at 9:55, arrives in Geneva at 19:44). On the way it stops at the attractions of the Savoie: Aix-les-Bains, Chambéry, Grenoble. Coming from Paris by TGV, you can meet it in Avignon or Montpellier. Service is still as good as it was when the train ran as a TEE. The new EuroCity night train, the *Pablo Casals,* is an excellent and convenient service from Bern in twelve and a half hours, taking the same time from Geneva as the day train.

The old *Hispania* moves more slowly but goes further, taking second-class couchettes from Basel, then sleepers and couchettes of both class from Geneva. Rougher travel than by Talgo: no food services in the evening and an early morning transfer at the border.

Paris—Lisbon

The classic way is with the Sud Express which, before the jet age, conveyed passengers to ships bound for South America and Africa, and later to the Clipper seaplanes with sleeping berths to New York. If you can spare 24 hours, it's still the comfortable way to go. Pack a picnic lunch before you leave Paris at 8:42: only snacks and drinks are served during the day. The dining car is attached at the Spanish border, just in time for dinner at 17:50. Second-class couchettes, put on broad-gauge bogies at the border, go right through to Lisbon, Porto, and Vigo. First-class passengers have to transfer but discover to their delight that they may spend the night in truly classic comfort aboard one of the vintage sleeping cars of the Portuguese Railways.

Madrid—Lisbon

You have a choice between a day and a night train. The afternoon *Luis de Camões* is a Talgo with bar car which takes a little over seven hours. At night, the ominously named *Lusitania Express* has no middle ground in sleeping accommodations: there are only second-class couchettes or first-class sleepers. Choose the sleeper unless you're desperately impoverished! The dining car runs all the way.

Crossing the Alps

Between rock walls roofed by snow and ice, the few paths weave through curving gorges and twist back to find a way around hill-sized boulders. The mountaineer's dream is the roadbuilder's nightmare. Although the Alps can't stop people who, like Hannibal, are determined to get through, they do slow them down. Engineers have been trying to widen Europe's worst bottleneck for over a century. But as soon as they push a tunnel through with great effort and expense, increased traffic begins to choke it. The Gotthard, Simplon, Lötschberg—each a promised solution to the problem—bulge with trains; plans now call for a Brenner Tunnel under the Pass.

Tunnels limit the view from a train, but their approaches—rising from lake country to foothill forests, hugging steep mountain sides, balancing on high viaducts—draw passengers to the windows. The richness of it overwhelms you on any of the Swiss–Italian crossings: from the Lake of Thun through the Lötschberg, or from the Lake of Geneva to Brig, then through the Simplon and to Domodossola; from the lakes of Lucerne and Zug through the Gotthard Pass to the lakes of Lugano and Como.

The Mont Cenis
(Paris–Modane–Turin–Genoa–Rome–Naples and Turin–Milan)

Few people would think of any passage outside Switzerland as Transalpine. But this classic road between Paris and Rome crosses the Alps, albeit their westernmost bulwarks, diving under the toughest ones through the Mont Cenis Tunnel.

The line passes some respectable mountains which you can see only with the *Mont Cenis*, the daylight train between Lyon and Milan. Other direct trains travel through Savoie and Piedmont in darkness; the long ride is timed for morning arrivals in both capitals.

The old express still plying this route is the *Palatino*, now upgraded to EuroCity. Departure is early in each direction, 18:47 and 19:10, arrivals around 10:00—provided that all goes well along the way in these two most strike-happy countries. At night the train carries only sleeping cars and second-class couchettes, first-class day cars between Rome and Turin. The meal service is a buffet car, meager for a train that leaves too early for dinner at the station and arrives well after breakfast time.

If you like camping, try the workhorse *Napoli Express* which takes sixteen and a half hours to Rome, nearly twenty hours to Naples. It has sleeping cars and second-class couchettes. The meal service is even poorer than on the *Palatino*: buffet on the Italian side but only trolley fare for dinner and breakfast in France. In the summer you can get into training for a ride on the Trans-Siberian aboard this train: Boulogne-Naples couchettes (second-class) get quite crowded, take over 24 hours, and have scarce food supplies. You live on your bunk with meals from the knapsack.

The EuroCity *Stendhal* runs between Paris and Milan with sleepers and second-class couchettes. No meal service, no interesting views. A businesslike train for business people in Turin and Milan.

The Simplon route
(Geneva–Lausanne–Brig–Milan)

Your first sightseeing choice is the EuroCity *Monteverdi* that leaves Geneva at 8:11 for Venice. Three more EuroCity trains, the *Lutetia*, *Cisalpin*, and *Lemano*, have two sections: TGVs of the same name run between Paris and Lausanne where you transfer to regular trains. Good timings, complete meal service, breathtaking views. If you miss them, there are as many as twelve day trains, most from Geneva via Lausanne and Brig to Milan.

Among the night trains the natural choice for Britons starting out on an Italian tour was the Calais–Venice Through Service—which is not always there when you want it, being subject to frequent cancellations. But with a change in Paris to the EuroCity *Galilei* you can step out next morning to the sight of the Venice's Grand Canal outside Santa Lucia station—or to the din of Florence traffic on Santa Maria Novella. The *Galilei* carries sleepers, couchettes, and a buffet.

The *Simplon Express* is an offspring of the Orient Express, similarly neglected, a slow people-mover from Paris to Belgrade. Only second-class couchettes and no food whatsoever for nineteen hours. You should get off at 6:45 in Venezia-Mestre.

The St. Gotthard route
(Basel/Zurich–Chiasso–Milan)

Basel is the crossroads of practically all trains running between the north (Amsterdam, Brussels, Frankfurt) and Italy through the Gotthard Tunnel. Day expresses leave about every two hours from Basel and Zurich for Milan. Most of these are EuroCity trains: the *Barbarossa* and *Herman Hesse* (Stuttgart–Milan), *Carlo Magno* (Dortmund–Genoa–Sestri Levante), *Colosseum* (Frankfurt–Rome), *Gottardo* and *Manzoni* (Winterthur–Milan), *Raffaello* (Basel–Rome), *Rossini* (Zurich–Milan), *Tiziano* (Hamburg–Milan). A wide choice of the best. The night trains don't offer more than getting you there. In Milan (or, northbound, in Basel) their through cars disperse in all directions. Make sure you're sitting in the right car or you may end up several hundred miles from your destination.

The station marshaller's nightmare is the triple combination of the Riviera and Italia expresses, plus the Calais–Roma service, merging and splitting in six directions. The passenger, however, gets a flexible assortment of cities and timings. The Italia comes from Frankfurt, the Riviera from Amsterdam and Brussels, the Calais–Roma via Metz and Strasbourg. Their assorted cars are sent through the Gotthard Tunnel in two batches to Milan, then to Bologna–Florence–Rome and to Genoa–Ventimiglia, the Italian end of the Riviera. The Holland–Italy Express bypasses all this with few stops between Amsterdam and Rimini.

The trains carry sleepers and second-class couchettes. Buffet cars run only between Milan and Rome.

The Glacier Express

St.Moritz–Chur–Disentis–Andermatt–Brig–Zermatt

The expressions 'armchair travel' and 'mountain climbing' gain new meanings here where you climb mountains in an armchair, sipping wine from a glass angled to prevent spilling on steep slopes.

If you want to go from Chur to Brig, you have two choices. Main line trains through Zurich and Bern take nearly seven hours with two changes. But the secondary narrow-gauge railway gets you there directly in four and a half hours and you'll wish it took longer. The *Glacier Express* runs across the top of Switzerland. Or, to be exact, it doesn't run, but chugs, crawls, climbs up and down slopes that other trains could never cope with and have to burrow through tunnels. The *Glacier Express* has its share of tunnels but it prefers to stay above ground, on bridges and viaducts, treating its passengers to the most spectacular views.

The name express may be a slight exaggeration for a train that has to resort to cogwheels to pull itself up a mountain at such speeds that it may easily be overtaken by a cow grazing a few feet from the tracks. But narrow-gauge does not mean some excursion dinky toy here. The meter-wide tracks carry almost full-width wagons; you may notice that the food trolley is slightly narrower than usual to fit through the aisle, but everything else is regular size. And a glance at a rail map tells you that this is a serious working train on the only route across the center of Switzerland. Until a few years ago the service was seasonal: sections of the tracks had to be taken up before winter and laid again in the spring because of the snow. But the new tunnel, the pride of the Furka-Oberalp-Bahn and the longest meter-gauge tunnel in the world, has made the route safe for year-round operation, to the joy of skiers.

Tourists congregate in the dining car which is often fully reserved weeks or months ahead. The food is not three-star but perfectly satisfactory, served at dazzling speed in order to cram three sittings into a single lunch time (if you haven't got a reservation your only chance to eat is at the third sitting). Wine is served in glasses that lean to the side on short stems to ensure that your drink will not spill when the table tilts as the train climbs up the mountainside. Don't forget to rotate the glass when the train goes around a curve. The highlight of the meal is the spectacular pouring of the digestifs: the head steward shoots streams of eau-de-vie into thimblesized glasses while raising the bottle over his head.

As a concession to visitors hanging out of the windows, feverishly photographing the scenery, there is a photo opportunity stop as the train emerges from the tunnel. The view of the glass-smooth lake surrounded by snowy slopes sends even the most jaded travelers scrambling for cameras. Yet the *Glacier Express* is not a tourist special. The complement of passengers includes school children munching sandwiches and local farmers talking more about the condition of the grass than the majesty of the mountains.

It's possible to ride the train on its entire seven and a half-hour journey that crosses the territories of three railways. The Rhätische Bahn pulls it from St. Moritz through to Chur. Here is the end of the main line from Zurich and a good place to join the train for its most spectacular run. At Disentis, the Furka-Oberalp-Bahn takes over. The next major stop is Andermatt, on top of the Gotthard Tunnel. If you want to go to Zurich or Milan, a rack railway will take you down to Göschenen where the main north–south trains stop. At Brig, less than two hours away, is the entrance of the Simplon Tunnel and a chance to change trains for Lausanne, Geneva, Bern, Basel or Milan. Here the *Glacier Express* is taken by the Brig-Visp-Zermatt Bahn up to the car-free village of Zermatt, at the foot of the Matterhorn. Passengers who rode the entire route receive a certificate and a slanted glass.

There are three departures a day in each direction during the summer, one in the winter. Parts of the route are not covered by Eurailpass. For information contact a Swiss tourist office; for tickets and reservations write Furka-Oberalp-Bahn, CH 3900 Brig or Rhätische Bahn, CH-7000 Chur, Switzerland.

The Orient Express

More than a decade after its official demise, the Orient Express is better known now than it was throughout its near century-long existence. A stack of books—from paperback mysteries to coffee-table photo albums—has been published about it, other trains revived its hallowed name, posters have been reprinted, boutiques sell wagons-lits paraphernalia. The Orient Express has become an object of nostalgia and symbol of the elegant old days.

Paris–Istanbul

It all started over a century ago, on October 4, 1883, when the world's first transcontinental train departed from Paris. Three days, nine hours and forty minutes later its passengers arrived on the threshold of Asia, in Istanbul. Admittedly, the train itself didn't travel quite that far: passengers were ferried across the River Danube and took an uncomfortable sea voyage to their final destination. Yet the trip was a triumph of technology and enterprise: a journey across national borders and railways in a politically fragmented Europe that didn't even have a coordinated time system. It was the work of one man, Georges Nagelmackers, a Belgian genius, who begged, bribed, and bullied bureaucrats, financiers and kings to let his distinguished passengers travel in uninterrupted luxury.

The next 94 years brought wars and revolutions both in politics and in technology. Dirigibles appeared and disappeared. Cars began to crowd the roads. The Orient Express was already 36 years old when the first commercial air service started with passengers sitting in open cockpits; when it ended its long service travelers were riding in jumbo jets. Wars stopped the train only briefly or merely diverted its route. It carried on in high style: a hotel on wheels with plush bedrooms, stewards to bring breakfast and shine shoes, a kitchen to supply the dining car with regional delicacies from pheasant to sturgeon, and a guarantee of the Compagnie Internationale des Wagons-Lits that nothing would discommode its illustrious passengers.

There were the occasional hitches, to be sure. In 1929 the express got stuck in the snow in the Turkish mountains for several days. The *chef du train* took foraging parties, getting out of the train through a tunnel dug into the snow, to scrounge food from a nearby village. He lost a few toes to frostbite, but kept his passengers fed—and kept his job. He only did what the Compagnie expected as his duty.

The King of Trains carried several crowned heads, as well as crooks, diplomatic couriers, arms dealers, spies, and high-class ladies of pleasure. No wonder that there have been tales, indeed legends, which grew into novels and later films. It was called the Train of Kings with good reason, not only because of the occasional royal passenger. Ferdinand I of Bulgaria had a hand in creating the train, having helped to build a section of the route through his country. He took a proprietary attitude which he occasionally expressed by insisting on driving the train himself. According to the regular engineer, he wasn't a bad driver but needed practice. The owners, Wagons-Lits Company, heaved a sigh of relief when Ferdinand abdicated after World War I. By that time, however, his son Boris had been bitten by the steam bug. As the new Tsar of Bulgaria he took control, literally. Clad in a custom-tailored white overall, he regularly climbed on the locomotive at the border, shouldered the engineer aside, and highballed the express into Sofia, with the steam pressure gauge past the red line most of the way. The passengers, falling about in the rocking carriages, were not amused.

Where is the Orient Express now? Rather, where are they, for there are more than one.

Paris–Stuttgart–Munich–Salzburg–Vienna–Budapest–Bucharest

Appearing under the old name in timetables, a skeleton of the original grand express still runs daily from Paris to Bucharest. Depleted, it's not even a through train. Day cars, sleepers and couchettes leave Paris at night. Next morning in Stuttgart more day cars are put on, as well as a mini-bar. The sleepers and couchettes are left behind in Salzburg. A few hours later Hungarian and Romanian day cars come on in Vienna, as well as a dining car (from Salzburg in the summer). In Budapest most of the Paris cars are exchanged for sleepers and a dining car to finish in Bucharest. One could, by switching nimbly from car to car, travel on the same train the length of the trip, but it really isn't the same train. And it isn't the old Orient Express.

Zurich–Istanbul

The first attempt to revive the glamour was made in 1976 by Albert Glatt, a Swiss entrepreneur, who first rented, then bought, some luxurious old wagons-lits, Pullmans and a dining car, built in the 1920s. These now serve on overland train cruises. The Nostalgic Orient Express runs between Zurich and Istanbul (with return by air) a few times a year. The rest of the time the cars ply the champagne route around Paris and Reims. They also go on some truly long-distance excursions into Russia as the Trans-Siberian Special, and into China as the Middle Kingdom Express; they cost a bundle, but passengers are treated to the fine handiwork of Swiss chefs in the kitchen, instead of *chai* from the conductress' samovar on the real Trans-Siberian.

London–Paris–Milan–Venice

The story of this Orient Express started in 1977, the year the old train died in its tracks. Some of the original cars were auctioned off in Monte Carlo and James Sherwood, president of Sea Containers, bought two sleepers. He went on to collect many more. Some cars were rescued from junk yards. All were brought up to current safety standards, then restored to their original beauty. New wiring and brakes were installed, and upholstery—faithful to original patterns—woven out of flameproof material. Inlaid wood paneling, brass and Lalique glass fixtures were recreated.

In 1982 the train began regular service, and received the crown, its own schedule in the Thomas Cook European Timetable.

The fare from London to Venice is over $1200. For this price the promotion promises perfect luxury. Unfortunately, this is not forthcoming. Staff, resplendent in 1920s uniforms, are poorly trained. The beautiful cars lack the comfort travelers have become accustomed to in the 1980s: in the earnest attempt to bring back the good old days, they were restored too authentically. The hot-water heating is nearly uncontrollable, the water taps clumsy, the ventilators noisy, the seats hard. The 1938 design suspension is inadequate for modern speeds. The cars bounce and rattle; it's difficult to sip your tea daintily out of the Limoges china. Was this really the ride once enjoyed by royalty?

Following the Oostende—Wien Express

London—Ostend—Brussels—Cologne—Frankfurt—Vienna—Budapest

London to Budapest in thirty hours? You could if you wanted to on this cross-Europe path that was carved out by the train that timetables list as having London and Budapest as its terminals. True, the boat train and the ferry bring passengers from London. But as the name modestly and correctly states, through cars run only between Ostend and Vienna, and between Aachen and Budapest in the summer. Sleepers and couchettes roll from the coast to the other edge of Central Europe in sixteen hours, which is reasonable for the distance but far too long to spend without a decent meal. Sadly, this is one of those dowager expresses that have come down in the world and lost their dining cars long ago. If you go non-stop, you'll have lots of time to sleep, but only if you pack something to stop the hunger pangs. The mini-bar trolley fare is certainly nothing to get excited about.

The Holland—Wien Express from Amsterdam follows this route from Cologne to Vienna. It departs at 18:56, leaving plenty of time for a picnic dinner if you came prepared with several *brotjes*. The trolleys come around till 23:00, then nothing until arrival in Vienna at 8:15. The long trip could be broken into segments east and west of Frankfurt.

Frankfurt—Ostend

The east-west service is poor, the only through train being the Wien—Oostende with a rudely early departure at 6:15 from Frankfurt. During the summer a train leaves here at 18:11 to reach Ostend after midnight for the overnight ferry to London. All other trains from Frankfurt or Mainz are intercities to Cologne where passengers must change for Brussels.

Going east is little better. The Oostende—Wien arrives in Frankfurt inconveniently at midnight. The additional summer train meets the overnight ferry from London in Ostend, leaving at 5:52, ending in Frankfurt at 13:11. All other trains from Ostend or Brussels terminate in Cologne. The bother of having to change trains there is balanced somewhat by the quality of the next leg: hourly InterCity trains with dining cars to Mainz. There are only a few direct ICs to Frankfurt, so you may need to change in Mainz to the S-Bahn or regular train.

Frankfurt–Amsterdam

The only convenient train with which you can reach the boat train for Britain is the EuroCity *Frans Hals* at 13:47.

Going east, the morning train is the EC-*Erasmus* which continues past Frankfurt on the Ostend–Vienna route, then down to Munich. The night-time Austria Express follows the same route. The train with the best timing is the EC-*Frans Hals* which leaves Amsterdam at 10:59, an hour and a half after the arrival of the boat train, to arrive in Frankfurt at 16:12.

Frankfurt–Vienna

At night the Holland-Wien Express at 23:35 is preferable (the Oostende-Wien leaves after midnight); it arrives in Vienna at 8:00, before you notice the lack of meal services. The journey is really too long for a day trip, but if you just want to take it in sections, there are two good EuroCity trains that stop in Würzburg, Nuremberg, and Regensburg—places worth seeing. The *Johann Strauss* leaves at 8:20, the *Franz Liszt* at 10:20. The latter continues past Vienna to Budapest.

From Vienna to Frankfurt the Wien-Oostende leaves at 20:45, the Wien-Holland at 21:20; these two long-distance runners arrive in Frankfurt at unattractive times, 5:15 and 6:05. If you have time for a day trip, start in Budapest at 6:45 with the *Franz Liszt*, or in Vienna at 14:05 with the *Johann Strauss*, both EuroCity trains with dining cars.

Walzing to Vienna

Paris–Basel–Zurich–Innsbruck–Salzburg–Vienna–Budapest

The Arlberg Tunnel opened the straight route from Switzerland to Vienna and lent its name to an express train, now old and slow. Although the far end of this route is really far, a EuroCity train covers the distance mostly in daylight. The EC-*Mozart* leaves Paris at 7:52, arriving in Vienna at 22:20, and sets off on the return trip at 8:38, arriving in Paris at 22:10. This train turns northwest at Salzburg, going via Munich instead of Innsbruck and Basel.

The overnight service from Paris is the Arlberg Express, originally one of the many versions of the great Orient Express. Sleepers and couchettes run only as far as Innsbruck, where you have to change cars for Vienna. You might as well change trains; you'll have an hour and a half for lunch at the station, then catch the EC-*Transalpin* and arrive in Vienna an hour before the Arlberg.

Coming from Basel you have the choice of two excellent EuroCity trains, both fast and well-served, carrying dining cars. The EC-*Transalpin* leaves at 8:27, the EC-*Franz Schubert* at 10:27, arriving ten and a half hours later in Vienna. The third train of their quality, the EC-*Maria Theresia*, runs from Zurich at 13:34, arriving at 23:00 in Vienna.

Finally, the night train, the *Wiener Walzer* offers convenient timings and good service. Going east, it leaves Basel after dinner time at 20:27, Zurich at 21:34, picks up the dining car for breakfast at 5:00, and arrives in Vienna at 8:35 for an hour's rest before continuing to Budapest. The return trip begins in Budapest at 16:25 or Vienna at 21:00. The Hungarian dining car stays on till midnight. You arrive in Zurich at a civilized 8:26, in Basel at 9:33. Sleepers run between Basel and Vienna, couchettes between Basel and Budapest.

On the blue Danube

Budapest–Vienna–Krems–Melk–Linz–Passau

The Danube looks brown in Vienna and grey in Budapest. The river will disappoint you in the cities. But if you follow it out to the countryside, to areas away from rail and road, ships will take you to its most beautiful stretches.

Between Budapest and Vienna the hydrofoils weave through green archipelagoes, hundreds of untouched islands, mostly bird sanctuaries. The Danube Bend appears as a large-scale Rhine: forest-covered mountains descend steeply to the shores at Visegrád where the walls of the royal summer palace, built in the Renaissance, still stand. The journey takes five and a half hours aboard a Hungarian hydrofoil or Austrian hovercraft. From April 1 till late September, two daily 'flights' go in each direction. Rail/ship combination tickets cost just slightly more than the regular return train fare.

Above Vienna lies the welcoming Wachau region. Krems nestles among vineyards that supply its cellars; at Melk the 900-year old Benedictine Abbey rises high above the river like a medieval fort. If you want more than a fleeting glimpse from a train window, you can take a ship from Vienna. Travel time is little over eight hours to Melk, a long day to Linz (from 8:00 till 22:45), but the return is shorter, coming downstream. You can continue to Passau after an overnight stay in Linz. The Austrian railway offers combination tickets (*Kombi-Karte*) for rail one way and ship the other. Eurailpasses are valid for free travel between Vienna and Passau.

For schedule information, tickets, and reservations contact ÖBB (railway) or DDSG (shipping) offices.

INDEX

For information concerning national railway systems, see under the relevant country in Travel Manual. Where there are several page references, numbers in **bold face** refer to the main entry.